HISTORY TEACHING, NATIONHOOD AND THE STATE

Also available from Cassell:

R. Aldrich *Education for the Nation*
J. Avis, M. Bloomer, G. Esland, D. Gleeson, P, Hodkinson *Knowledge and Nationhood*
G. Haydon *Teaching about Values*
D. Leinster-Mackay *Education and The Times*
J. Slater *Teaching History in the New Europe*

History Teaching, Nationhood and the State

A Study in Educational Politics

Robert Phillips

CASSELL

Cassell
Wellington House
125 Strand
London WC2R 0BB

PO Box 605
Herndon
VA 20172

First published 1998

British Library Cataloguing-in-Publication Data
A catalogue record for this book is available from the British Library.

ISBN 0-304-70298-6 (hardback)
   0-304-70299-4 (paperback)

Typeset by York House Typographic Ltd, London
Printed and bound in Great Britain by Redwood Books, Trowbridge, Wiltshire

Contents

Acknowledgements

This book would not have been written without the help, support and advice of many people. I would like to thank colleagues in the department of education at the University of Wales Swansea, particularly Wendy Cunnah and Mike Rowe, and to mentors associated with the PGCE course, notably Ian Kilcoyne, Paul Thomas, Lana Picton and David Thomas. I am also indebted to the library and secretarial staff at Swansea. I am grateful to various people over the years who have provided intellectual stimulation such as Richard Jones, Peter John, Martin Jephcote, Keith Jenkins, John Furlong, Gareth Elwyn Jones and Roy Love. Two people in particular gave me invaluable advice over earlier drafts of the book, Richard Aldrich and Terry Haydn. The book would not have been possible without the help of people who gave up their time to be interviewed by me, especially former working group members, civil servants and teachers. I am particularly grateful to the Department for Education and Employment and to the Schools Curriculum and Assessment Authority for permission to use various documents for the purposes of the research. Thanks also to everybody at Cassell for seeing the book into print. Finally, it is dedicated to three 'heroes' of mine who, sadly, died as the book was being written, namely my father, my friend James Lowe, and the great Raphael Samuel. I am confident that they all, for different reasons, would have been pleased to see it published.

Abbreviations

CCW Curriculum Council for Wales
CSE Certificate of Secondary Education
DES Department of Education & Science
DFE Department for Education
ERA Education Reform Act
ESRC Economic & Social Research Council
GCE General Certificate of Education
GCSE General Certificate of Secondary Education
HA Historical Association
HCA History Curriculum Association
HCW History Committee for Wales
HMI Her Majesty's Inspectorate
HTG NCC History Task Group
HWG National Curriculum History Working Group
INSET In-Service Training
KS Key Stage
LEA Local Education Authority
NC National Curriculum
NC/HWG National Curriculum History Working Group Minutes
NC/HTG NCC History Task Group Minutes
NCC National Curriculum Council
NSG Non-Statutory Guidance
OFSTED Office for Standards in Education
PESC Political, Economic, Social, Cultural
SAT Standard Assessment Task/Test
SCAA Schools Curriculum & Assessment Authority
SCHP Schools Council History Project
SEAC Schools Examinations & Assessment Council
SHP Schools History Project
TES *Times Educational Supplement*
TGAT Task Group on Assessment & Testing
THES *Times Higher Education Supplement*
TVEI Technical & Vocational Education Initiative

Chronology of History in the National Curriculum: 1989–1995

1989:
Jan: History Working Group begins work
Jun: Interim Report completed
Aug: Publication of Interim Report (DES, 1989a)

1990:
Jan: Final Report completed
Feb: National Curriculum Council History Task Group begins work
Apr: Publication of Final Report (DES, 1990a): period of 'extra' consultation begins
Jun: Letter to MacGregor from SEAC confirming HWG's assessment proposals
Jul: Publication of History for Ages 5–16 ('MacGregor proposals') (DES, 1990b); sent to NCC
Dec: Publication of NCC Consultation Report (NCC, 1990)

1991:
Jan: Publication of Draft Orders for History; Clarke's interventions
Jan-Mar: Last minute changes to Orders
Mar: Publication of Statutory Orders for History (DES, 1991a)
Sep: Implementation of Statutory Orders

1992:
Publication of *Teacher Assessment at Key Stage 3: History* (SEAC, 1992b)

1993:
Mar: Publication of *Pupils' Work Assessed* (SEAC, 1993)
Apr: Patten announces Dearing Reforms
Jul: Publication of Dearing's Interim Report (Dearing, 1993a)
Dec: Publication of Dearing's Final Report (Dearing, 1993b)

1994:
May: Publication of Draft Proposals for History (SCAA, 1994b)

1995:
Jan: Publication of new NC Orders for History (DFE, 1995)

Chapter 1

The Battle for the Big Prize:
History Teaching, the State and Policy
in the Late Twentieth Century

> Margaret Thatcher has fought many historic battles for what she sees as Britain's future. Few of them, though, are as pregnant with meaning as her current battle for control over Britain's own history ... The debate is a surrogate for a much wider debate about the cultural legacy of the Thatcher years. It is about the right to dissent and to debate not just history but a whole range of other assumptions. If the Prime Minister can change the way that we are taught history, she will have succeeded in changing the ground rules for a generation to come. It is a big prize. (Martin Kettle in the *Guardian*, 4 January 1990)

The struggle for the 'big prize' explains why history became such a controversial subject within the National Curriculum (NC) (Phillips, 1992a). It initiated fundamental discussions in educational and political circles and became public property, provoking literally thousands of articles, letters and editorials in the quality and tabloid press between the establishment in January 1990 of the National Curriculum Working Group for History (HWG) and the publication of the revised Statutory Order for history which was published in 1995 (Department for Education (DFE), 1995).

Other subjects within the NC, of course, initiated similar debates. Music, for example, could justifiably be interpreted as a struggle for culture (Shepherd & Vulliamy, 1994). Similarly, the English NC attracted as much controversy in the press as history (Cox, 1995). Even the making of the physical education NC involved the politics of pedagogy (Evans & Penney, 1995). Similarly, it would also be unhistorical to claim that the debate over history at the time of the NC was entirely unique in the 'history of history' in Britain. Thus Elliott (1980; 1992a; 1992b) has written on the failure of history curriculum reform in England between the wars and the 'crisis' over history teaching and examining in Scotland. Marsden (1989) has shown the degree to which both history and geography were subject to politicization in the nineteenth and early twentieth centuries, particularly at patriotic high points, one of which formed the basis of a study by Betts (1990). In particular, the work of Aldrich (1984) and Aldrich & Dean (1991) show that debates over the teaching of history have occurred at various times in the twentieth century.

Similarly, it is parochial to imply that the debate over history in the NC was a particularly British phenomenon. Andersson (1991) has described the struggle over history in Finland's schools during the second half of the nineteenth century. Wegner's (1990, 1992) important work on the intense discussions over the teaching of history in pre and post Nazi Germany is particularly important for reminding us of school history's capacity to shape both individual and collective minds. Moreover, an interesting parallel to the struggle over the history NC in England and Wales has been occurring in the United States (Nash *et al.*, 1997; Nelson, 1992), summarized in a collection of essays stimulated by the work of the Bradley Commission (Gagnon & the Bradley Commission, 1989). Moreover, at the time of the creation of history in the NC, vibrant dialogues were taking place on the teaching of history and prescribed syllabuses in the emerging small nation states of the New Europe (Slater, 1995). At the time of writing, these debates are continuing in South Africa (Sieborger & Alexander, 1996) and in other parts of the world (Dickinson *et al.*, 1995).

However, in terms of the profound public, political and professional interest it evoked and in the sheer volume of printed literature it initiated, the 'great history debate' within the NC has a particular significance. This is reflected in the surprisingly extensive list of references to it in *Hansard*, in the memoirs of Thatcher (1993) and of Baker (1993), and in political analyses of the Thatcherite era (Letwin, 1992). In addition, the debate is cited in books such as those exploring the relationship between education and the state (Turner, 1996), on the concept of citizenship (Heater, 1990) and anti-racism (Troyna & Carrington, 1990), on comparative European education systems (Coulby & Jones, 1995) and pupils' perceptions of Europe (Convery *et al.*, 1997). It also appears in an undergraduate text exploring the concept of British cultural identities (Storry & Childs, 1997) and on the first page of a book concerned with 'that elusive, displaced notion of Englishness' (Schwarz, 1996). These final references are particularly significant and apposite, for at the heart of the debate over history in the NC was the issue of cultural and national identity, centred on the often vexed question of what it meant to be British at the end of the twentieth century (Carrington & Short, 1995).

Kettle's article, cited at the beginning, was stimulated by the publication of the HWG's *Final Report* (Department of Education and Science (DES), 1990a). He is accurate in his assertion that the debate over history in the NC should be viewed within the context of a hegemonic struggle over cultural transmission and heritage (Phillips, 1992b; Crawford, 1995). For the history debate centred on important questions relating to state formation, patriotism and nationalism (Clark, 1990; Gilroy, 1990; Marks, 1990; Robbins, 1990). These issues have long been of interest to historians (Hobsbawm & Ranger, 1983) but also to social anthropologists and sociologists and political scientists (Billig, 1995; Tonkin, 1992). History is, after all, essential for the creation of the collective memory (Alter, 1989; Phillips, 1996a); it is the essence of the 'horizontal comradeship' of the 'imagined community' which is the nation (Anderson, 1991).

It should therefore be no surprise to find that governments have at various times become interested in what history is taught in schools. As Baldwin (1996, p.132) has suggested 'the opportunity to discuss and understand the formation of identity ... is what makes history an essential and controversial part of any curriculum'. Berghahn & Schissler (1987) demonstrate, in a collection of essays analysing the nature of textbooks in Europe in the nineteenth and twentieth centuries, that school history has been used at various times in Europe as a means of state socialization, geared to the teaching of the national past to generate an identification with the nation and the state (see also Gilbert, 1984). Thus, in a description of the connection between national identity and history in the NC, McKiernan uses Anderson's analogy to symbolize the substance of the debate, for the NC was a 'national imagining' which involved 'different groups with different national imaginings … competing to define it' (McKiernan, 1993, p.34). This is perhaps what Tosh had in mind when (in a symbolic year) he wrote that school history was a political battleground because the 'sanction of the past' is useful both for 'upholders and subverters of authority' (Tosh, 1984, p.8).

Aldrich (1990a) has argued that historians in the future will be particularly fascinated with the history debate. This stems not only from the personal interest and direct interventions in the history debate by Kenneth Baker, Kenneth Clarke and Margaret Thatcher (see Graham with Tytler, 1993) but also from the important light it sheds on the complex national soul of Britain in the 1980s and 1990s, a period of intense cultural, ideological, economic and social changes. Yet at a time of intense change in the present, it seems curious to contemplate that British society in the late twentieth century should be obsessed with the past. In his thought provoking *Mythical Past, Elusive Future*, Frank Furedi (1992, p.3) suggests that contemporary uncertainty at the end of the twentieth century caused 'anxiety about the future' which in turn 'stimulated a scramble to appropriate the past'. Like Kaye (1991, 1996), Furedi describes attempts by governments and elites throughout the world to reinvent national histories, also emphasizing that history has become a subject in demand by a range of groups concerned to find identity in a changing, uncertain, often troubled world; there is thus no longer 'a history with a capital H; there are many competing histories' (1992, p.8).

History was no longer the preserve of historians, teachers or government; rather, in the late twentieth century there were a wide range of 'claims' upon the past, 'all being affected by local, regional, national and international perspectives' (Jenkins, 1991, p.66). The reference here to 'regional/national' goes some way towards explaining why Wales has its own history NC (Welsh Office, 1990, 1991, 1995), and why the constituent parts of the United Kingdom have very distinctive history curricula, developments which may have implications for future debates over nationhood (Haydn, 1995; Phillips, 1996a, 1996b; Phillips, 1997a). For at the heart of the NC debate was the struggle over 'other histories' (Hastrup, 1992). This also provides a challenge to those who have suggested that history is at an end (Fukuyama, 1992).

In addition to being a focal point for the politics of identity, 'the great history debate' also centred upon pedagogy, focusing for example upon the relative importance of educational skills versus historical content, a debate which had been vibrant within the history teaching profession in varying degrees throughout the twentieth century (Aldrich, 1991; Little, 1990; Roberts, 1990). It also went to the heart of epistemological discussions relating to the nature of historical knowledge and historical disciplines (Gardiner, 1990). The history debate was thus also concerned with the notion of autonomy and power, centring upon the methods of teaching history – *how to teach it* – and perhaps even more importantly, about the selection of and justification for history – *what history to teach and why teach it* (Beattie, 1987; Phillips, 1991). All of this may be said to be part of what Gathercole and Lowenthal (1990) have termed 'the politics of the past', what Osborne (1995) calls 'the politics of time' and above all, what Slater (1989) has termed 'the politics of history teaching'. Yet the debate over history in the NC cannot be fully understood without reference to the educational politics and policies of the period.

Educational Politics in the 1980s and 1990s

When Margaret Thatcher took office in 1979 few could have predicted the scale and pace of educational policy legislation which would be introduced in the following two decades. In some ways, of course, these reforms continued the 'great debate' over education. Yet the period since 1979 was a major break from the past in a number of fundamental ways, partly resulting in an education system 'transformed' (Chitty, 1992a). The 1988 Education Reform Act (ERA), in particular, initiated a fundamental change in the ways that schools are organized, managed and controlled (Tomlinson, 1993). The Act 'altered the basic power structure of the educational system' (MacLure, 1989, p.v). The legislation was an attempt to change the power relationships which had governed education since 1944; in the words of Salter & Tapper (1988) it was an attempt to 'reverse the ratchet' of post-war education policy.

Through the Act, government sought to shift power and control of education in contradictory ways, either by offering alternative centres of influence in the locality through, for example, grant maintained schools and local financial management or, significantly for the purposes of this book, by increasing the centralizing influence of the state through the NC (Chitty, 1988; 1992b). The NC was controversial from the start (Haviland, 1988) mainly because it was stimulated, in part, by the belief that teachers had enjoyed too much autonomy in the 1960s and 1970s, particularly over the control of the curriculum. The proposals were first announced during the election year in 1987 by Kenneth Baker, Secretary of State for Education; they found their way on to the statute books within the ERA in 1988 and were then described in various DES publications in the following year. The NC prescribed core and foundation subjects across the 5–16 age range which was divided into four key stages. History was included as a foundation subject across all key stages.

Each subject would be assessed on the basis of the proposals put forward by the Task Group on Assessment & Testing, involving attainment targets and a complex ten level scale of assessment. Bench-mark tests in the shape of Standard Assessment Tasks (SATs) would ensure the maintenance of high standards. Crucially for the purposes of this book, the Act also established advisory systems and consultation processes. The content or programmes of study for each subject, as well as the attainment targets, would be drawn up by subject groups whose proposals would go out for statutory consultation to be conducted through the National Curriculum Council which would also provide the Secretary of State with advice on the form which the legal basis of each subject – the Statutory Order – would take.

Many scholars have identified the role here of the ideology of the New Right in influencing education policy in the 1980s and 1990s (Johnson, 1991a, 1991b; Jones, 1989; Quicke, 1988; Lowe, 1995; Carr & Hartnett, 1996). Chitty (1989) describes the New Right as a collection of educationists, philosophers and economists whose writings influenced successive Secretaries of State for Education and Prime Ministers. Chitty and others have stressed that although the New Right claimed to have a coherent strategy of economic, moral and educational post-war regeneration, its suggested strategies and solutions for this were sometimes contradictory. For New Right ideology consisted of 'enterprise and heritage' (Corner & Harvey, 1991), as well as 'choice and control' (Lawton, 1989b), a mixture of neo-liberal market individualism and neo-conservative emphasis upon authority, discipline, hierarchy, the nation and strong government (Levitas, 1986; Whitty, 1989).

Although the concept of a mandatory statutory curriculum had been proposed by New Right groups such as the Hillgate Group (1986) as a means of reforming education and holding teachers to account, the NC also posed challenges. On the one hand, many New Right activists saw the need for intervention by the state as a means of 'reversing the ratchet' of declining standards and progressive teaching methodologies, both of which were the product of a teacher-dominated educational 'establishment' which had to be challenged. On the other hand, the details of the proposals caused considerable unease amongst its neo-liberal elements. As Jones (1989) has emphasized, many of the New Right regarded the NC as a betrayal, for many of those practitioners whom it had been attacking since the publication of the *Black Papers* in the 1960s and 1970s 'were now being invited through the front door of the DES to devise a curriculum for all state students' (p.30).

Given these circumstances, it is hardly surprising that the NC – and history in particular – became a source of cultural struggle, contest and conflict. One of the aims of the book is to demonstrate how neo-conservative elements within the New Right sought – with varying degrees of success – to influence the policy process relating to history in the NC in the late 1980s and 1990s. Before embarking upon this account, I first want to make reference to some of the analytical and methodological influences which have shaped the book.

Politics, Reform and Education Policy Research

Given their pace, scale and nature, it is little wonder that the education reforms mentioned above should have stimulated profound interest amongst academics. Consequently, a rich, wide ranging literature emerged in the 1980s and 1990s which, in an 'illuminative' way, sought to 'find out how things are and how they came to be that way' in relation to education policy (Ozga, 1987). Thus Lawton's (1980) study of the 'politics of the curriculum' analysed the ways in which the curriculum was a source of ideological conflict; his portentous prediction that central government would intervene to influence the direction of the curriculum in the 1980s and 1990s was subsequently described in other works (Lawton, 1989a, 1992, 1994). Similarly, Chitty (1989) analysed the complex relationship between the DES, Her Majesty's Inspectorate (HMI) and politicians over the creation of curriculum policies between 1944 and 1989. Salter & Tapper's (1981) empirical study of the role of the DES was important for examining the nature of the education policy making apparatus of the central state. From a more theoretical perspective, Dale's (1989) important analysis of the relationship between education and the state re-emphasized the complexity of the different components of the central state for shaping policy.

This theme of the complexity of the creation of education policy at the central state level was given most prominent attention by Stephen Ball who drew upon a range of analytical perspectives to cultivate an 'applied sociology' to explain it (Ball, 1994a). In the introduction to his influential *Politics and Policy Making in Education: Explorations in Policy Sociology*, Ball (1990a) made it clear that he was using the ERA as a case study to trace the formulation of education policy. The book analysed the ideological origins of the ERA and the consequent struggles over its constituent parts, particularly the NC, and concentrated upon the work of the DES and the working groups established by Kenneth Baker to advise on the form which the NC should take. Ball emphasized that an appreciation of the ideological origins of policy was essential for appreciating policy outcomes within what he called the *context of influence*. Using the work of Foucault (see Ball, 1990b), he emphasized that education policy was:

> a discourse, a construct of possibilities and impossibilities tied to knowledge and practice. Control of the discourse and thus of its possibilities is essentially contested in and between arenas of formation and implementation. As texts, policies can be subject to a variety of readings, they will have a different affectivity in relation to different groups of readers ... the ERA is a half-written text, a story outline; its detail, meaning and practice lie in on-going struggles relating to the interpretation of its key components. (Ball, 1990a, p.185)

Significantly, Ball also made reference to the New Right *discourse of derision* as applied to education which acted to 'debunk and displace' specific words and meanings in relation to education and to influence the policy process (see Kenway, 1990). A large section of the book was devoted to what Ball called the 'hand to hand fighting' that went on in association with the production of documentation by the various working groups established by the ERA for each of the NC subjects: Ball referred to this aspect of the policy process as the *context of text production* and utilized data generated from policy makers themselves in order to shed light upon the macro politics of the period.

Although Ball recognized that the ERA was the product of a 'profound distrust of teachers' and that one of the major intentions behind the NC was to cause teachers to be 'reduced to agents of policies which are decided elsewhere' (Ball, 1990a, p.171), he also acknowledged that at all stages in the policy process the NC was open to struggle, contestation and re-constitution as policy was interpreted and disputed in ways which were 'unanticipated by the initiators or formulators of the Act' (ibid, p.135). As the various elements of the ERA began to be implemented at a micro level, therefore, Ball returned to his ethnographic roots by publishing, with Richard Bowe & Anne Gold, *Reforming Education & Changing Schools* (1992) describing empirical work concerned with the actual implementation of the NC in secondary schools. It was in this book that Ball and his colleagues further utilized the notion of discourse and highlighted the gap between policy intent (at macro levels) and actual implementation (at micro/meso levels) within the third policy arena, *the context of practice*. Ball and his colleagues emphasized that although the government ultimately relies upon teachers for the actual delivery of policy, the loosely coupled relationship between schools and the state allows scope for teacher initiatives, creativity and 'ad hocery', thus encouraging Ball and his colleagues to question whether the NC represented 'state control over school knowledge' (Ball & Bowe, 1992, p.99).

The work of Ball and his colleagues has been recognized by scholars for shedding light upon the complexities of the education policy process in the highly charged political context of the 1980s and 1990s (Chitty *et al.*, 1991; White & Crump, 1993). Yet it has also not been without its critics, particularly in connection with its tendency to underestimate the role of the central state in the determination of policy at a micro level (Dale, 1992; Hatcher & Troyna, 1994). In response to the charge of theoretical eclecticism and post-structural optimism, Ball himself has defended his work as essentially a pragmatic attempt to describe the 'real world' of education policy (Ball, 1994b).

As far as my own book is concerned, Ball's claim that the education policy process is cyclical, unpredictable, open to interpretation, conflict, compromise and 'slippage' seems applicable to the 'great history debate'. Similarly, the three policy 'contexts' is regarded as a useful theoretical, conceptual and organizing framework with which to explain the extraordinary and complex struggles over history in the 1980s and 1990s. To borrow Ball's own language, the book describes the 'real world' of history in the NC. Before describing how the following chapters are organized, it would be useful at this point to clarify what the book is and what it is not about.

The book is an attempt to describe the ideological, educational and political events surrounding history in the NC in England, from its origins in the late 1980s to its reform under the Dearing Review between 1993 and 1995 (see Chronology on p.viii). Given the richness of the data being described, it focuses mainly upon macro politics, although it does consider the professional response at a micro level using data from my own studies of NC implementation (Phillips, 1991, 1993a, 1993b) and thus concentrates mainly upon debates over the teaching of history in secondary schools. Moreover, the final chapter speculates about how teachers will 'recontextualize' the NC in the future.

Although the 'great history debate' provided the focus for discussing a range of different identities, such as those centred upon gender (Osler, 1994), I decided to concentrate upon the issue of nationality, as it provided the most dynamic and contested concept of the period. It needs reiterating that the book focuses exclusively upon the peculiarities of the history debate in England, for as was indicated earlier, Northern Ireland, Scotland and Wales have distinctive history syllabuses and therefore different 'imaginings' which merit separate accounts (Phillips, 1997a). Furthermore, the book is written from the perspective of somebody who has monitored debates over Englishness with some interest (Phillips, 1997b) and who is not therefore part of what M. Phillips (1996, p.317) has derided as a 'self-hating English intelligentsia'.

By describing in detail the macro politics of history teaching in the 1980s and 1990s, it is hoped that the book will be of interest to a range of readers. Historians may find it useful for the light it attempts to shed upon 'the national soul' in the late twentieth century but also for explaining why their subject became such a source of bitter debate, reminding us once more that history is, after all, 'always for someone' (Jenkins, 1991). It therefore seeks to provide, so to speak, a contemporary 'history of history teaching'. However, by drawing upon some of the theoretical and analytical tools mentioned above, it is hoped that sociologists may also be interested in the way the book attempts to make the connection between history, ideology and identity; in this sense the book can usefully be described as a 'sociology of history teaching'. Educationalists – particularly curricular historians and scholars working in education policy – may find some utility in the book for it is a study of history as policy (Silver, 1990). The 'great history debate' is used to provide insight into the ways in which education policy in the turbulent last quarter of the twentieth century was conceived, created and contested.

Contesting History: Pedagogy, Derision and Conflict

Chapters 2–4 examine the ideological roots of the history debate, centring upon discourses constructed by professional organizations (including teachers), pressure groups and the press around government, politics and the legislative process prior to the establishment of the NC. Influenced by Goodson's (1987) claim that in order to understand curriculum reform we need to 'develop a sense of history' about school subjects, Chapter 2 provides a 'history of history teaching' by tracing the development of history teaching in secondary schools in England in the twentieth century; thus the major 'subject traditions' which shaped history teaching prior to the NC are evaluated, for example the impact of the 'new history'. In particular an attempt is made to analyse the major pedagogic discourse relating to history teaching on the eve of the NC. Using some of the theoretical and empirical work done in the 1980s and 1990s on history teachers' conceptualization of their subject, this provides the opportunity to evaluate the dominant and prevailing discourses relating to history teaching on the eve of the creation of the NC. The impact of the GCSE and the new history are regarded as particularly important in this respect.

Chapter 3 describes the New Right discourse of derision in relation to history teaching. By analysing a number of important and well publicized New Right texts, it focuses upon attempts to deride the state of history teaching in schools prior to the establishment of the NC. The chapter explains why the New Right took such an active interest in the teaching of history and, in the process, New Right ideas specifically relating to history teaching are placed within a wider context of discourses on culture, nationhood and education. In this chapter and throughout the book, following Codd (1988), Kenway (1990) and Wallace (1993), particular attention is devoted to the linguistic devices of rhetoric, metaphor and image to legitimize New Right texts.

This provides the opportunity in Chapter 4 to illustrate the ways in which discourses of derision and pedagogical discourses competed within the crucial context of influence prior to the establishment of the NC History Working Group (HWG). Influenced by the need to consider Goodson's (1988) other claim that it is important to scrutinize 'the motives and aspirations of the individuals and interest groups that structure and restructure schooling' (p.xii), the chapter assesses the mediating impact of the Historical Association (HA) as well as the contributions by government ministers (including Kenneth Baker) and other agents within the state – such as HMI – to produce texts on history teaching.

Chapter 4 also focuses upon the ways in which one of the most contentious issues relating to history teaching in the late twentieth century – the debate over the teaching of historical empathy – was contested in the press. Social scientists have for some time recognized the importance of the discursive and ideological influence of the press (Fowler, 1991). Similarly, educationalists have recently noted the significance of the relationship between education and the press in the twentieth century (Cunningham, 1992), particularly the ways in which the media have helped to 'frame the debates about education policy' (Wallace, 1993, p.322). Thus, throughout the book, attempts are made to show the ways in which the media created what Baker (1994) calls 'two dimensional' debates over history, and in the process simplified extremely complex issues. Even more significantly, through the process of polarization, as well as what Wallace calls 'myth making', it can be argued that the press actually contributed to the formulation of policy, for the media:

> provide a bridge between the context of influence and the context of text production within the education policy process. The mass media are centrally implicated in the context of text production. They influence the range of written texts and their oral and visual equivalent that in varying degrees come to represent education policy. (Wallace, 1993, p.334)

Making History: Ministers, Mandarins and Mavericks

Influenced by Ball's (1990a) desire to 'explain policy making via what it is that individuals and groups actually do and say in the arenas of influence in which they move' (p.9), Chapters 5–8 analyse the work of the major 'text production' bodies relating to history in the NC between 1989 and 1991. These chapters draw upon a combination of documentary evidence, data generated from interviews with elite interviewees and the role of the press. It is important at this point to comment upon some of the methodological, practical and ethical challenges relating to this aspect of the work which was concerned with 'researching the powerful' (Walford, 1994) in relation to history in the NC for a brief reflective account of how the research for the book was conducted also reveals the part played by ad hocery and good fortune in the process (see Phillips, 1998a for wider discussion of this).

Like many teachers at the time, I was conscious of the challenges likely to be faced by the curriculum groups established by Kenneth Baker under the ERA to advise him on the form which the NC should take. The significance and symbolic nature of the task facing the HWG and the other NC history groups was not lost on me either. Here were bodies being asked to 'make history' at a time when history in Eastern Europe, South Africa and elsewhere in the world was 'being made'. Like many other history teachers, I was interested to know who these people were, I wanted to find out about their backgrounds in order to establish their ideological disposition and, in the highly charged political context of the Baker/Thatcher era, establish how and why they had been selected (see Blum, 1990). Between 1990 and 1996, therefore, I conducted over 50 interviews with individuals directly related to history's 'text production': these included former working group members, civil servants and government ministers. The vast majority of these interviews were taped and transcribed, although some questions were answered through correspondence. This data is referred to at various times throughout the book, beginning in Chapter 4 with reference to Baker's views on history.

Researchers concerned with other elements of the ERA have commented upon the helpfulness provided by elites in the conduct of policy research in education (Whitty & Edwards, 1994). Yet elite interviews only reveal a picture which is partial and incomplete (Fitz & Halpin, 1994). This is what Kogan (1994) has called 'the truth problem' in elite settings.Thus an over-reliance upon the testimony of interviews alone would have provided only a partial (albeit interesting and valuable) picture of the story of history in the NC. However, during the course of my research, I was given access to the working documentation of the various 'text production' bodies associated with the NC. Access was provided on the understanding that, in the process of writing up my research, the anonymity of individuals was safeguarded. Unsurprisingly, the documentation provided a rich, often fascinating insight into the work of the groups. In addition, it provided a means by which the 'truth problem' could at least partially be overcome through cross-reference between interview data, official documentation and other published sources such as accounts of the policy process by policy makers themselves.

Chapters 5 and 6 provide a detailed analysis of the work of the HWG, utilizing a triangulated combination of interview data, the information provided in the minutes of the group (which were voluminous, detailing most aspects of the HWG's eighteen-month lifetime) and semi-autobiographical works done by former working group members themselves (e.g. Guyver, 1990; Prochaska, 1990; Jones, 1991). Chapter 5 begins by analysing the composition of the HWG and then considers the circumstances leading to the production of the group's Interim Report (DES, 1989a). This chapter mainly uses the data provided in the minutes in order to maintain a narrative flow for the reader; this is continued in Chapter 6 which evaluates what was arguably the most important NC history text, namely the HWG's Final Report (DES, 1990a). The chapter ends with an analytical account of the HWG's work utilizing the interview data in order to consider the degree of political influence exerted upon the group. This section also makes reference to an interview conducted with Kenneth Baker which is cross-referenced to his own memoirs (Baker, 1993) and to those of Margaret Thatcher (1993).

The next chapter (Chapter 7) evaluates the response to the Final Report and analyses the discursive mediating role of the HA and the important events leading up to the production of the MacGregor proposals (DES, 1990b). The chapter considers the role of Margaret Thatcher in the history debate: interview data, correspondence, press accounts and some secondary sources are used to 'illuminate' this period of text production. Chapter 8 is devoted to the work of the next chief player in the policy process, namely the NCC's History Task Group (HTG). This chapter gives particular prominence to the degree of direct political interference in the debate again by using interview data cross-referenced to minutes, as well as references to the claims made by Graham with Tytler (1993) concerning the interventions in the debate by Kenneth Clarke. These educational/political circumstances are used to account for the eventual policy outcome, namely the original Statutory Order, the legal text of history in the NC which was to be implemented in schools in 1991 (DES, 1991a).

Changing History: Implementation, Reform and the Future

The final two chapters are concerned with history teaching past, present and future. Chapter 8 begins by considering history teachers' initial reactions to history in the NC and therefore touches upon the 'context of practice'. Using references to my own empirical work which was concerned with evaluating the views of history teachers in secondary schools during the period 1990–95, it evaluates teachers' perceptions of the policy process by focusing particular attention upon the reactions of history teachers to the policy texts produced between 1989 and 1994. This chapter (and the previous one) scrutinizes the claim that there was a degree of 'consensus' over the NC at this time (Roberts, 1990). By making reference to the problems associated with implementing the NC in general (content overload, bureaucracy, an over-complicated system of assessment) and which applied specifically also to history, the chapter describes the circumstances leading to the review of the NC conducted by Sir Ron Dearing. Chapter

8 therefore analyses the politics of the Dearing reforms relating to history, when the subject took centre of the political stage once more. The history review group established under Dearing to advise on the ways in which history in the NC could be reformed turned out to be one of the most controversial text production bodies of the period, as it became riddled with bitter divisions and in-fighting, publicly played out in the press. The chapter evaluates the committee's work and the circumstances surrounding the creation of the reformed Statutory Order (DFE, 1995).

The final chapter offers a retrospective analysis of the 'great history debate' by considering the extent to which the study of the educational politics of this period sheds light upon the complex relationship between education and the state during the 1980s and 1990s. In the process, it considers some of the messages that can be derived about educational policy formulation. Returning to the connection between the past and the future which was referred to at the beginning of this chapter, it places the debates over history, identity and nationhood at the end of the twentieth century within the wider context of speculation about the direction of history teaching and the role of history teachers in the twenty-first century.

Chapter 2

History, History Teaching and the Shaping of a Pedagogic Discourse

The major purpose of this chapter is to describe the development of professional discourses relating to history teaching in the 1970s and 1980s. By 'pedagogic discourse', I have in mind a regulation system which 'creates, maintains and legitimates' certain pedagogical practices and forms (Bernstein, 1986, p.209). This is what John (1991) calls 'the professional craft knowledge of the history teacher' or what Haydn (1993) has termed 'the chemistry of history lessons'. By describing the pedagogical ideologies, practices, beliefs and values which constituted a prevailing dominant pedagogic dis-course relating to history teaching immediately prior to the NC, it is then possible later in the book to determine the precise nature of the 'discursive gap' created by the 'alternative possibility' of the NC (see Edwards, 1995). It is important to stress here that what I shall be describing are the stated aims, ideas and values which were perceived to be constituting the most appropriate or desired practices relating to history teaching prior to the NC. There may, of course, be a 'gap' of a different (but equally significant) sort between stated aims and actual practice in this respect.

'Consensus' Over History Teaching in the Twentieth Century?

The creation of a NC was in some respects a novel departure, for throughout most of the twentieth century a tradition had emerged in English secondary schools of non-interference by the state in the details of what was actually taught in history classrooms (Gordon & Lawton, 1978). Early regulations in the twentieth century asserted teacher autonomy and variation of practice, particularly in relation to history teaching. Thus Aldrich & Dean (1991) refer, in a summary of the development of history teaching in the twentieth century prior to the NC, to the Board of Education's report of 1910–11 which advised that the history syllabus, more than other syllabuses, should be based upon the interests and initiatives of individual teachers; they also quote from the Board's *Handbook of Suggestions* of 1929 which stated that:

> The history syllabus, even for schools in similar circumstances, may properly vary accord-
> ing to the capacity and interests of the teacher. It is undesirable that all schools in any

particular locality should follow the same syllabus. Each teacher should think out and frame his own scheme, having regard to the circumstances of his own school, its rural or urban environment, its staffing and classification, and in some measure also to the books and the topics which most appeal to him. (Aldrich & Dean, 1991, pp.97–8)

A similar picture of teacher autonomy for the determination of history syllabuses existed in the secondary schools which had been established under the 1902 Education Act. Even though the regulations of 1904 listed the subjects to be taught (a list which have an 'uncanny air' of similarity with that of the NC: see Hargreaves, 1989, p.64; also Aldrich, 1990b), no specific requirements were laid down for history. Again, Aldrich & Dean refer to the 1908 Circular which declared that history was a subject 'in which perhaps more than any other there is room for the greatest variety of treatment' (ibid, p.98), encouraging them to conclude that 'history became a matter for historians and history teachers, both as individuals, and as interest groups' (ibid, p.99).

Other writers have emphasized the degree of autonomy afforded to history teachers in relation to the choice of historical content throughout the first three-quarters of the twentieth century (Gordon & Lawton, 1978). A major explanation of the lack of direct state involvement lies in what was actually taught in schools which had its roots in earlier traditions. Marsden (1989) has shown that throughout the nineteenth century, geography and history lessons had always had the intention of producing the 'good citizen' rooted in anti-papist Protestantism. Imperial developments in the 50 years or so prior to the First World War, as well as the impact of social Darwinism, promoted patriotism, heroism and racism (Tomlinson, 1990). The Boer War and the First World War increased patriotic fervour to new heights; thus Betts (1990) describes an attempt by Lord Meath to encourage patriotism in the school curriculum between 1902 and 1918.

The horrors of 1914–18 caused a reaction to jingoism. Grainger (1986), describing the nature of patriotism between 1900–39, states that 'while it was accepted that love of country might be properly derived from history lessons, doctrinal patriotism which stimulated hostility to other countries was discountenanced', contrasting this with other European countries, particularly France, where it 'was the nurse of patriotism' (Grainger, 1986, p.34). As Marsden (1989) has demonstrated, the inter-war period saw the first attempts in geography and history lessons to generate international under-standing and even 'sympathetic understanding' (the beginnings of empathy?). Significant also was the establishment of the League of Nations, formed in 1918 to encourage international understanding and citizenship. It tried to promote in history classrooms 'peace and war, cooperation rather than antagonism, culture rather than destruction, international rather than national ideals' (Aldrich, 1984, p.216).

Yet patriotism and Anglocentricism prevailed in the inter-war period, reflected in the 'lack of grasp that Anglocentric attitudes and the desire to promote a sympathetic understanding of other people were not necessarily congruent: thus the notion still prevailed that patriotism and imperialism, so long as they were of the British variety, were the keys to world understanding' (Marsden, 1989, p.522). This partly explains the lack of interest in the League of Nations publication *History Teaching and World Citizenship* in 1938. This contrasted with the popularity of a publication a year later which advocated a line of development or chronological approach to the teaching of British history which would, it was claimed, provide a sensible path towards good citizenship (Jeffreys, 1939).

As far as history teaching methods were concerned in the early twentieth century, the work of Aldrich (1984) and Aldrich & Dean (1991) have highlighted some of the innovative aspects of history teaching, citing Keatinge (1910) and Happold (1928) as evidence. Yet a commitment in some relatively isolated instances to creative teaching methods was balanced by a more conservative tendency to cultivate 'good citizenship' and traditional academic study due to two main reasons. First, Steele (1980) suggests that throughout the nineteenth and for most of the twentieth centuries, history teaching had been bedevilled by a lack of coherent theory underpinning the subject. Second, Elliott (1980) suggests that history teaching suffered from ineffective teacher training in the subject.

Aldrich & Dean (1991) emphasize that by the 1950s, some three-quarters of grammar schools were following a broadly chronological, English-orientated history course (plus some European history) with an emphasis upon modern history for examination purposes. Slater could parody the immediate post-war history syllabus in the following manner:

> Content was largely British, or rather Southern English; Celts looked in to starve, emigrate or rebel; the North to invent looms or work in mills; abroad was of interest once it was part of the Empire; foreigners were either, sensibly allies, or, rightly, defeated. Skills – did we even use the word? – were mainly those of recalling accepted facts about famous dead Englishmen, and communicated in a very eccentric literary form, the examination length essay. It was an inherited consensus, based largely on hidden assumptions. (Slater, 1989, p.1)

It is important not to overstate the 'inherited consensus' which prevailed in post-war history classrooms (Booth, 1969). Nevertheless, there was enough consensual belief both within and outside education that government should leave the 'secret garden' of the curriculum alone. It was not as though central government felt obliged to promote, through the history classroom, a sense of citizenship rooted in English Protestantism. Essentially, history teachers in England did it for them.

The Demise of 'Consensus'?

Any notion of 'consensus' – real or imaginary – which had developed over history teaching by the 1950s began to disintegrate from the 1960s onwards. A number of factors account for this. First, the growth of post-war immigration and the subsequent cultural diversity caused urban schools in particular to re-evaluate the orientation of their history syllabuses. Secondly, the growth of social science, with its emphasis upon conceptual analysis and social constructivism caused a consequent development of relativism. This was given greater resonance with Britain's relative decline on the world stage. Thirdly, significant historiographical developments caused a re-evaluation of the social focus of history; it was no longer the preserve of the 'great men' or 'history from above'. Finally, the most important factor in the move towards changes in history teaching was the growth in the 1960s of new subjects in the secondary sector such as social science and the development of integrated curricular approaches sponsored by the Schools Council (Schools Council, 1972; Blyth *et al.*, 1976). A combination of these factors caused a perception that the place of history in schools was under attack.

This perceived attack on the place and status of history in schools stimulated a number of polemical responses. Mary Price (1968) in a famous article declared that history was 'in danger' and that many history teachers were in a state of 'pessimism and perplexity' about the state of the subject. She claimed that history was disappearing from the timetable as a subject in its own right in the drive towards integration and social studies. Even more serious was the research evidence generated by the Schools Council in 1966 which showed that many pupils questioned the relevance of the subject and regarded it as 'useless and boring', causing a situation whereby 'history could lose the battle not only for its place in the curriculum but for a place in the hearts and minds of the young'. Price gave a number of reasons, stemming partly from the syllabus, partly from the methods of teaching, why history was apparently 'losing the battle' to other subjects. Firstly, the history syllabuses had not changed since the turn of the century: world history had made little headway because the history syllabuses remained 'obstinately a survey of British history'. Secondly, there was the 'deplorable' belief that history was only suited to more able pupils. Thirdly, the most serious charge was that history teaching relied far too heavily upon note taking and rote learning. Following this she called for a more efficient network for the dissemination of views on history teaching and the setting up of a Nuffield or Schools' Council type project to research the subject.

'New' History and the Role of the History Teacher

Price's call for greater networking did not fall upon deaf ears with the establishment, in 1969, of the HA's *Teaching History* which provided a forum for a debate over the nature of school history initiated by Price's warnings (see Wake, 1970). Central in this was discussion over what became known as the 'new history'. In some ways the new history was not new at all as the work of Keatinge (1910) and Happold (1928) cited by Aldrich (1984) testify. The debate over new history is important not only because it pre-empted many of the issues raised during the NC debate itself; its significance, as we shall see, lies in the impact it had upon shaping pedagogic discourse prior to the NC.

New history arose from the attempt to adopt rigour, theory and method to the teaching of history which was, according to Booth (1969), Price (1968) and Steele (1980) severely lacking. One advocate of new history pointed to the 'major problems' associated with defining the subject, such as the:

> patent lack of agreement about the basic propositions upon which history as a subject is constructed. Another is the great mass of information – facts – of which history is composed. Yet another is the methodology to be adopted (which) in practice too frequently follows the traditional lines of chronologically organized textbooks. (Jones, 1973, p.11)

The late 1960s and early 1970s witnessed a range of books and articles which were preoccupied with these and other issues. According to Gunning (1978) new history was heavily influenced by theories on child psychology. Hallam (1970) described the application of Piagetian theory for history teaching, particularly the importance of preoperational, concrete operational and formal operational thinking for the ways in which history teaching should be planned. Bruner's (1960) work also emphasized the importance of conceptual understanding; particularly important in this respect was the emphasis upon the spiral curriculum, namely that the cultivation of conceptual appreciation should start early in a child's career, albeit at a simple level and that this conceptual understanding should be cultivated in different contexts as the child develops. The application of Brunerian theory to history teaching was vital in the way that it placed emphasis upon method, process and skills. Pupils should therefore be introduced to the methodology of history and be made aware of history as a discipline with unique features, processes and structures.

Finally, the taxonomic work of Bloom encouraged teachers to explore the existence of a possible hierarchy of skills in history which could be taught in a progressive manner. Thus Coltham & Fines (1971) drew up their influential *Educational Objectives for the Study of History* which showed teachers the importance of being aware of 'what a learner can do as a result of having learned' and listed a whole series of 'learning outcomes' which history fostered, including attitudes such as attending, responding and imagining, through to skills and abilities such as vocabulary acquisition and reference skills, as well as more complex skills such as analysis, extrapolation, synthesis, judgement and evaluation. Thus Roberts (1973) described the application of the Coltham–Fines approach to his history department.

Whereas, as we have seen, for most of the twentieth century history teaching had little or no 'theory' to under-pin it (Steele, 1980) and relied instead upon academic history for its organizing influence (Aldrich, 1984), the application of educational theories to history teaching caused a fundamental re-conceptualization of the subject from that described by Jones (1973) above. Moreover, this process was given further articulation and intellectual force through teacher training departments and colleges (Pendry, 1990) which, as Elliott (1980) remarked, had been another obstacle to reforming history teaching in the inter-war period. Above all, the development of a theoretical base for the subject allowed history teachers to draw a distinction between 'school' and 'academic' history:

> There is an academic discipline called 'History'. There is also a school subject called 'History'. There is no self-evident reason why they have to do the same. If we are teaching fourteen-year-olds, we should subject everything we want to teach them, whether a fact, a concept or a skill to this question: 'Of what use, or potential use, is this knowledge to them?' We should not ask, 'Is this piece of knowledge, or this skill, part of the equipment of an academic historian?' because the vast majority of our pupils will never be academic historians. (Gunning, 1978, p.14)

Here was the emergence of a discourse centred on the relevance of the subject to pupils, not academic historians.

The implications of the application of theory through new history to the teaching of the subject in the 1970s were significant in a number of respects. The most obvious implication was the stress upon enquiry, method and innovative teaching styles (Garvey & Krug, 1977; Steele, 1976). More significant, perhaps, is that it led to a re-evaluation of the selection of historical content. As Chaffer (1973) argued, history teachers needed to think seriously and explicitly about their rationale for choosing to teach certain historical events. An over-emphasis upon chronology and the consequent tension upon the need to 'get through' the syllabus could be reduced through 'patch' or 'thematic' approaches to the selection of content. This therefore had the significant advantage of allowing the teacher to concentrate more precisely on the teaching methods that could be used. In addition, content should be selected on the basis of relevance to pupils; hence the development of world history (Chaffer & Taylor, 1975). It was therefore vital that 'history teaching must break out of the narrow nationalistic strait-jacket in which it has lived for so long' (Ballard, 1970, p.5).

For history teachers, the new history provided an opportunity for breaking out of another 'strait-jacket', namely the influence of academic history. The rationale for the selection of content, for example, represented a challenge to academic justifications for the teaching of certain elements of history (Elton, 1970). It is also interesting to note the language and points of reference in a number of the books cited above (and below), for the emphasis was upon the creative role of history teachers in shaping not only teaching methods but the actual selection of historical content. Thus, both the opportunities and responsibilities for designing history courses were the teacher's (Chaffer, 1973). The teacher had to be the 'pioneer' in curriculum development (Chaffer & Taylor, 1975, p.48). The importance of the teacher's role could not be under-estimated for 'ultimately the attitude and knowledge of the individual teacher hold the key to the future' (Steele, 1976, p.5). The history teacher was in an 'enviable position because the teacher can control the syllabus and the teaching method with few external constraints' (Jones, 1973, p.13) particularly as far as lower school syllabuses were concerned. External examinations still provided constraints for curriculum development but even here there were opportunities (Milne, 1973). The potential for history teachers to take responsibility for the future direction of history teaching was significant because:

> While in many countries the direction of the syllabus is under state control, either of the state or representative teachers, in Britain the onus for change lies squarely on the classroom teacher. (Ballard, 1970, p.11)

The Schools Council History Project and its Impact

The new history clearly had implications for the Schools Council for Curriculum and Assessment. In March 1972, four years after Price's call for research into history teaching, it announced that it was to fund a curriculum project on history, to be based at Leeds University, starting the following September. As was stated in *A New Look at History*, the object of the Project was to provide 'stimulus, support and materials' to help teachers 'revitalize their own practice in general and in particular to encourage greater "pupil participation" in the subject' (School Council History Project (SCHP) 13–16, 1976, p.8). It also had more fundamental intentions, there was a need for a project which:

> would help teachers to reconsider the place of history within the changing curriculum and especially its role in the various forms of inter-disciplinary studies which were currently being developed in schools. It also stressed the case for a project which would consider the problems of examining in history and promote models which would examine understanding rather than ill-digested rote-learning ... The Project began with a conscious attempt to re-think the philosophy of teaching history in school. (ibid, p.8)

Again, the precise language used in the above extract is interesting. Teachers were to be 'helped', not 'told' (discourse which, as we shall see, contrasted markedly with documentation published twenty or so years later). Basing its pedagogic strategies, philosophy and assessment procedures on some of the psychological research work cited above, the SCHP focused attention upon the process of history, stressing that history should be viewed as a distinct body of knowledge, requiring the cultivation of precise skills – for example the ability to evaluate evidence – in order to understand it. Moreover, it paid more precise attention to the definition of historical concepts such as change and continuity or causation. Its authors were concerned to make history generally more accessible across ability ranges; it was thus child-centred, gearing its aims explicitly at the 'needs of the adolescent'. History, said the SCHP, should enable pupils to understand the world around them and should assist their quest for self-identity. It was also concerned with stressing the variety of history and historical approaches. Thus, SCHP courses included social, economic and cultural history as well as political history. Historical events and periods were chosen for specific purposes: the history of medicine (a study in development), the American West (a study in depth), the Arab–Israeli or Northern Ireland conflicts (understanding of contemporary problems) and so on.

Slater (1989) has claimed that it was 'the most significant and beneficial influence on the learning of history and the raising of its standards to emerge this century' (p.2). Its importance, according to Sylvester (1994), lies in the ways that it provided a coherent philosophy and a rationale for the subject, widened the content of history in schools, established new ways of assessment (including teacher-assessed coursework) and influenced classroom methodology and aims. Yet there is sometimes a tendency to over-emphasize its achievements. One of its detractors in the 1980s (see Lang below) called it 'sacred cow history'. By the time of the NC debate, it still only accounted for just over a quarter of GCSE syllabuses. This may be because Schools History Project (SHP) (re-named after the abolition of the Schools Council in 1984: see Plaskow, 1985) represented a radical attempt at reforming secondary school history, perhaps too radical for the majority of teachers. There was also the problem of translating the theory of new history into practice (Rogers, 1984). SHP was certainly subject to critical scrutiny by teachers in the 1980s. Lang suggested that it was having more of a negative than a positive impact upon innovation in history teaching (cited in Williams, 1986). Using examiners' reports, Williams (1986) questioned whether SHP had an effect upon teaching methodology at all; he conceded that the project had 'done much to liberate school history from its former obsession with the transmission of a corpus of factual information' but questioned whether it encouraged a sufficient sense of chronology. In addition, he accused the Project of inertia in its selection of historical content. More significant was his claim that although teachers often selected SHP as a 'soft option', in fact in many ways it was too complex and as a result he concluded by suggesting that SHP had failed to alter the way history is taught in schools.

Similar themes were explored by Holmes (1986) in a study of history departments in one Local Education Authority (LEA) which suggested that the SHP's influence on history teaching amongst 13–16-year-olds was more limited than commonly believed at the time. Only 12 per cent of the schools in his study followed the SHP's *What Is History?* course through to examination, and he found that it put too much pressure on teachers. However, in contrast to Williams, Holmes' research indicated that SHP was having direct and indirect effects on the aims of history departments, including those who were not using SHP materials directly. This confirms Patrick's research (see below for detailed discussion) illustrating the more general impact that new history had upon ideas relating to the aims and objectives of history teaching in the 1980s.

New history and SHP had important influences in other ways. Two highly influential collections of essays on historical understanding and history teaching articulated much of its philosophy (Dickinson & Lee, 1978; Dickinson, Lee & Rogers, 1984). More significant, perhaps, is the influence over HMI; as early as 1977, HMI had suggested that the curriculum should be based upon eight areas of experience, to include history. Interestingly, the document placed emphasis upon evidence and historical skills, as well as the need to appreciate the views of people in the past (DES, 1977). This was given greater articulation in the 1985 publication *History in the Primary and Secondary Years* (DES, 1985a) which suggested that history courses should be planned around the needs of pupils. It did not specify the precise historical content to be taught, but offered broad suggestions that there should be a balance of British, world and local history and that history courses should be designed to cultivate conceptual appreciation and under-standing in history (Slater, 1991). Significant as these influences were over HMI, new history's real importance lay in its impact upon the GCSE (General Certificate of Secondary Education).

The Introduction of the GCSE

The introduction of the GCSE saw the beginnings of the government's involvement in the debate over the teaching of history, represented by Sir Keith Joseph's speech to the HA on 10 February 1984 (Joseph, 1984). Whereas Joseph was prepared to express his views on the nature of the curriculum, including history, and established the admin-istrative machinery at the DES to effect the reforms, his own neo-liberalism meant that he was not prepared to establish a system which prescribed what was actually taught – that would be left to his successor. Thus the working group set up by the DES to determine the new criteria for the history GCSE (the principle of a 'working group' was not an exclusively NC innovation) specified only general rather than specific content criteria (DES, 1985b). Given the tradition within history teaching for an eclectic array of syllabuses and approaches which had emerged since the 1970s this was under-standable. The time was simply not yet apposite for a detailed prescription of what should be taught in the history classrooms of England and Wales; therefore the GCSE criteria for history stated that it was 'in the professional tradition of the discipline and inherent in its nature that candidates should be able to study history in its varied contexts', reflected, for example, in the wide variety of CSE and GCE syllabuses. Thus the criteria stressed that examining groups should continue to provide a 'wide range of options to give freedom to innovate and to reflect local interests' and therefore it was 'not desirable to stipulate a minimum core of content' (DES, 1985b, para 4.1).

Thus, examining boards, not central government, would be given the opportunity to determine the precise content requirements of GCSE history syllabuses. Although the criteria affirmed that pupils should have the opportunity to study British history, it was suggested only that examining boards should offer at least one syllabus which helped pupils towards an understanding of the 'intellectual, cultural, technological and polit-ical growth of the United Kingdom'. In contrast, the criteria suggested that in their deliberations over content, the boards should 'bear in mind the linguistic and cultural diversity of society', an echo of the Swann Report published in the same year.

Moreover, the criteria embraced many of the principles of new history and the SHP.

In *A New Look at History*, SCHP had claimed that whereas 'most examinations in history test primarily the ability to recall information', it was putting forward a case 'for an additional assessment in history, not so much of the knowledge acquired as a result of studying the syllabus given but of the abilities pupils have acquired to think historically' (SCHP, 1976, p.53). Encouraged by the research of Booth (1980) and particularly its own research officer (Shemilt, 1980), it stressed the need not only for teaching but assessing historical concepts such as change, causation and empathy, as well as the process skills of evaluating historical evidence. The GCSE criteria thus specified that pupils should be able to recall historical knowledge but also that they should gain the ability to 'evaluate and select' knowledge and 'deploy' it in a coherent form. Pupils should thus be encouraged to develop a 'wide variety' of skills concerned with evaluating historical evidence.

Even more significant, perhaps, was that pupils were to be encouraged to empathize through the 'ability to look at events and issues from the perspective of people in the past'. The suggestions that history should provide a 'sound basis for further study and the pursuit of personal interest' and that the subject should encourage pupils to understand the present were also, as we have seen, SHP corner-stones. Another symbolic aspect of the criteria was that all teachers, not just those who taught SHP, should be encouraged to use teacher assessment (20 per cent of the new examination would be based on coursework) and differentiation by outcome through levels-related criteria. The criteria recognized that this was a new development for teachers and that therefore 'new developments and experimentation ... will be encouraged'.

In theory at least, teachers were being encouraged to enjoy more, not less, autonomy through the new examination. The story of GCSE implementation contrasts markedly with the ways in which the NC was conceived and implemented. GCSE actually confirmed the tradition of diversity and regional variation, albeit within a flexible national criteria and gave considerable ammunition to its critics (North, 1987); the most notoriously contentious issue concerning GCSE in this respect was the teaching and assessment of empathy.

The Debate Over Empathy

As Booth *et al.* (1986) have pointed out, volumes have been written on the nature of historical empathy, a reflection not only of the complexity of the concept but an indication also of the passions which it initiated. The GCSE's definition of empathy as 'an ability to look at events and issues from the perspective of people in the past' had its origins in the Ministry of Education's Pamphlet 23 of 1952 which urged teachers to cultivate in pupils 'a quality of sympathetic imagination ... humility about one's own age and the thing to which one is accustomed, a willingness to enter a different experience' (quoted in Aldrich & Dean, 1991, p.99). Knight (1989) has traced its origins through the long tradition of attempts by historians to understand (rather than sympathize) with the objects of their study by considering as objectively as possible the circumstances in which they lived and thus the factors that motivated them.

Even though history teachers as long ago as Keatinge and Happold had always encouraged pupils to think 'empathetically' in one form or another, this was done implicitly through imagination, reconstruction and understanding. Teachers were now being asked to teach empathy explicitly and, more significantly, they were being expected to assess it. This was particularly demanding given that empathy was concerned with the affective rather than cognitive domains (Low-Beer, 1989). Research had been done on empathy (Shemilt, 1980, 1984) but inevitably there was uncertainty amongst many teachers who had no direct experience of teaching it; thus there was confusion between empathy and 'historical imagination' (Lee, 1984). Booth *et al.* (1986) suggested that empathy could be encouraged through effective questioning, reconstructive techniques such as role play and the use of historical fiction, as well as the full range and variety of historical evidence. Yet they also highlighted the differences between 'everyday', 'stereotypical' and 'differentiated' empathy and in the process emphasized the challenges of teaching empathy effectively, stressing that 'good historical empathy' was 'difficult to achieve' (p.8).

Given these demands, little wonder that examiners' reports and surveys in the late 1980s should emphasize that empathy was causing teachers great challenges (Brown, 1989; Daugherty *et al.*, 1991). Truman (1990) has shown that the teaching and assessment of empathy was in a state of development even by the late 1980s, that some teachers viewed it with 'hesitancy' and that their approach to empathy was 'less than perfect'.

The Emergence of a Discourse?

The above sections considered the historical and professional factors which shaped history teaching, particularly since 1972. By making reference to research studies undertaken in the 1970s and 1980s, it is now possible to consider the nature of historical pedagogic discourse on the eve of the NC debate.

Two studies in the mid-1970s demonstrated the apparently limited impact of new history on influencing teachers' philosophy of history teaching. Thus, history was still 'content-based, chronologically arranged, nationally-biased, politically orientated, formal in learning methods, limited in resources, and deficient in attention both to objectives and their evaluation' (Davies & Pritchard, 1975, p.114). A survey of 60 primary teachers and 60 secondary teachers conducted in 1973 concluded that there was little consensus on the purposes of school history. The most popular purpose identified in the survey was to 'develop understanding of how the present evolved', followed by 'interest and enjoyment' and the 'cultivation of human understanding'. Yet less than a third of the secondary teachers in the survey identified 'the development of thinking skills' as a chief aim of their teaching (Harries, 1975).

Despite the controversy over new history and empathy within the GCSE, much of the available research on the nature of history teachers' views conducted in the late 1980s demonstrate support for the philosophy of the GCSE and the principles underpinning new history. Patrick's important ESRC (Economic & Social Research Council) sponsored research conducted between 1985 and 1987 on the aims of history teachers demonstrated the indirect influence new history had over teachers' conceptualization of their own pedagogical practice (Patrick, 1987, 1988a, 1988b). The research focused upon two main areas: the historical content taught in secondary schools, and the aims and justifications which were articulated by history teachers in its defence. With regard to historical content, the research showed that in the lower years history was organized broadly around a chronological outline, although not rigidly so, through a selection of topics and patches. In year one, ancient and early British history was common but had virtually disappeared by year three where there was greater variety than in earlier years. The industrial revolutions, modern world history, the world wars and revolutions predominated. At years four and five, over half the schools chose modern world history at examination level, with a third offering either SHP or social and economic history (Patrick, 1988a).

Patrick's evaluation of history teachers' aims showed that the most common justification for the teaching of the subject was that pupils would find the subject enjoyable and interesting, and that it could be used to gain an insight into the present. History teachers also justified the subject on the grounds that it cultivated skills such as the ability to use evidence, to detect bias, to think in a logical, critical and analytical manner and to formulate an argument. The subject was also justified through the conceptual understanding that it encouraged of ideas such as causation, change, continuity, chronology and empathy. The data revealed that three-quarters of the teachers in the survey 'expressed views favourable' to the list of aims of history teaching as outlined in the 1985 HMI document (DES, 1985a), namely: an awareness of the nature of evidence, an appreciation of change and continuity, an understanding of cause, historical empathy/imagination, an ability to pose historical questions, a sense of chronology and time and language skills. Patrick therefore concluded 'that most of these teachers would broadly support the "new" history with its emphasis on skills-based, evidence-based work' (Patrick, 1988, p.12).

Patrick also went to pains to emphasize that although these types of aims 'predominated', the research also demonstrated diversity and variety in the articulation of the justifications for the subject. Thus, overall more than a 100 'distinct aims' were identified in the research. She also noted that 'the teachers had no difficulty in describing their aims but found it more problematic to explain how they translate them into practice' (Patrick, 1987). This may, of course, be a good example of the contrast between the rhetoric of *stated* aims and the *actuality* of classroom *practice* (see introduction to this chapter). This aspect of the research was interesting: it showed that although it is difficult to talk about a precise, carefully defined pedagogic discourse which had emerged by the mid-1980s, nevertheless it is possible to suggest a degree of emerging unanimity regarding the purposes of school history teaching based upon the aims of new history.

Other surveys and research conducted during the late 1980s demonstrated the impact of new history and the GCSE. An Historical Association survey on the early impact of the GCSE report that schools had adopted an 'evidence based approach to learning' which was 'less didactic' and 'more open' in its approach to teaching and learning (Brown, 1989). The survey also revealed that a lack of adequate In-Service Training (INSET) provision had led to difficulties relating to assessment; teachers were often confused and unsure about many of the new assessment techniques such as differentiation, criterion referencing and coursework management. Nevertheless, even this survey which analysed the early period of GCSE implementation demonstrated support for the new examination and 'that though there may have been concern about the administrative procedures of GCSE most respondents felt that the examination had been beneficial and successful' (ibid, p.35). These findings broadly confirmed those articulated in other surveys (Kingdon & Stobart, 1988; DES, 1988), including Daugherty *et al.*'s (1991) extensive study of GCSE implementation which found an 'overwhelmingly positive response' from all those from whom research evidence was obtained to the changes which the GCSE had brought about.

In terms of evaluating, then, history teachers' conceptualization of pedagogic discourse in the late 1980s, the conclusion from the available research evidence would suggest that on the eve of the NC, most history teachers in secondary schools preferred 'to marry (or have come to accept) traditional and new history practices rather than change radically their everyday procedures and established opinions solely on the merits of either ideology' (Truman, 1990, p.10). Despite tensions existing over assessment, particularly with regard to empathy, it seems that a broad pedagogic discourse had emerged in schools about the nature and purposes of history teaching. This discourse or 'professional craft knowledge' (John, 1991) held the view that school history, or the 'chemistry of history lessons' (Haydn, 1993), should be interesting, enjoyable and accessible to pupils; that history teaching should not be exclusively associated with the transmission of knowledge and content but that it should be taught in a way which cultivated a range of intellectual skills and historical concepts through a predominantly evidence-based approach (Patrick, 1987, 1988a, 1988b). To Truman, this 'practical and philosophical balance between old and new perspectives' involved:

> a genuine desire to be able to develop critical thinking skills and an understanding of historical methodology in pupils without abandoning cherished characteristics for their former rationale and practice such as chronological perspective, editorial skills, an appropriate depth of content and the opportunity to use the dramatic storyline. (Truman, 1990, p.16)

This set of complex pedagogical history was influenced more by the qualified relativism of Carr (1961) than by the historical certainty of Elton (1967). It was essentially what Evans (1994) has referred to as a combination of 'scientific' and 'relativist/reformer' pedagogical traditions in the USA which placed emphasis upon:

> use of competing interpretations, the teacher as guide rather than arbiter of truth, and emphasis on thinking about important questions from history . . . these teachers have found that the spirit of inquiry, the spirit of questioning, when played out in their classrooms, serves to stimulate student interest in activity, and thought. (pp.186–7)

Crucially, this was also a discourse rooted in a perceived notion of professional autonomy, for research such as that conducted by Brown (1989) showed that heads of department enjoyed relative autonomy with regard to the selection of historical content as a consequence of the GCSE. Similarly, as we have seen, Patrick's research illustrated the variety of history courses on offer in lower school syllabuses within a broad, chronological framework from Ancient Civilization to the Second World War, with modern world history predominating in the upper school (even here there was a broad choice of syllabuses: see Tyldesley, 1983). This variety reflected the importance of local decision making. The need to be sensitive to the local needs and requirements of schools explained the general criteria of the GCSE (Roy, 1986) and reflected the view that they 'should be allowed, within a broad framework, to construct their own syllabuses according to local needs and interest' (Brown, 1989, p.33). Furthermore, although influenced by wider academic views of history, there were substantial conceptualized differences between the highly complex and situated knowledge of the 'chemistry of history lessons' and 'the academic view' of history (Haydn, 1992b). In this respect, 'there are ways in which schools history has its own agenda' (Hake & Haydn, 1995, p.21).

How much 'real' autonomy was actually enjoyed by teachers during this period is subject to debate (see Lawton, 1980; Blenkin, Edwards & Kelly, 1992; Scarth, 1987), yet its importance lies in the fact that it was *perceived*. Professional autonomy in regard to the selection of historical content was closely connected with the notion of creating the 'chemistry' for effective learning. After all, historical skills or conceptual understanding could not be effectively acquired if they were not 'related to content that has some inherent interest and appears to relate to the lives of the pupils' (DES, 1985a, p.12). According to Haydn (1992b, p.9) by selecting 'uninteresting' content, the history teacher ran the risk of 'not engaging the commitment and enthusiasm' of pupils which seemed to contradict the whole notion of pedagogic activity in the history classroom; after all, 'interest, relevance and accessibility are the *sine qua non* of teaching history in ordinary schools'.

This notion of syllabus construction within a broad framework based upon local contexts and needs is vital for appreciating the nature of pedagogic discourse on the eve of the NC and explains the subsequent reaction by history teachers to the imposition of centrally prescribed content. The heated debate over the 'common core', for example, within the 5–16 curriculum prior to the announcement of the NC showed the sensitivities over this issue (see Chapter 4). On the eve of the NC debate, Truman could write:

> Significantly, at this point in time, teachers are concerned about both the explicit definition of content by central government and the quality of contextual knowledge which may be deemed appropriate to uphold the integrity of historical study in the schools of the twenty-first century. (Truman, 1990, p.12)

He went on to state in a portentous manner that 'notwithstanding the teacher's classroom autonomy' to resist 'the influence of central control', he warned that it was inevitable that the government through the NC would 'prescribe a detailed description of the content, skills and processes which will be seen to satisfy some, antagonize others and strait jacket the rest of the teachers of history' (ibid).

Chapter 3

Discourse of Derision:
The New Right and History Teaching

This chapter analyses a vital aspect of the political context in which the debate over history teaching in the NC took place. Firstly, it considers the nature of conservatism in the 1980s and 1990s, focusing attention upon the ideology of the New Right (Eatwell & O'Sullivan, 1989). Secondly, it describes some of the strategies and tactics employed by the New Right in pursuit of its political and educational aims. Thirdly, and crucially, by concentrating in detail on the words of some prominent activists, it analyses the nature of the New Right's derision of history teaching in the 1980s, thus illustrating its contribution to the 'context of influence' on the eve of the NC.

Neo-Conservatism, Nationhood and Education

Reference was made in Chapter 1 to writers who have stressed that New Right ideology combined neo-liberalism and neo-conservatism, involving both 'competition and compliance' (Levitas, 1986) as well as 'enterprise and heritage' (Corner & Harvey, 1991). These were hardly natural bedfellows and often caused tensions which themselves were reflected in policy. As Belsey (1986) has demonstrated, whereas neo-liberals have emphasized the market, the individual and *laissez faire* as their major ideological goals, neo-conservatives by contrast placed stress upon authority, discipline, hierarchy, the nation and strong government. As Hall & Jacques (1983) have stressed, what united them under Thatcherism was a belief in the need for a strong state, albeit for different reasons. Neo-liberals did not value a strong state in itself but saw it as a means of creating a strong economy. By contrast, some neo-conservatives saw a strong state as an end in itself to create order and stability through institutions like the family and the school (Quicke, 1988).

The growth of neo-conservative thought in the 1970s and 1980s was associated, like neo-liberalism, with the growth of new associations and pressure groups (Griggs, 1989). An important feature of the most important neo-conservative groups was that they were often formed by academics. Two of the most significant were the Conservative Philosophy Group (1975) and the Salisbury Group (1977). They produced a number of influential publications, two of the most significant being *Conservative Essays* (Cowling, 1978) and the journal *The Salisbury Review* edited by Roger Scruton (Scruton, 1988a, 1988b). Scruton, of course, has become well known as a dedicated proponent of neo-conservatism with regard to the 'politics of culture' (Scruton, 1981). I want to argue that his work was influential in shaping the intellectual climate within which the debate over history in the NC was conducted. Moreover, by analysing the fundamentals of neo-conservative thought itself, we can see how and why history and history teaching in schools (particularly the type of history teaching described in the previous chapter) became such a focus for derision.

Neo-conservative ideology can be summarized under the headings of authority, hierarchy and nation. Neo-conservatives saw themselves as engaged in a cultural struggle in the 1970s and 1980s; in a struggle against social welfarism, cultural relativism (including multi-culturalism and anti-racism), permissiveness, lawlessness, disorder and anarchy. This has encouraged writers such as Hall & Jacques (1983) and Seidel (1986) to stress neo-conservatives' hegemonic intentions. Gramsci (1971), of course, stressed the importance of ideology in the process of class domination. The dominant ideology works on and within a range of social institutions – including education – to define a certain set of values and culture which is regarded as correct and normal. Crucial in the process is the role of intellectuals in their work to define and justify the main features of the dominant culture. Thus, as Seidel (1986) points out, both the British and French New Right were engaged in a cultural battle against the post-war social democratic consensus. Education provided a vital field for this sort of cultural struggle. Quicke (1988, p.8) describes this process as an attempt to 'to conquer the hearts and minds via a slow drip feed into the nation's consciousness' through education. Other writers have also noted the educational arena as the focus for cultural struggle (Apple, 1993; Aranowitz & Giroux, 1986; Giroux, 1992).

It is difficult to over-estimate the contribution and influence of Scruton in the construction of this neo-conservative discourse. In the pages of *The Salisbury Review* and in important books such as *The Meaning of Conservatism* (1980) Scruton offered an intellectual and scholarly articulation of conservative beliefs. Yet (ironically like all good Gramscians) Scruton was also active in the popular sphere – he wrote a remarkably large number of newspaper articles, particularly for *The Times* in the 1980s and contributed to radio and television programmes too. This populist element was characteristic of neo-conservatism in the 1980s and, as we shall see, became a particularly important factor in the debate over history. In *The Salisbury Review*, Scruton was able to give voice to a wide range of intellectuals – including philosophers and writers and (more significantly) educationalists and historians – whose views were then given prominence in the press by Scruton himself; for example, Honeyford's essay on *Education and Race* (1984) was warmly supported by Scruton in *The Times*.

To Scruton, the conservative disposition placed obligations to the nation above individual autonomy and the rights of man (Scruton, 1980). This obligation to civil society stemmed from shared inheritance rooted in a sense of nationhood, for the 'nation state is the state at the extreme of self-consciousness' (ibid, p.185). According to Jones (1989), one of Scruton's strengths in the 1980s, unlike other intellectuals, was his ability to portray himself as having a close association with the intuition, prejudices and instinctive reactions of the citizens of 'the nation'. This came from his belief in a common, natural, unifying culture, a sort of 'inner knowledge' which only those who have shared its unique customs, habits and rituals understand and appreciate.

As Seidel (1986) and others have shown, the crucial agent in the construction of this notion of 'nation' was the idea of a common, inherited past, a belief in Enoch Powell's 'rootedness' and a 'continuity' with the past or a 'shared' heritage. She cites Powell's belief that a nation which abandoned its 'common status' in favour of the 'non-identity' of multi-culturalism is on the road to oblivion. This 'elision of nation, culture and race' was a constant theme running through neo-conservative discourses in the 1980s. One of the best examples was Casey's 'One nation: the politics of race' (Casey, 1982). Like Powell, Casey despised the 'invasion' by foreign culture of British homogeneous culture; the only solution to this 'problem' was either assimilation into the true 'common' culture or, if this was unacceptable, repatriation. Significantly, this argument was justified on the grounds of history and tradition. Thus British and English history could not be understood without respect for 'sentiments of patriotism' which went with a 'continuity of institutions, shared experiences, language, customs, kinship' (quoted in Seidel, 1986, p.112).

According to Scruton (1986) all this stemmed from the belief in a particular culture because without it the nation's citizens would not have the sense of 'belonging' within a 'common enterprise'. Vital in the process of achieving a 'common culture' was the role of history; it followed that:

> The first concern of the history teacher must be to teach the history of Britain, so that a child may understand the past in terms of its present and observable residue ... (which creates) ... that informed awareness of history as a living process, a form of communication with the past and the future, which stems from an awareness of the 'pastness' of everything one touches, and of the evolving nature of existing social and political arrangements. (Scruton, 1986, pp.134–5)

The Salisbury Review attacked multi-culturalism and anti-racism and the progressive ideology which under-pinned it for undermining the promotion of the idea of a 'common' culture through education. To Scruton, anti-racism was diametrically opposed to the homogeneous, 'common', 'practical knowledge' culture which was the legitimate foundation of the British nation. Education had become corrupted by those influences which the natural conservative disposition so passionately opposed: modern progressivism and relativism questioned cherished principles, values and institutions. In 1985 he contributed to *Education and Indoctrination* in which he highlighted the threat to cultural unity posed by relativism (Scruton, Ellis-Jones & O'Keeffe, 1985). Following Powell and Casey above, the argument presented was essentially that anti-racism posed a threat to the whole notion of Britishness. It was an affront to claim, as anti-racists did, that the values of imperialism had inculcated British schools. Deep scepticism was held of the attempt to 'invent' a multi-cultural history for Britain: such an attempt was unnatural and dangerous because of the threat it posed to the 'true' British identity. Not only were such attempts perceived to be anti-educational but posed a totalitarian threat through indoctrination and overt politicization. At the root of the neo-conservative detestation of multi-culturalism and anti-racism was the opposition to relativism (Scruton, 1986).

Scruton contributed to one of the most important New Right pamphlets on education in the 1980s, namely the Hillgate Group's *Whose Schools? A Radical Manifesto* (Hillgate Group, 1986). Its importance lay not only in the arguments that it presented (much of which, as we have seen, was endorsed in the ERA) but in the language and rhetorical devices used in the process to debunk alternative educational voices. In this sense, it provided a particularly illustrative example of the New Right discourse of derision and it is for that reason that I want to devote attention to it in some detail here.

As Quicke (1988) has indicated, a common feature of New Right discourse was the stress on crisis, that the education system was in turmoil, that 'consensus' over education had broken down, that parents could no longer have any faith in a system which was geared towards the needs of producers (teachers and LEAs) and not the consumers (parents and pupils). *Whose Schools?* was a good example of this sort of argument. Thus, according to its authors, the 'crisis' had arisen because the educational system had been corrupted by progressivist trends such as 'curriculum reform' or 'child-centred learning', the product of years of 'egalitarian propaganda' initiated by departments of education in universities. The 'traditional curriculum' had been 'displaced' in favour of a 'politicized' curriculum consisting of 'artificial' or 'soft' subjects such as integrated studies, which led inevitably to a decline in standards, particularly in comparison to other countries. All this had 'undermined the attempt to preserve, enhance and pass on the precious heritage of our culture, replacing tried and lasting subjects with spurious alternatives' (Hillgate Group, 1986, p.3).

One of the main solutions offered by this neo-conservative tirade was unashamedly neo-liberal, thus illustrating the close relationship between the two ideological strands within the New Right. Schools should be opened to the market, owned by individual trusts and not LEAs or 'self appointed experts' so that their 'survival should depend on their ability to satisfy their customers', managed effectively by headteachers. Again, the neo-conservative tension relating to state intervention was expressed. According to the Hillgate Group, in an ideal world education should not be the responsibility of the state but it had to interfere in order to maintain standards and uniformity. Intervention of some sort was particularly needed to ensure that teaching should have as one of its main priorities 'the survival of knowledge and culture'. In order to do this, teachers needed to be subject to much more precise regulation, after all 'consensus has broken down' and it was 'no longer possible to leave so much to the conscience of the individual teacher' (p.9). The main solution according to the Hillgate Group was a 'national curriculum' which would ensure 'the values of a traditional education' with, at its core, reading, writing and arithmetic but also the 'proven' subjects such as foreign languages, history and literature, part of a tested curricular of the 'lore and tradition of our country'. After all, these ensured 'a testable and coveted body of knowledge' which it was 'the duty of any educational system to pass on from generation to generation' (p.7).

The NC would have to be backed up by an 'exacting examination system' designed to 'test children's knowledge and aptitudes', unlike the 'dangerous and unjustified' GCSE which was a product of 'egalitarian thinking' and had led to a 'decline in standards'. Examination results, along with any other relevant information, needed to be published, thus allowing parents the opportunity to 'choose' the best schools for their children. Schools could be inspected not by HMI who had been 'subverted by the bureaucratic self-interest and fashionable ideology of the educational establishment' but by 'independent' inspectors, subject to parliamentary accountability.

What united neo-conservatives like the Hillgate Group and neo-liberals such as those from the Institute of Economic Affairs, for example Sexton (1987), was the belief in the primacy of the parent-as-consumer over the teacher-as-monopoly producer. Teacher collectivity, autonomy and control through trade unions and LEAs needed to be swept away in favour of the free market through 'choice' and 'competition'. What distinguished Sexton's purely Hayekian free market solution from the Hillgate agenda was the latter's propensity towards interfering in the educational arena to ensure that certain sacred values were upheld. Thus, in a follow-up to *Whose Schools?* published in the following year, the Hillgate Group articulated in greater detail their justification of state involvement in education (Hillgate Group, 1987). Without state interference, 'the knowledge, skill and culture upon which our society' had been been founded would be 'irretrievably lost' due to the teaching of the 'misguided relativism' of multi-culturalism which threatened the 'traditional values of Western societies' (p.3). The aim of the state through education had to be to ensure that minorities were integrated into 'the national culture, and to ensure a common political loyalty' (p.4).

Explaining the Effectiveness of New Right Discourse: the Impact of Authoritarian Popularism

I now want to draw breath slightly and offer an analytical explanation for the New Right's success in the field of education. Inevitably, I shall be referring not only to the success of New Right in this respect but to the more widespread popular appeal of Thatcherism in the 1980s. Thatcherism's appeal and success confounded intellectuals at the time and initiated a vigorous debate within left intellectual circles (see for example, Hall, 1985; Jessop *et al.*, 1984). Hall (1979) explained Thatcherism's appeal by stressing the hegemonic nature of a New Right which was pragmatic and politically astute enough to be able to embrace both neo-conservative and neo-liberal elements. Thatcherism was effective, according to Hall, because it acquired an 'authoritarian popularism' which combined a respect for 'nation, family, duty, authority, standards, traditionalism' with neo-liberal competition, the market and anti-collectivism. This ideology often involved 'applying simplifying analytic schemes to complex events' (Hall & Jacques, 1983, p.22), for example, in the field of education. Authoritarian populism was not simply a rhetorical discourse aimed at winning short term political gain but appealed (and still appeals) to real lives, to real people and connected with their real, lived experiences, people who in the uncertain 1970s and 1980s felt confused, concerned and worried about seemingly bewildering changes in economic, social, cultural and political life. In presenting straightforward solutions to this crisis, the New Right sought to appeal directly to people's intuitive notion of 'common sense' (Hall, 1985; Hall, 1988). Popular authoritarianism thus offered a rich, varied mixture of issues and themes with a long history – hierarchy, nation, standards, the family – all of which have a sense of appeal during a time of uncertainty (Smith, 1994).

The application of these sorts of ideas in education had their origin, of course, in the *Black Papers* of the 1960s and early 1970s, written by an eclectic collection of academics, teachers, philosophers and writers. In this sense, the later works of the Hillgate Group and others were simply re-iterations of earlier themes and ideas. The first *Black Paper* accused progressive educational ideas of causing a decline in educational standards and values; the demise of the grammar school in favour of comprehensive schools was particularly lamented (Cox & Dyson, 1969a). The second initiated the idea of a 'crisis' in education (Cox & Dyson, 1969b). Although these early papers were essentially defensive in nature and were regarded by many as eccentric, they gained a considerable degree of circulation, with the first three copies selling nearly 80,000 by 1971 (Salter & Tapper, 1988).

The *Black Papers* had established a populist, authoritarian discourse on education which was expressed by various New Right groups such as the Hillgate Group, the Centre for Policy Studies and the Social Affairs Unit in the 1980s which themselves had an impact on the Tory Party (Knight, 1990; Lawton, 1992, 1994). Yet the real significance of popular authoritarian discourse lies in the impact it had upon wider public perceptions of education. Dale (1989) thus described ways in which New Right activists sought to elevate 'common sense above theory' and the 'people against the experts' in education. Such experts and educational theory had merely betrayed the 'true' interests of the people, the William Tyndale affair being a good example. Dale notes that one of the main reasons for the success of this popular authoritarian discourse was the use of the popular press (p.85).

Authoritarian populist discourse, then, held in contempt the theories and concepts of trendy experts which have merely corrupted true education. What was needed was a return to fundamentals, to tried and tested methods of pedagogy and to traditional subjects and values. I now want to examine, more precisely, the ways in which these sorts of New Right discourses contributed to ideas on history teaching. To what extent, for example, did neo-conservative views on nation, authority and hierarchy impact upon debates over history teaching in the press in the 1980s? How did the populist authoritarian distrust of research and innovation result in a call for a more 'common sense' approach to history teaching? Crucially, to what extent and in what ways did these sorts of discourses contrast with the 'pedagogic' discourses outlined in the previous chapter?

'Setting the Pace and the Agenda': The Genealogy of New Right Discourses on History Teaching

It was hardly surprising that New Right activists became intensely interested in two areas of the curriculum in particular: English and history. According to Jones there were a number of reasons why the Right saw a need to intervene in these 'chosen battlefields':

> The kinds of understanding of culture prevalent on the right led it towards these areas, and it was there that its political project could most easily take hold, in developing themes of identity and nation. It was also the case that English and history were strongpoints of opposition, where radical ideas were deeply embedded ... History in schools, with its relativistic methods and increasing bias towards the social and the economic reflected the work of Marxist and radical historians in creating what one critic called 'a shop steward syllabus' of modern history. (Jones, 1989, pp.64–5).

Similar points are made by others who stress the New Right's hegemonic intentions in the UK (Phillips, 1992b; Crawford, 1995). In the USA, inspired by such intellectuals as Bloom (1987) and Ravitch (1985), the New Right also intervened in debates over the teaching of history (Cornbleth, 1995; Seixas, 1993; see also Gagnon & Bradley Commission, 1989). Thus, Shor described attempts by American conservatives to restore 'Standard English, a traditional reading list, and cleansed versions of history (the

"American Heritage")' and the call for a core curriculum, rejecting the 'ideological diversity of the protest era' (Shor, 1986, p.13). Kaye (1991) has shown the similarities between the British and American New Right in these respects, in particular, the influence of New Right ideology upon academic historiography. I now want to describe in considerable detail the specific 'discourse of derision' as applied to history and history teaching which emerged in the UK in the 1980s prior to the establishment of the HWG.

The previous sections described the outburst of polemics on education from various New Right pressure groups, such as the Hillgate Group, the Social Affairs Unit and the Centre for Policy Studies. All had neo-liberal connections but articulated conservative and populist sentiments on history teaching. The Centre for Policy Studies, in particular, was to prove particularly active in attacking the philosophies relating to history teaching described in Chapter 2 (see Lawlor, 1995). I now want to suggest that the significance of these New Right groups lies in the ways they were able to raise the profile of history teaching from the professional to the public domains. This, of course, was no mere coincidence: a characteristic feature of populist authoritarian discourse, as we saw in the previous sections, involved publicization, mainly through the press. This was a conscious attempt to wrestle debates away from a monopolistic 'establishment' to a wider public arena and in the process construct a discourse around it. In doing so, New Right intellectuals utilized a series of social and political networks and often were members of more than one pressure group (see Griggs, 1989). Later, as we shall see, some of them were to be invited into the policy making process itself.

The Centre for Policy Studies, in particular, was able to cultivate powerful allies. Margaret Thatcher, for example, even wrote the introduction to one of the first of the Centre's publications on history (Thatcher, 1979). Slater (1989) argues that by consequently publishing no less than seventeen pamphlets on education, five dealing exclusively or predominantly with history, the Centre for Policy Studies set the 'pace and agenda' for the debate over the history curriculum in the late 1980s and the subsequent debate over the NC. One of the first of these publications thus mourned the loss of 'strong and powerful visions of the past which inspired the nation as it went about its daily life' (Thomas, 1979, p.6). The reason for the decline in faith in 'our institutional and cultural heritage' was, according to Thomas, 'a range of foolish misconceptions' about the past such as a 'distorted' view of imperialism. All of this was part of a wider attack upon the principle of capitalism; 'strong and powerful visions of the past' (p.6) were needed because they were 'fundamental to free enterprise' (p.7). Other Centre for Policy Studies publications attacked the new GCSE examinations, particularly in history (Hiskett, 1988). These proved to be preparatory attacks prior to the wholescale denunciation of history in the NC (see Lawlor, 1989, 1990, 1991).

The following sections describe this discourse of derision relating to history teaching by analysing the texts of four of the most significant and high profile contributors of the 1980s. This is done in order to illustrate the utilization of language and the use of 'words and concepts as an integral part of cultural struggle' (Seidel, 1986, p.107). Three of these expressed their views through Centre for Policy Studies publications (Beattie, 1987; Deuchar, 1987, 1989; Kedourie, 1988); the fourth is the extraordinary contribution of Partington (1986) to a collection of essays on education produced by the Social Affairs Unit. This essay was extraordinary not only in the claims that it made and in the particularly robust language that it employed, but also in the ways that it contrasted so markedly with Partington's earlier moderately liberal (and highly perceptive) views on the history curriculum (Partington, 1980a; 1980b).

Partington was also exceptional in comparison to the other writers selected for attention in that he was the only one who could be said to have been part of the 'educational establishment'. He had been a headteacher, an education officer, an examiner and a lecturer in education. Beattie was a history lecturer but certainly did not regard himself as part of the establishment which he set out to attack. By contrast, Helen Kedourie's credentials for contributing to the debate over history was that she was studying at the College of Law in London, and had formerly been educated at St Paul's Girls School and at King's College London (Kedourie, 1988). Yet of all the many campaigners and polemicists against the educational establishment and the developments in history teaching in the 1970s and 1980s, few contributed more significantly and energetically to highlighting the perceived faults in the system than Stuart Deuchar. By his own admission, Deuchar had limited experience of teaching history: he was a 'small farmer' and had taught history in a private school for two years (Deuchar, 1989). Yet this limited educational experience goes a considerable way towards explaining his motivation and his objects of derision. Deuchar was both a member of the Campaign for Real Education and a Centre for Policy Studies pamphleteer. His contempt for the educational establishment, his bitter opposition to the progressive methodology and conceptual frameworks represented by the SHP and his calls for a return to traditional history and pedagogy epitomized the 'common sense populist' strand of New Right thinking in the 1980s and which had its origins in the *Black Papers*. Unlike many other rightist polemicists, Deuchar was never afraid to articulate his views directly with teachers themselves. Thus, he attended many HA and SHP conferences throughout the country in the 1980s and early 1990s. Deuchar was the Mary Whitehouse of the history world: keeping a concerned eye on the moral barometer of the subject, which had became corrupted by the trends and fanciful whims of the 'new history' which had pervaded school history over two decades.

As we shall see, each of the writers had particular objects of derision – for Beattie it was the 'politicization' and watering down of academic history; for Kedourie it was the 'evils' of 'new history'; for Partington it was the hi-jacking of history teaching by 'neo-Marxists'; for Deuchar it was above all the demise of British political history in schools. Yet all touched upon some common, fundamental conservative themes, centred around an attack on the development of 'new history' and the SHP in particular. The common, unifying themes of these discourses as well as the solutions offered are summarized below.

When 'History was History': The 'Cultural Crisis' and the 'Flight from British History'

As we saw in the previous chapter, a characteristic theme of conservative restorationist discourse is the belief in the sanctity of the past, a sort of 'golden age', a time when education was based upon sound, certain principles which worked. Therefore, the complexity and research-driven philosophy of the 'new history' contrasted markedly with the past when, in Deuchar's words, 'a school was a school and a teacher was a teacher and history was – more or less – history' (Deuchar, 1987, p.1). Beattie mourned the loss of a period when 'Once upon a time, most British children were introduced to history by looking at the British past' (Beattie, 1987, p.17). Partington contrasted the 'mild socialist consensus' on history teaching in the 1950s and 1960s with the politicization of history in the 1970s and 1980s (Partington, 1986, pp.63–4).

The result of this politicization was that history had become a subject very different from that which had been taught to parents (Kedourie, 1988, p.5) This was because it had become distorted in many ways, not least in the way that it had been complicated through a preoccupation with concepts and the cultivation of skills. Attempts by the SHP to give precise, rigorous instructions in relation to its 'Study in Depth' were thus ridiculed by Deuchar (1987, p.9) as nothing less than 'six paragraphs of gobbledygook'. Beattie (1987, p.6) claimed that 'history was in peril' because what was being taught in school now was not 'proper' history at all: it was essentially watered down 'contemporary history' or 'current affairs' (p.17).

The certainty of the past was contrasted with the contemporary crisis. Deuchar (1989) therefore referred to the 'cultural crisis'; Kedourie (1988) described the 'serious situation' which had arisen as a result of, in Partington's (1986, p.81) words, the 'sedulous attack on the central traditions of the West'. For at the core of this restorationist discourse, as we have already seen, was the sense of loss of a common heritage. Deuchar's (1989) 'cultural crisis' had come about because of the 'flight from British history' (p.4), the 'wilfully perverse dismissal of historical content and facts' inspired by an intellectual movement which had brought about 'a fundamental loss of faith in our civilization' (p.5).

Partington (1986) denounced the 'systematic denigration of English (later British) history' (p.72) which amounted to a well-orchestrated campaign to 'subvert the teaching of history and to preach contempt and hatred for the central political and cultural traditions both of Britain and the western civilisation of which it is part' (p.81). He lamented the tendency to decry the belief that history should be used to foster 'pride or reverence in the study of our national past' (p.70). Similarly, Deuchar (1989, p.4) denounced those teachers who believed that the teaching of British history had the potential to be 'nationalistic' and those syllabuses that had caused 'the loss of a huge slice of our national heritage. There is no feeling in these syllabuses that we are talking about our own history' (Deuchar, 1987, p.4). Nowhere was this better illustrated than in the syllabus of the SHP which elevated world history above our 'own history' which was so 'rich and varied' (Kedourie, 1988, p.14).

The Attack on the 'Two Headed Monster': A 'Host of Malignant Sprites'?

Of all the objects of derision, nothing came in for more attack from polemicists as the SHP, for it represented everything that the New Right detested. With the exception of Beattie, all the writers selected for particular analysis in this section devoted large tracts of their publications to a determined denigration of what SHP and the 'new history' stood for. Kedourie's paper in particular was devoted to a wholesale denunciation of SHP, the philosophy of 'new history' and those who conceived it. To Deuchar, Kedourie and Partington, the whole rationale and philosophy of SHP and 'new history' was not only misguided and flawed but overtly politicized and ideologically sinister. Both Kedourie and Partington were contemptuous of the SHP's avowedly child-centred approach which regarded the 'needs of adolescents' as paramount. According to Partington, these needs were not 'desirable qualities to be fostered', merely 'needs which adolescents consciously avow' (p.66). Kedourie (1988) favoured a history syllabus which pampered less to the needs of the child but a 'scheme which their elders believe best for them' (p.6). Like Beattie, she believed that history should not be concerned with explaining the modern world but that it should be taught merely for its own sake (p.7). Similarly, Deuchar found 'deplorable' the way in which SHP through its pursuit of 'relevance' encouraged pupils to view the past as a means for the pupil to 'get out of it for his own personal benefit or gratification' rather than a respect for 'our civilization, its institutions and its values' (Deuchar, 1989, p.4). It was a 'two-headed monster' (p.1).

To Deuchar, Kedourie and Partington, SHP was both confusing in its methods and wildly ambitious in its aims. Deuchar again referred to the 'gobbledygook' language employed within SHP materials, while Kedourie believed that SHP was a 'nightmare' for the 'conscientious teacher'. In contrast, the coursework elements allowed the faults of the 'bad teacher' to be masked (Kedourie, 1988, p.17). A major reason for SHP being portrayed within this discourse as having no substance and no rigour was that it had an apparent contempt or disregard for historical knowledge. Thus the 'new history holds that, since nothing is ultimately knowable, and the historical record is selective, subjective and inevitably biased, the actual historical content of history is almost valueless' (Deuchar, 1987, p.2). By arguing that the pursuit of historical knowledge was 'unimportant' in comparison to the philosophical and methodological aspects of history, SHP did not teach real history or 'the subject itself' merely the 'nature of the subject' (Kedourie, 1988, p.8). Apparently, this had come about because 'new history' had been influenced by the 'Neo-marxisms' which 'promoted the view that objective knowledge of the world is not possible' (Partington, 1986, p.70).

This contempt for knowledge and content stemmed from what Partington termed an 'unconditional relativism' found in the works of Collingwood (1946) and Carr (1961). This 'relativistic rejection of the propriety of cross-cultural comparisons' explained why SHP subverted respect for British culture (Partington, 1986, p.70). This was unacceptable because it rejected the fundamental liberal principle namely the 'pursuit of truth'; for there was, after all, a 'core of knowledge' of British history which pupils had been denied. Traditional history, by concentrating on this core of British history 'gained breadth of knowledge and a respect for the past, even a sense of gratitude towards those people from whom we have deservedly inherited this amazing civilization . . . and came to some understanding of our institutions, traditions and values' (Deuchar, 1989, p.3). This also explained Deuchar's contempt for the variety of syllabuses offered by the examination boards which did nothing to promote 'our national heritage' (Deuchar, 1987, p.5). Rather, SHP was pre-occupied with the detection of 'bias' in everything, again, distracting from a 'search for the truth' (Deuchar, 1989, p.8).

An important feature of the discourse here was its precise, Eltonian perception of history. To Deuchar particularly, historical knowledge refers unproblematically simply to the 'facts' and should be studied accordingly. Similarly, Kedourie criticized SHP's emphasis upon understanding history as a distinct 'form of knowledge' rather than 'inalienable facts' (Kedourie, 1988, p.10). This dismissal of the notion of 'historical understanding' was to be a crucial issue in the NC and a theme which Deuchar was to re-visit during the debate over the NC itself (Deuchar, 1992).

The departure of 'new history' from content and knowledge was explained by its critics as an obsession with the cultivation of historical skills and concepts. Kedourie lamented the trend towards teaching 'concepts', 'key ideas' and 'grand themes' through a 'process-based' approach at the expense of 'narrative', 'chronology' and the 'past itself' (Kedourie, 1988, p.10). This was not only laborious but misguided, for SHP expected pupils to do what trained, professional historians take a lifetime to achieve. For Deuchar, source evaluation dominated 'new history', it was not really a 'skill' because it did not encourage judgement and ignored knowledge. His major criticism was that it did not 'encourage pupils to think for themselves outside the historical context'. Pupils were merely coached by teachers into making the 'correct' statements that examiners were looking for. In this sense, the skills based approach of SHP was merely a 'parlour game' which 'distorts and diminishes history' (Deuchar, 1987). This obsession with skills and the failure by SHP to 'look at content' meant that a 'host of irrational and malignant sprites flew into the ideological vacuum created by the lack of serious discussion about heritage and tradition' (Partington, 1986, p.69).

Empathy was singled out for particular derision in this respect. It epitomized everything that Deuchar, Partington and Kedourie detested about the 'new history'. It was, after all, a key SHP 'concept' but one which was merely 'generalized sentiment-ality' without historical knowledge (Deuchar, 1987, p.15). Again, empathy was too 'complex': empathetic understanding was simply too difficult a process to be achievable either in the classroom or the examination. It stemmed from what Kedourie con-temptuously called the 'verbal algorithm' of SHP that history was about people and that empathy made history appear more relevant to pupils by encouraging them to see that history was about 'ordinary people like themselves'; this 'denies the richness of history for it dismisses the achievements of people in positions of power ... to belittle the role of those labelled as great is to take a partisan and impoverished approach to history' (Kedourie, 1988, p.12). Again, empathy, like relativism, was dangerous because it deflected attention away from 'our' heritage and historical situation, it was 'in a terrible hurry to be sympathetic towards everybody else's predicament before making sure that we have a clear idea of our own standpoint' (Deuchar, 1987, p.15).

A characteristic feature of the New Right discourse of derision was to focus attention upon personalities and selected examples. Dennis Shemilt, formerly Director of SHP, was singled out for particular contempt by Deuchar, Kedourie and Partington. Deuchar (1989) described Shemilt's 1980 study of the Project's implementation as 'vintage cant' while Partington (1986) accused Shemilt of exaggerating the strengths of SHP over traditional history. Kedourie seemed to devote the majority of her paper towards a denigration of Shemilt and SHP: thus through 'misplaced ambition' Shemilt was denying children opportunities to 'see the worth of history textbooks' (p.8); the project team wanted nothing more than to treat history as a 'pastime' (p.9).

The Solutions: British History, Certainty, the State and the Teacher's Role

As Bosanquet (1983) has indicated, although New Right discourses are dominated by 'antithesis', it is also possible to detect a 'thesis'. Similarly, we can recognize a set of proposals and envisaged 'solutions' within Deuchar, Kedourie, Beattie and Partington to the 'crisis' in history teaching which had emerged in the 1970s and 1980s. Given that at the heart of these discourses was the belief that school history had tried 'deliberately to deny to British children the legitimate pride in themselves and their cultural heritage which is their birthright' and that 'our civilization is threatened not only by cultures with different attitudes and values, but by destructive tendencies within ourselves' (Deuchar, 1989, pp.13–14). School history should teach instead at its central core the history of Britain because 'the presumed payoff comes in the shape of cultural heritage, shared values, common loyalties' (p.5), for 'our home-grown western-civilization remains the only viable option' (p.14). This is in contrast to those who have a 'nasty-looking axe to grind' when advocating 'criteria for the selection of content' (p.13).

It is important here to examine more precisely what was meant by 'British' and 'our home-grown civilization'. Deuchar went to pains to stress that he was not envisaging a 'narrow nationalism' in this respect. But on occasions a more precise definition of the concept of 'our' appeared. 'Our' within a British and western context turned out, in fact, to be Englishness. Thus, in describing the multiplicity of GCSE syllabuses in England and Wales, Deuchar allowed his true vision of heritage and identity to be revealed. The syllabuses had contributed to:

> ... the loss of a huge slice of our national heritage. There is no feeling in these syllabuses that we are talking about our own history. It is always referred to impersonally as 'the past'. This does not apply to the Welsh Joint Education Committee Syllabus, which robustly aims 'to promote an awareness of our [presumably Welsh] national heritage ... ' There is nothing in the Aims of the English Examining Boards which might suggest a desire to promote an awareness of our English national heritage. (Deuchar, 1987, pp.4–5)

Using Apple's (1989) references to 'binary oppositions', the 'we' in the British context applies to 'us', namely the 'English', in contrast to 'them', in this instance the 'Welsh'. This also explains Partington's indignation at 'the systematic denigration of English (later British) history' (Partington, 1986, p.72).

The second identifiable 'solution' within the discourse related to methodology. Clearly, Deuchar and company rejected the Carr/Collingwood notion of relativism, instrumentalism and the tentative nature of evidence and interpretation, particularly its implication of bias, in favour of the Eltonian/Oakeshott faith in neutrality, objectivity and the sanctity of the past. Thus, according to Kedourie, following Elton, the simple aim of school history should be to 'induct a child into the past. The past, by its very nature, cannot be altered except by new evidence and new interpretations which simply change our view of the past' (Kedourie, 1988, p.7). According to Beattie, the aim of school history should be 'the reconstruction of the past for its own sake' for this had the additional advantage of being 'what goes on' in university history departments (Beattie, 1987, p.9). After all, 'suitability of a subject depends entirely upon the historical criteria of quality of evidence and susceptibility to detailed, chronological narrative' (p.16). The aim of the history teacher was therefore simply to introduce pupils to the reality and certainty of the past as it existed.

Finally came the most important and obvious solution of all. At the core of the discourse was a profound distrust of the teacher-as-producer and faith in the 'common sense' of parent-as-consumer. Parents, after all, knew what was best, they 'would like their children to be taught history in much the same way they were taught it themselves' (Deuchar, 1989, p.11). This, however, had been corrupted by the arrogance and cleverness of the producer monopoly who claimed to know better. The traditional New Right solution to educational problems was, of course, recourse to the cleansing power of market principles even though, as neo-conservative populists, they recognized that these had potential problems. Thus Beattie (1987) pointed to the potential difficulties for the position of history in schools if market forces were allowed to dominate what was taught. Mindful perhaps of the 'conservative modernizers' and 'privatizers' within the Tory party and of the vocational intuition of parents, he suggested that history in a free market could be superseded by the hated 'relevant' subjects in the quest for economic growth. Yet the problem of teacher monopoly and dominance had to be dealt with. The second albeit reluctantly accepted solution, therefore, was intervention by the state. Beattie pointed out that the British education system had been free from any types of control, particularly government control and had become instead a sort of closed shop. Part of the solution envisaged by Beattie was a closer involvement by the universities in the construction of syllabuses and the increase in parental interest in the teaching of history, fraught as this was with difficulties. It did, however, lead to 'greater accountability through participation in educational decisions by a wider range of interested parties (which) has the advantages of weakening the grip of organized teachers' (p.31).

However, Beattie's neo-liberal instincts made him reluctant to advocate direct control over history syllabuses by the government. Whilst also recognizing the dilemma, Deuchar found it easier to reconcile himself with the proposed solution for he would 'sooner trust politicians who are chosen by the people than an educational establishment' (Deuchar, 1989, p.14). Whatever the precise nature of the solution – the imposition of market principles, parental control or direct state involvement – one thing was clear, teachers' stranglehold on history had to be broken. The following extract from Beattie was crucial:

> ... the authority of the teacher has ended. He has no more authority (*qua* teacher or historian) to decide the weight to be given to different but equally respectable aspects than (say) have parents or politicians. To the extent that what is taught as history has been changed in pursuit of 'wider social ends', and to the extent that ideological preferences have shaped the character of the history curriculum, then to that extent have teachers exceeded their authority. On these questions, teachers and historians are (or should be) merely one element in a debate in which there is wider public interest. They have no special, privileged status. (Beattie, 1987, p.19)

The subsequent debate over the NC saw an unprecedented 'wider public interest' and intervention by historians in what was taught in the history classrooms. In many ways it appeared that the 'authority of the teacher' had indeed ended.

Chapter 4

Competing Discourses?
History, Empathy and Politics in the 1980s

The previous two chapters described the development of discourses relating to the teaching of history. This third and final chapter on the 'context of influence' relating to history in the NC considers the extent to which the tensions between these discourses manifested themselves in the 1980s. The chapter provides the opportunity to introduce other important contributions by government, academic and professional organizations to the debate over the teaching of history; one of the most important in the 1980s came from the Historical Association which acted both as a mediating influence and as a curriculum pressure group, a role which was significant in the subsequent NC debate itself. By analysing the controversy over the GCSE and the teaching of empathy in particular, the chapter shows the elevation of the profile of history teaching from the professional to the public and political arenas. This is important for considering the circumstances in which the HWG was established. Finally, important sections in the chapter are devoted to direct interventions in the debate by Secretaries of State for Education during this period: Kenneth Baker's views on the teaching of history are given particular scrutiny.

Keith Joseph, 'British History' and 'Shared Values'

In 1984, rather portentously, Tosh could write that:

> There are signs that the history syllabus in British schools is about to become a bone of contention once more, as conservatives and radicals shape up for a struggle for control. History is evidently still too powerful a force in our consciousness to be shrugged off as an intellectual pastime ... Society requires a usable past, and different conceptions of the social order produce rival histories. Many historians have been proud to enlist on one side or another, believing that they have a social responsibility to promote this or that group identity, or to reinforce the authority of the state. (Tosh, 1984, p.8)

The 1980s began with a flood of articles in *Teaching History* re-iterating the warnings of Price and Booth of the dangers facing history in schools (Baker, 1981; Fisher, 1982; Moore, 1982). Foster (1989) noted the growth and development of organizations such as the History at the Universities Defence Group, the establishment of a national association of history advisers, as well as various HA initiatives (see below) signalling continued concern about the future of the subject. Formed in 1982, the Defence Group's object was 'to work with and through the Historical Association' to defend the scope of history in British universities and monitor the impact of financial cuts upon the teaching of history in the university sector (Davis, 1983). Cannadine (1987) at the time of his own departure to the USA painted a particularly bleak picture of the 'state of British history', the product of familiar pressures: inter-disciplinary studies at school and university, the growth of world history, the decline of Britain from the world stage and so on, both the cause and the product of, a 'weaker sense of national identity'.

It was in these circumstances that the government signalled a direct interest in the teaching of the subject, with Keith Joseph's (Secretary of State for Education) speech on 10 February to the HA (Joseph, 1984). Joseph's neo-liberal reputation was well established but sections of this carefully crafted speech could well have been taken out of *A New Look at History* (SCHP, 1976). Mindful of his audience, Joseph emphasized the 'unique role' history had to play in the school curriculum; he even admitted that history was vital for developing skills such as analysis and criticism, sometimes in situations 'in which there cannot be a right answer'. He also recognized the changed nature of British society in the 1980s in social, cultural and ethnic terms. But the bulk of the speech echoed familiar New Right themes. The teaching of predominantly British history as opposed to 'Roman, American or Caribbean history' was vital because of the 'shared values distinctive of British society'. Of course, he said, there were cultural differences but it was 'the commonality that defines us as a society'. Influenced perhaps by Thomas (1979) and Hayek (1954), Joseph lauded the liberty of individualism in the law and institutions of the country: without a secure knowledge of British history pupils would not be able to take a 'proper pride' in these institutions 'bequeathed to us ... for the benefit of our successors'. Like Deuchar three years later, Joseph insisted that he was advocating 'national' as opposed to 'nationalist' history. After all, British history would enable pupils to 'understand the development of the shared values which are a distinctive feature of British society and culture and which continue to shape private attitudes and public policy'.

According to Berghahn & Schissler (1987) Joseph was concerned by the impact of new history which, in his eyes, had concentrated too much on 'history from below', as well as on multi-culturalism, both of which undermined feelings of patriotism at the sensitive time of the Falklands War. Joseph had sympathy with those elements of new history (such as the cultivation of transferable skills) which appealed to his neo-liberalism but his problem (like others within the New Right) was how to reconcile these benefits with the apparent disrespect for national culture. The speech signalled a vigorous debate over the teaching of the subject to which the HA contributed in significant ways (Lewis, 1987; Foster, 1989). Given the importance of the HA's role in this and more particularly in the debate over the NC, I want to spend some time describing the HA's background, including its image amongst teachers.

The Historical Association: 'Government Poodle' or Representative 'Power House'?

At the height of the NC debate in 1990, the HA had a membership of between 7,000 and 8,000, approximately half of whom were teachers (Roberts, 1990). The rest consisted of academics, teachers' trainers, advisers and members of the general public. Since its creation, in 1906, it had been concerned with 'guarding the quality and status of history' (HA, 1957, p.53). The manner of the HA's inception in the universities, however, meant that it developed an elitist image causing some to lament its unwilling-ness to encourage closer links with schools (Coss, 1988). Yet before the 1960s there was little need for the HA to involve itself greatly in school matters, due to the fact that the position of history in schools seemed secure. The threat to history in schools from the 1960s onwards caused the HA to change; it established, for example, *Teaching History* in 1969 which in its first volume hoped that 'it may encourage teachers of history to be adventurous in devising new ways of tackling the exciting possibilities of the subject' (*Teaching History*, 1(1), p.1). Yet the elitist image continued and it was not until 1975 that the HA established an Education Committee.

The highly charged educational/political context of the 1980s meant that the HA had to play a more interventionist role in curriculum matters (Robbins, 1981). Foster (1989) has shown that it became more active in school initiatives, establishing, for example, an advanced certificate in the teaching of history in 1984, initiating three inquiries to evaluate the nature of history in schools, as well as forging links with the History at the Universities Defence Group (see above). However, despite these initiatives, they hardly give credence to Foster's claim that the HA was becoming a 'power house' pressure group. Shortly after Joseph's speech, a meeting at the House of Lords between academics, HMI and HA members called for history to be given greater prominence in schools. The HA responded with the establishment of the 'Watchdog Committee', created to guard against the threats to history and to campaign for inclusion of history as a compulsory element within a core curriculum. Lewis describes this as a 'momen-tous decision' and that the HA was 'uniquely placed' to take on this kind of role, being the 'only national body to represent historians which requires selection of its repre-sentatives' (Lewis, 1987, p.133). Lewis also describes further attempts at raising the profile of history in schools, including another House of Lords meeting in January 1986.

In fact, the HA's record of 'representing teachers' views' before the NC was fraught with difficulties and tensions. Lewis himself quotes from a *Times Higher Education Supplement* (THES) editorial which accused the HA of still being dominated by 'old style historians'. In defence of the HA, Lewis identified a core element of the HA's attitude towards school history, one which was to remain fairly constant not only through the debate over the GCSE but in relation to the NC also:

> The THES had missed the point that the school-teacher members of the HA were not concerned about aspects of content so much as the fact that in some schools history had disappeared altogether from the curriculum or, that in those where it continued to exist, it was often submerged within integrated programmes which made historical content or method difficult to identify. (Lewis, 1987, p.131)

Yet this is only partially true. In 1986, in response to requests from Keith Joseph, the HA published *History for Life* which was a suggested core syllabus for the 14–16 age range, concentrating predominantly on British history (HA, 1986). It seemed curiously at odds with the non-specific content criteria as outlined in the GCSE and a subsequent meeting with the new Secretary of State, Kenneth Baker, led to the presentation of the HA's *Proposals for a Core Curriculum in History* (HA, 1987; Foster, 1989; Roberts, 1988). These attempts to define the nature of a core history curriculum infuriated many teachers who were angered by attempts to put forward an apparently arbitrary, prescriptive selection of historical content with an anglocentric emphasis. Some observers called upon the HA to go in the 'opposite direction' (Lamont, 1988); others described the HA's moves towards a content-led history curriculum as 'dangerous' and 'ridiculous' (Fines, 1988). There seemed considerable justification for the charge that the HA was still elitist and that it seemed 'unable, or unwilling, to purge itself of outmoded attitudes which date from its inception' (Coss, 1988, p.177).

Caught Between Two Stools? The Historical Association and the Development of a Professional Arbitration Discourse?

The HA did indeed seem out of touch with the views of classroom teachers who evidently bitterly distrusted a list of prescribed content. Lewis (1987) himself quotes examples of letters to the press from teachers labelling the HA as a 'self-appointed cabal', a 'mixture of interested amateurs and academics', the 'establishment view'. At the Birmingham HA Conference in October 1987, a group of angry teachers declared that the HA was 'discredited' and that it was 'vital that teachers have a voice of their own' (TES, 23 October 1987). The article went on to describe the 'ugly and vitriolic scenes' caused by teacher anger against the HA which seemed to be 'giving in too readily to demands for a content-orientated approach and being too prescriptive in its recommendations'. The most damning accusation of all was that the HA was simply the 'government's poodle'. Consequently, the HA's proposals for the 7–14 age range, published in *Teaching History* in February, 1987, were less prescriptive and suggested that there should be a balance of British, world and local history. Yet again, however, the HA was accused of anglocentricism.

How are these developments to be explained and what are their significance for the debate over the NC? The controversy relating to the HA and the common core debate stemmed from differences relating to the selection of historical content. As we saw in Chapter 2, teachers had been afforded flexibility through the non-content specific criteria of the GCSE, allowing them to select from a wide range of GCSE syllabuses offered by the examination boards; these selections were made on the basis of local interest and expertise. By prescribing specific content, the HA seemed to be contradicting the philosophy underlining GCSE. After all, 'it stood out in making firm proposals on content' (Foster, 1989, p.215). Teacher autonomy over the selection of historical content at a local level was clearly not its major priority; the defence of the subject at a national political level was. Moreover, according to the HA, more precise justifications for the construction of history syllabuses were required, other than teacher or pupil needs. It was no good arguing that because of the lack of time available to teach the subject, teachers should be given freedom to select what was most appropriate for their pupils because 'the danger is that the claims on time are so persuasive that they become a justification for any content selection on the grounds that a teacher must have freedom to choose on the basis of his, her or pupils' interest' (Lewis, 1987 p.136).

This contrast in perception over the selection of content, then, stemmed from the HA's major priority, namely the vigorous defence of history in schools. Parents needed to be convinced of history's worth; moreover, recent interventions by Joseph and Baker had suggested that their support could only be gained through more substantial justifications. As Lewis put it 'there is a danger that the public at large and politicians may conclude that, if the professional historians cannot agree amongst themselves, then this is a justification for the downgrading and possible elimination of history from the curriculum' (ibid, p.135).

Yet in the 1980s and as we shall see, throughout the NC controversy, by attempting to please everybody, the HA ran the dangerous gauntlet of pleasing no one (Phillips, 1992a). Thus, the HA 7–14 proposals were criticized both for their anglocentricism by teachers and for their lack of anglocentricism by the press! A sympathetic Foster has noted that the HA seemed to be stuck between 'those who see content as the key to selection for what goes into the history curriculum and those who see methodology, historiography, skills and concepts as being the fulcrum for selection' (Foster, 1989, p.216). An even more loyal Lewis complained that it 'found itself recast in the role of arbiter between the extreme protagonists of a skills approach to history teaching on the one hand, and the protagonists of a content-centred approach to syllabus concentration on the other' (Lewis, 1987, p.134).

These tensions existed against a background in which history teachers had been 'expected to regard themselves as lesser professionals, a cadre of demi-priests standing between the public and the universities' (Coss, 1988, pp.177–8). Within such circumstances proposals such as *History for Life* seemed to be endearing themselves to the likes of not only Joseph and Baker but even Deuchar who decreed that the HA's 'suggestion of a core of British history 14–16 aimed at our voters of the future deserves our full support' (see Deuchar, 1987, p. 17). Little wonder that the HA's credibility amongst teachers was fragile; yet the HA's actions can be explained by a desire to adopt a mediating influence between government and their extra-parliamentary supporters on the one hand and the interests of teachers on the other. In seeking out a role of this sort, the HA was indeed in danger of falling between two stools. It was a dilemma which stayed with it throughout the debate over the NC. Attempts by the HA to construct a 'consensus' (see Roberts, 1990) amongst teachers around the NC were, as shall see, fraught with difficulties which, it could be argued, had their origins in HA tactics in the 1980s.

Competing Discourses?

This was the context within which the discourses of derision described in the previous chapter were initiated. Between the establishment of GCSE in 1986 and the announcement of the HWG in 1989, these New Right publications had the effect of further promulgating the history debate into public and political circles. I now want to evaluate their impact and consider the response to them amongst teachers. As Quicke (1988), Griggs (1989), Lowe (1995) and others have emphasized, and as was discussed in Chapters 1 and 3, a major reason for explaining the popular appeal and impact of New

Right discourses in the 1980s was the prominence given to them in the press. A characteristic feature and tactic of organizations such as the Centre for Policy Studies was the cultivation of the media through press releases. An article in the *Independent* shortly after the publication of Deuchar (1987) could report that 'children have little or no historical knowledge because of the fashion for imparting skills rather than facts' and went on to describe other aspects of the pamphlet in detail, including those sections which described the debasement of culture and heritage. Similarly, an article which described the publication of Hiskett (1988) claimed that GCSE examinations were 'perverting the course of history'. The article gave prominence to Hiskett's claims that GCSE syllabuses were selective in their choice of historical content and that some were nothing more than 'shop steward' courses. The article went on to contrast the merits of 'traditional history' which provided a 'backbone of key dates' with the faults of the new examinations which 'leaves wide gaps' in children's knowledge. The article quoted the criticisms of history teachers at Eton and Rugby of GCSE and also used examples to denigrate empathy. Pupils, it said, were being encouraged to imagine they were Hitler or a supporter of Castro.

New Right contributors used even more direct methods to elevate their views. Deuchar wrote numerous letters to the press on his favourite themes. A letter to the TES on 4 September 1987 denounced 'new history' and claimed that traditional history teaching methods were more effective and less expensive in the process. History teaching, said Deuchar, should not be obsessed with evidence work and the cultivation of skills, rather it should have as its major priority 'the honest pursuit of truth'. In the TES on 29 January 1988 he claimed that 'new history' was a 'manifestation of our post-colonial neurosis', there was 'widespread dismay' at the teaching of concepts and empathy and he repeated his demand that history should be concerned with the pursuit of truth. A thorough inquiry was needed on 'new history' which should be scrapped in favour of a return to 'traditional history'. He also defended his views in *Teaching History* (Deuchar, 1988).

Deuchar's contributions and others from the New Right initiated indignant responses from teachers; these contributions shed further important light on the nature of teachers' views on history teaching (discussed in Chapter 2) prior to the establishment of the NC. A Wiltshire head of humanities attacked Deuchar for claiming that education should be concerned with the 'mere passing of "facts" from one generation to another'. Rather, the function of history was to develop the ability amongst young people to 'rationalize, analyse, interpret, empathize and thus to develop reasoned opinions' (TES, 18 October 1987). A head of history in a school in Berkshire offered a critique of Beattie's claim that knowledge in history had been relegated in favour of a skills-based approach which was 'at best laughable and at worst a gross and disturbing parody of what is actually happening' (TES, 11 December 1987). He also denounced the tactic of quoting empathy tasks 'out of context', defending, instead, activity-based approaches on the grounds of utility, relevance and understanding. Pedagogic devices such as these did not conflict with the search for knowledge, rather they were 'arrangements for the purpose of conveying understanding and without which illumination could not take place at all'.

Significantly, other responses from teachers sought to show that the New Right had over-emphasized the distinction between 'skills' and 'facts'. Thus, a head of history from Newcastle believed that 'the key to successful history teaching is a judicious blend of traditional and modern methods' (TES, 18 September 1987). The members of a history department in Hounslow condemned the 'content versus skills' debate as facile and contrived, claiming that 'without content, it would not be possible for pupils to engage in the skills' (TES, 10 July 1987). They also emphasized that the variety of activity-based teaching, using debate, role-play, discussion and other techniques provided stimulation and accessibility to a range of pupils. Here, they raised an issue which would be an important one during the NC debate itself, namely the link between teaching methods and genuine historical understanding:

> Having exposed pupils to the rigour of the discipline and the factual content, it becomes possible to differentiate between those who understood the content, when they have to interpret it in an empathetic reconstruction, and those who have learned or remembered but have not understood. (ibid)

A head of history from London defended new history's attempt to 'start at the front end of enquiry and not fetter itself to the product' (TES, 19 February 1988). A teacher from Ipswich denounced Deuchar for attempting to 'return history in schools to a passive and uncritical view of the past' (TES, 19 Feburary 1988).

Empathy, Popularization and the Academics

Discussions over GCSE and empathy signalled the highly significant intervention by Professor Robert Skidelsky, who was to play a crucial role in the debate over the next few years not only in the extra-parliamentary and academic contexts but within government also. He was a much respected academic historian: he was an expert on Britain in the inter-war years and his subsequent biography of Keynes was to receive particular acclaim. But by his own admission (Skidelsky, 1993a), he had a wide range of 'interests and obsessions', one of which was the history of progressive schools in England. Not surprisingly, therefore, he had a reputation (intellectual as well as in political terms) in his early career as liberal progressive. Yet, as a consequence of his own personal experience, his ideological position seemed to shift; thus as the history debate progressed and at the height of the NC controversy itself, he had gained a reputation (rightly or wrongly) as one of the chief representatives of New Right views on history teaching.

Skidelsky's personal involvement in the debate over history came in the mid-1980s. His children had attended Lewes Priory School in East Sussex. On 31 January 1988, *The Sunday Times* reported that the history teachers at the school, Chris McGovern and Dr Anthony Freeman, had entered the pupils privately for the 'more traditional' Scottish Ordinary Certificate because of their profound reservations on GCSE, particularly the lack of British history and about empathy. Shortly afterwards, Skidelsky declared his public support for the teachers in an important article entitled 'History as social engineering' (*Independent*, 1 March 1988) in which he accused those who had designed the GCSE of adopting misconceived criteria for the selection of historical content leading to a preponderance of world rather than British history and for being obsessed with the cultivation of skills rather than the teaching of historical content. He called for an immediate review of the GCSE and for academics to become involved in the debate.

Significantly, they did. One of the characteristics of the GCSE and NC debates was, as Tosh had predicted, the contribution from academics of a variety of ideological persuasions, but dominated mainly by those from the right. Professor Norman Stone, for example, in populist style, demanded only a few days later in *The Sunday Times* that 'we' should 'Put nuts and bolts back into history' (13 March 1988). Stone, like Roger Scruton, wrote regular columns in the newspapers, particularly *The Sunday Times* and was also to play an influential role in the debates.

Skidelsky's article provoked an extraordinary and an unprecedented public response in the letters pages of the *Independent* and other newspapers, including the TES. Letters came not only from teachers but parents, academics and even pupils themselves. An analysis of the letters in the *Independent* following Skidelsky's article is important for the purposes of this thesis for they reveal the contrasting discourses in relation to history teaching: pedagogical but also public/populist and academic discourses. Thus, letters from members of the general public were generally supportive of Skidelsky's thesis. White (3 March 1988) claimed that 'the dangerous and pervasive' argument that skills were more important than knowledge had come about because it was easier to teach and assess skills than knowledge. The next day another contributor lauded over the days when 'tables, spelling and grammar, passages from the poets, the genealogical tables of the kings and queens of England, the dates of the great battles of the world: all used to be learned by rote' (4 March 1988). The contributor turned out to be Marjorie Seldon of the Institute of Economic Affairs. The response from academics was less uniform but broadly supportive of Skidelsky's views. Professor David Cooper of the Department of Philosophy, University of Durham, supported Skidelsky for drawing attention to the 'flaccid relativism about knowledge, truth and value' which the 'misguided', 'fanatical', 'multiculturalist' ideology was encouraging in schools (4 March 1988). Anthony Seldon (Co-Director of the Institute of Contemporary British History) agreed with Skidelsky about 'limiting the factual knowledge taught' (5 March 1988). Iain Smith, from the Department of History at the University of Warwick, rehearsed the criticism that empathy was merely encouraging pupils to 'invent feelings in the present and to project them on to fictitious stereotypes in the past'; this, he said, was the 'antithesis of what the study of history should be about' (9 March 1988), a view supported by an editorial in the newspaper (10 March 1988).

Yet Skidelsky's views were attacked by pupils. Edward Klevan praised the GCSE as a 'massive move forward from the repetitive and tiresome note-taking which previous generations have suffered' (11 March 1988). Judith Feuchtwanger described the empathy work which she had been asked to do as 'enjoyable and interesting' and that it showed her 'both sides of the coin' of historical interpretations (5 May 1988). There were correspondingly fewer contributions from teachers but Pamela Johnston, a teacher from Hampshire, criticized Smith for his claim that empathy was merely about imagination, on the contrary 'our students are specifically told they must not project present-day feelings on to fictitious stereotypes' (14 March 1988). One of the most indignant responses came from the Chairman of the Secondary Examinations Council. He knew of 'no GCSE examiner who would disagree' with Skidelsky's assertion that knowledge was vital. After all, he said, 'History is not history if there is no knowledge base. The skills of the historian cannot be practised in a factual void' (14 March 1988).

The New Right, the 'Content Question' and HMI: A Change of Direction?

Given such high profile discussions in the media, Slater (1989) is justified in his assertion that the New Right set the pace and the agenda for debates over the teaching of history in the 1980s. New Right influence can be seen in a number of ways. First, it had managed to elevate the teaching of history from professional to public and political domains; the contexts for discussion had shifted from classrooms, teacher centres and examination boards to newspapers, political conference halls and even parliament itself. Secondly, by stressing the characteristic theme of 'crisis', New Right activists, aided by academics such as Skidelsky, had effectively discredited features of history teaching such as empathy; in addition, SHP, which had appeared vibrant and dynamic in the late 1970s, appeared curiously on the defensive by the late 1980s. Thirdly, perhaps more importantly of all, through a combination of populist argument and derision, New Right discourses on history – expressed publicly through the press – had managed to create an artificial polarization of the 'skills versus content' and the 'traditional versus new' debates.

As we have seen, issues relating to the selection of historical content had proved to be extremely controversial. History teachers' sensitivity over this matter explains the HA's difficulties over such documents as *History for Life* and the acrimonious regional conference debates of 1987. Yet in responding to New Right attacks on new history, for example, teachers indignantly rejected the assertion that they disregarded content in pursuit of skills, process and concepts (see above). Some also conceded that teachers had sometimes over-emphasized skills. A London head of history admitted that 'many teachers did go too far in trying to teach the skills associated with handling evidence' but suggested also that 'the pendulum is swinging back towards a consideration of content' (TES, 19 February 1988). Similarly, in a review of Kedourie (1988), Brown argued that:

> This pamphlet is designed to put the clock back rather than progress forward into the 1990s. It makes the valid point that some history teachers may have neglected the question of content at the expense of developing pupil skill in using the sources of the past. But the two are not mutually exclusive. No history teacher today would argue that content is irrelevant or that pupils should not, through their study of the past, develop a sense of chronology ... This pamphlet ... contributes nothing to the current debate on the place of history in schools. It erects a demonology ... in which good is contrasted with evil, orthodoxy with error ... Is the logical irrationality of the witch-hunt to have veracity in the education of the 1990s? (Brown, 1988, p.42)

Brown and other teachers were articulating the fear that as a consequence of polarization, many of the gains achieved in history teaching as a consequence of 'new history' and GCSE would be lost in the re-emergence of content-driven criteria for the planning and teaching of history. Yet on the eve of the NC, it seemed that this was the direction in which HMI, at least, were proceeding, as reflected in the important publication entitled *Curriculum Matters 5–16: History* (DES, 1988). This document was significant for three reasons: first, it demonstrated the shift in HMI thinking from general to more specific criteria for planning and organizing history syllabuses; second, by considering teachers' responses to the document, it shed light on teachers' views in relation to selection and criteria on the eve of the NC debate; third, most important of all, the discourse articulated in the document proved an important influence over the HWG itself and provided a framework for planning the subsequent NC reports.

The document's chief architect, Roger Hennessey, had been appointed staff inspector for history in 1987. His appointment came as something of a surprise both within HMI circles and amongst the teaching profession, for David Sylvester, a well known advocate of SHP had been expected to succeed John Slater. Moreover, Hennessey was a relative 'outsider' having worked mainly in the area of social studies as an HMI. His appointment was therefore significant as his views on content contrasted slightly with Slater's. This was illustrated in 1988 when he gave the annual address at the Association of History Teachers in Wales Conference. The title of his speech – 'The Content Question' – gave a useful insight into his thinking. He questioned the tendencies in the 'early days of the new history' to 'decry contentism'. In contrast, Hennessey re-asserted the importance of historical content on three grounds. First, there was a need for 'chronological structure, of a framework within which past events, developments and episodes could be set'. Secondly, he accused new historians of being 'sociologically naive' to deny the importance of content for influencing young people's views as, thirdly, content need not necessarily become pre-occupied with 'events'; rather, 'Content has to address the really long term changes in not only our own, but in world, society'. As an important pointer for the future, Hennessey reminded his audience that:

> It is no longer sufficient to claim . . . that the content does not matter so long as the skills are developed – this kind of assertion will not hold water with the increasing number of people who are asking tough questions about what justifies the presence of a subject on the school curriculum . . . content is dynamite and it is for that reason that so many countries pay assiduous attention to the content issue. Whether or not the choice of content should be left to chance in England and Wales is increasingly an academic question in the era of the national curriculum, but it remains an intriguing question as to why so great an issue was left to chance for so long. (Hennessey, 1988, p.4)

The subsequent publication of *Curriculum Matters 5–16: History* late in 1988 (DES, 1988) had the hall-marks of Hennessey's thinking (and perhaps even more significantly, Kenneth Baker's: see below). It defined history as a combination of 'a body of knowledge', 'process' and 'concepts'; it also emphasized that history should be taught in a way which encouraged children to 'interpret their history critically' but at the same time it stressed that the history curriculum 'provides one of the fundamental ways in which a society transmits its cultural heritage to new generations'. The most significant section of the document gave advice on the planning of history courses. Planning should begin with a careful consideration of the selection of historical content which 'has to be continually re-assessed and re-cast' according to what is perceived as important within the contemporary context. In sections 10 and 11 the document argued that the following factors should be considered in the selection of content:

> a. Breadth: content should include not only political but social, economic, religious, cultural, scientific and technological elements.

> b. The development of concepts: both general concepts (such as cause and effect) and specific (such as 'feudalism' and 'Renaissance').

> c. The development of historical understanding: expressed through a sense of time, familiarity with historical terminology and historical reconstructions, with the important proviso that they be 'based on evidence – they should not be uncontrolled flights of imagination'.

> d. The development of skills: from being able to detect the personal standpoints of past writers to the ability to recall information.

e. British history: to include not only England but also Wales, Ireland and Scotland; it was impossible to study all of British history but certain selections could be made such as the development of British institutions and democracy.

f. Contemporary themes in an historical context: such as the changing status and contribution of women, the long-standing ethnic diversity of Britain.

g. History of other peoples: to enable pupils to gain understanding of peoples with different experiences.

h. The location of the school: local history was a sensible starting point for young children particularly.

Other important statements gave an insight into HMI thinking. The document went on to stress that content should be organized around a respect for chronology, for there 'are serious risks inherent in ignoring' it. It recognized that although integrated humanities courses were useful as a means of managing content, they should protect the 'heartlands' of history and other subjects. As far as teaching methods were concerned, there should be a 'central place in history' for 'story and narrative', as well as evidence and the ability to pose questions relating to it. A questioning approach to history would allow pupils to appreciate motives, situations and standpoints of people in the past and thus promote an 'objective truth' of the past. Moreover, history lent itself to a wider range of teaching modes, from whole class to group work. The document emphasized the need for progressive assessment, not only of skills and concepts but also the 'testing of knowledge content' which 'presents fewer difficulties' than skills. Assessment could be undertaken in a variety of forms and contexts.

The most significant section of the document (section 16) related to the outcomes of a 5–16 history course. Here the document suggested that by the age of sixteen pupils should know of a range of historical content from early civilizations to the Normans and the Early Modern World, as well as various aspects of modern history. Although the document stressed that it was not advocating 'a step-by-step' syllabus, it could nevertheless be interpreted as an important shift in emphasis away from the relatively non-content specific HMI document published three years earlier. The 1988 document was, of course, a product of changing contexts; it attempted to synthesize the important features of 'new history' with a re-affirmation of the need to select content carefully according to the criteria set out. As an editorial of *Teaching History* made clear the document was 'patently a child of its time ... a wily political document, intended as much for those outside the classroom as for those within' (*Teaching History*, April 1989).

The subsequent 'reading' of the 1988 text by teachers is useful not only as an indication of the ways in which texts are interpreted but for the light it shed on teachers' views on history teaching in the late 1980s, particularly in relation to the selection of content. A number of history teachers contributed responses to the document in the April 1989 edition of *Teaching History*. The responses showed that general aspects of the document were welcomed. The document was thus described as a 'welcome contribution to the debate about history in schools' and provided 'food for thought' prior to the NC. Teachers noted that it was 'balanced and thoughtful' in the ways that it recognized the combination of skills and concepts. By providing useful criteria and objectives for the teaching of history, the themes in sections 10 and 11, it was felt that the document seemed to 'represent good practice'. In this sense, it said 'little that well-read history teachers will find new'.

Yet the positive interpretation relating to the document's broad statements in relation to sections 10 and 11 contrasted markedly with teachers' views on other aspects of it. The main criticism here was that it was difficult to reconcile the criteria in sections 10 and 11 with the 'outcomes' of section 16. These seemed 'out of place', 'contradictory' and 'paradoxical'; the content outlined in the section appeared to be 'prescriptive' and 'undermining of teachers' autonomy'. The content itself was regarded as 'Anglocentric' and 'ethnocentric'. The editorial concluded that support for the 1988 document was 'unenthusiastic'. The major reason for this was the apparent mismatch between the general criteria set out in sections 10 and 11 with the specific content highlighted in section 16 or 'the dissonance between the historical processes it purports to support and the list of outcomes it expects'.

The debate over the 1988 document was a pre-cursor to the NC debate itself. The central issue in 1988–89, as it would be between 1989 and 1991, centred upon the fundamental question relating to the selection of historical content, namely 'who selects and why'? As one of the respondents to the 1988 document phrased it:

> This surely lies at the heart of the content debate – a good case can be put forward for the inclusion of far more topics than the allocation of time in the curriculum will ever allow. Can there ever be consensus? In the absence of consensus who will prescribe content and on what authority? (*Teaching History* April 1989, p.37)

I now want to end this chapter by considering an important aspect of the development of history in the NC, namely the 'policy context' of the establishment of the HWG in 1989. An important element of this involves the aims and intentions of the architect of the NC, Kenneth Baker; some of my analysis below (and in some subsequent chapters) is derived from data generated through my own interview with him.

The Policy Context of 1989: Kenneth Baker, Centralization and the National Curriculum

Scholars agree that the appointment of Kenneth Baker as Secretary of State for Education represented a turning point in the centralist tendencies of Tory education policy. Knight (1990) describes the tensions within the Tory party over education immediately prior to Joseph's departure; this perceived confusion stemmed from Joseph's own intellectual turmoil about the direction in which policy should proceed. Joseph's period in office has been interpreted as 'wasted years' (Morris & Griggs, 1988). In Chitty's (1989) words the 'real break' in post-war Tory education policy came with the appointment of Baker 'the supreme pragmatist'. Like all political opportunists, Baker's approach to policy making was eclectic for Baker was influenced by both neo-liberal and neo-conservative elements of New Right thought.

This might explain some of the tensions which emerged between Baker and Thatcher. As both of them indicate in their memoirs (Baker, 1993; Thatcher, 1993) they had fundamentally different views on what form the NC should take. Thatcher's neo-liberal instincts favoured a minimum core curriculum as advocated by the Centre for Policy Studies (Lawlor, 1988). Baker was convinced, however, that a radical overhaul of the curriculum could only be achieved through strong state centralization and the establishment of a broad entitlement curriculum of which history would be a central part. Baker managed to persuade Thatcher of his case, a decision which she grew to regret. In this sense, Baker 'won the battle – but not the war' (Lawton, 1994, p.61).

Rumours about the establishment of a NC had been rife throughout 1986. Finally, in January 1987 at the North of England Education Conference, Baker officially declared the intention of the government to introduce a national core curriculum following the election. Baker emphasized that England had adopted an 'eccentric' approach which had left the school curriculum to 'individual schools and teachers' which contrasted with the centralized system in Europe. Pointing to the weaknesses and apparent failure of the English system, he indicated that greater central control was necessary (DES, 1987a). A few days later Baker claimed that this would not compromise profession-alism; indeed, the proposed national curriculum would therefore allow 'schools and teachers to use professional enterprise and judgment' in applying the national criteria which would be established by government appointed working groups (DES, 1987b).

Baker saw no contradiction between ending teachers' capacity to devise their own curricula and the establishment instead of groups who would take over that responsibil-ity. The irony, however, was not lost amongst the New Right (see Letwin, 1992) who, as was indicated in Chapter 1, perceived this as a betrayal (Jones, 1989). It seemed that the enemies of the New Right – HMI, DES bureaucrats, teacher organizations and educational experts – were being given a free hand to institutionalize the hated practices of the old system. It was not surprising, said Jones, that pamphlets from the Centre for Policy Studies criticized Baker for his 'reliance on the functionaries of the old regime' (ibid, p.30), particularly HMI.

New Right activists realized that any plans to overhaul radically the education system could be circumvented if they failed to influence the NC working parties charged with creating it. In this sense, the institutional machinery created by Baker to establish the NC was potentially disastrous for the New Right. For those with a particular interest in history, their aim of reforming the history curriculum depended not only upon the actual composition of the HWG but in their capacity to influence it.

Baker and History

As Baker himself notes in his memoirs, he had a special interest in history, having studied the subject at Oxford (Baker, 1993). He published in 1988 an *English History in Verse*: in the introduction he outlined the rationale for an anthology which could offer:

> a true sense of the narrative flow of our history. It is important for people living today to understand how they came to be what they are, to appreciate the forces and events that have shaped the institutions which guide and govern us, and generally to recognize how our rich and complex past has shaped what we think of as our national identity. (Baker, 1988, p.xxi)

Baker's views on history were more sophisticated than perhaps some commentators have given him credit for (see Lawton, 1994). Baker was no straightforward 'grand narrative' Whig historian as the reference to the 'complex past' above suggests. Thus, he claimed in the same anthology that 'at one level the story is of kings and queens, of wars and battles, of famous victories like Trafalgar' but it also involved 'the lives of ordinary people of England' (Baker, 1988, pp.xxi–xxii). Included in the anthology, therefore, were pieces of poetry from the Peasants' Revolt and contributions by George Loveless and 'unknown' contributions from factory workers and victims of the blitz. Baker saw history – in all its variety – as essential for appreciating how 'the national character' had been shaped and defined. In his speech to the Society of Education Officers on 23 January he therefore claimed, like Joseph before him, that history was essential for preparing pupils for adult life. Yet Baker did not envisage a history syllabus that promoted blind allegiance to the status quo. He justified history on the grounds that it enabled pupils 'constructively [to] criticize the institutions of our country'. This is why they needed a 'developed sense of our national past'; yet the speech also went on to justify teaching the history of other countries as well as 'the contributions made over the centuries by those who have settled here from other lands' (DES, 1987b). This apparent commitment to an informed, 'constructively critical' view of history might explain Baker's veiled criticism of Thatcher's perception of history as 'a pageant of glorious events and significant developments, with our small country having given the world parliamentary democracy, an independent judiciary and a tradition of incorrupt administration' (Baker, 1993, p.206). As an historian himself, Baker perhaps had a more perceptive appreciation of history's complexity, as the following extract from my interview with him reveals:

> I have tremendous respect for Margaret but she wasn't a historian. I think probably Margaret's view of history was the kings and queens of England and probably a Whig view of history also! But history is much more than that, it's the full rounded nature of how our country got from there to here and that's much wider and quite difficult do to properly. (Interview)

Nevertheless, Baker was clearly concerned about the state of history, particularly in relation to the teaching of historical knowledge; thus, in his autobiography, Baker recalls that he wanted to ensure that pupils left school with a 'real knowledge' of history over the past 1000 years. This, he claimed, was not happening in schools because in those he had visited he found children studying dinosaurs for the second or third time. A 'more helpful preparation for life' would have involved studying Charles I and Cromwell, the Victorian Age or the Second World War (Baker, 1993 p.193). Although he conceded that empathy was 'an important part of historical understanding' nevertheless children 'had not been given enough basic factual information to enable them to perform this complex task' (ibid, p.206). He explained his perception of empathy to me as follows:

> I remember going to some classes, seeing children trying to imagine that they were living in a medieval village dealing with medicine. Now I am not against that, history does require some imagination, the greatest historians have that imagination ... the writing of history does require imagination, it doesn't just require the analysis of existing documents, it requires an imaginative interpretation to try and see what the different figures were really getting at ... but to say to a child 'imagine what medieval medicine was' you have to have a lot of knowledge to know what medieval villages were all about ... you have to have that background before you can possibly say to young children 'now let's think about medieval medicine' ... therefore I believe very strongly that history should to a very large extent be concerned with the knowledge of the period. (Interview)

This explained why Baker described himself as one of those 'who stood in the ranks of those who saw the systematic and disciplined acquisition of historical knowledge as the essential basis of this curriculum' (Baker, 1993, p.206). The problem for Baker was the perennial problem for all historians and history teachers and which is a recurring theme throughout this book, namely, the criteria for selection of historical content:

> There is far more history that deserves to be taught in our schools than there is likely to be time to teach. So the selection is crucial. My concern is that so much of the selection is unbalanced and that pupils leave school without an adequate mental map of those things which have led us to where we are now and without the wherewithal to form even a preliminary judgment on what was good or bad, glorious or inglorious. (DES, 1987b)

Baker's desire for a history syllabus which ensured a 'more disciplined acquisition of historical knowledge' accounts for his request at a meeting with the HA, on 19 December 1986, for proposals on the type of history which the HA would wish to see included in a national curriculum (Lewis, 1987). Yet there was evidence that Baker was sympathetic towards New Right views on history. An article in *The Daily Telegraph* (25 April 1988) announced that empathy was 'a thing of the past' and reported a letter from the Secondary Examinations Council to Chris McGovern (one of the Lewes Priory teachers) which said that 'ministers' shared his concerns over empathy. Subsequently, Angela Rumbold (the education minister) met McGovern and his colleagues on 4 May. In interview, Baker's recollections of his perceptions of the Lewes teachers were hazy but he did comment that:

> I was sympathetic towards what they were doing because they seemed to me to be attempting to bring back a degree of rigour into history teaching; although I had differences of opinion with Margaret on what should be contained in history, I did believe that there should be a degree of rigour in teaching and they represented the rigour in teaching as opposed to the 'Imagine you are living in a medieval village and you are ill' approach. (Interview)

More alarming for the HA and for the majority of teachers was the claim that Baker had asked Skidelsky, McGovern and a number of famous academics (among them Beloff, Elton, Stone and Thomas) to draw up an 'alternative British history syllabus' entitled *The Making of the United Kingdom* which could be used for the GCSE (*The Sunday Times*, 13 November 1988; see Beloff *et al.*, 1989). Did this represent, to use Chitty's (1989) phrase, a 'Victory for the New Right?' Would the HWG also be 'captured by the discourse?'

On 13 January 1989 a press release announced the establishment of the HWG; asserting that 'history is the foundation stone of citizenship and democracy' it gave details of the group's composition (DES, 1989b). This was the group which was to have the major responsibility for shaping the history curriculum for generations to come: not an inconsiderable task! In my interview with him, Baker recalled what his major intentions had been when setting up the HWG:

> I wanted to embed in the future understanding of children in our country the love and understanding of the past. I wanted them to feel that this was not an alien territory which they only watch through costume dramas on BBC1, that they are all part of this great continuum and that I wanted them to get the feeling that they are not just kids of the late twentieth century, created out of nothing and created instead out of this day and age. Children must have a sense of being part of a great tradition, a great flow of events that has brought them to where they are today. (Interview)

Essentially, the rest of the book considers the extent to which Baker was able to achieve his aims.

Chapter 5

'Making History':
The National Curriculum History Working
Group and the Interim Report

This is a central chapter in the book and is one of four devoted to an evaluation of the *context of text production* relating to history in the NC during the period 1989–95. It analyses the complex factors which shaped the production of the HWG's Interim Report (DES, 1989a). Given its importance for shaping the subsequent debate and policy process, it is worth first summarizing the 'context of influence' (described in the previous chapters) within which the HWG and other groups would have to work in the months and years ahead.

History's 'Context of Influence' in 1989: A 'Thankless Task'?

It was argued in the previous chapters, then, that the debates over GCSE, empathy and a 'common core' of historical content had been the product of competing and some-times mediating influences. It was suggested that the influence of the New Right was particularly significant for publicizing and politicizing history. As a consequence of this influence and the role of the media, it was shown that the history debate had become polarized around the issue of 'skills versus content'. The recognition of the need to justify the teaching of the subject of history in relation to *specific* as opposed to *general* criteria for the selection of historical content was reflected in attempts by the HA, academics and government to suggest and sometimes define what history should be taught. This culminated, for example, in the production of the 1988 HMI document (DES, 1988) which, although offering general critera for organizing history syllabuses in schools, also suggested some of the historical content which could form the basis of a 5–16 history course.

The previous chapters emphasized the difficulties associated with attempting to offer a precise definition or description of teachers' collective view of history teaching; nevertheless using research evidence and teachers' own contributions to the debates in the 1980s, it is possible to detect the emergence by 1988 of a broad pedagogic discourse relating to history in secondary schools which had been influenced by new history and the GCSE. Teachers' 'readings' of the 1988 HMI text suggested that teachers were sensitive to attempts by central government to prescribe historical content. The complexity of these circumstances combined with the challenges and difficulties of the HWG's task ahead was summarized at the height of the NC history debate as follows:

> Imagine for a moment (in an unfashionably empathetic way) that you are a member of the history working group. You have been chosen to identify history courses which will improve on best practice and win and sustain the confidence of teachers, parents, governors and Parliament. However, you have been selected by a government famous for its ideological conviction and for its distaste for much of the contemporary professional practice at a time when teachers themselves seem both acutely sensitive about their professional autonomy yet fiercely argumentative about the best way forward for their subject in schools. And of all the major subjects of the National Curriculum, history is the one most easily influenced by political values. You only have a year to prepare the report while keeping up with your normal job. Can you imagine a more thankless task? (Martin Roberts, TES, 20 April 1990).

The Establishment of the HWG: Biographies, Agendas and Influences

The perceptive and eloquent comments above articulated the complexity of the 'context of influence' within which the HWG would have to operate when it started work in January 1989. The combination of teachers, advisers, teacher trainers and local authority representatives on the HWG at first glance seemed to suggest that the New Right's fears that the groups would be dominated by the 'educational establishment' appeared justified. A more precise analysis of the composition of HWG suggests that Kenneth Baker was conscious of the need to attempt to placate such disparate interests as the New Right and teachers. Interviews conducted with former members of the HWG and with Kenneth Baker revealed that all except one had been interviewed by Baker and/or Rumbold themselves. At the time of the establishment of the HWG, speculation in the press was high that Baker (mainly under Thatcher's influence) would pack the group with New Right appointees. A brief biographical account of the members of the HWG is important not only for speculating at Baker's intentions but for establishing the likely direction the HWG would eventually take.

Baker appointed only two teachers, one of whom (Carol White) had been moderately critical of aspects of SHP; the other, Robert Guyver, had for some time been committed to the teaching of 'discrete' history in the primary sector. The teacher 'representation' increased with the co-option of Chris Culpin (from 23 October 1989), a well-known author of school textbooks, and Dr Tim Lomas (from 10 July 1989), a history teacher with a reputation for being an expert on assessment. The HWG contained two teacher trainers: Anne Low-Beer, who had raised doubts about historical empathy, particularly in relation to its assessment (Low-Beer, 1988, 1989) and was also a lower years specialist. The second, Gareth Jones, was to have a vital coordinating role between the HWG and the History Committee for Wales (HCW); in the 1970s he had argued for a fusion of 'traditional' and 'new' history (Jones, 1978). The HWG also contained three members with LEA backgrounds, one of whom, Henry Hobhouse, was described in the DES (1989b) press release as an 'author'. He had recently published a book entitled *The Forces of Change: Why we are the way we are now*. Its main thesis was that 'modern history has been shaped less by the actions of mankind than by three natural forces: population growth, food supply and disease' (Hobhouse, 1989).

The original two academics appointed had contrasting backgrounds. John Roberts was a high profile academic; by their own admission, members of the HWG emphasized the importance of Roberts' influence in the early stages of HWG's lifetime. This was understandable given that his academic pedigree was formidable: two of his books, *The Triumph of the West* and the single volume *History of the World* had made him famous. Formerly Chancellor of the University of Southampton, he was, in 1989, Warden of Merton College, Oxford, a post to which he was profoundly committed. Indeed, the dual task of sitting on HWG and running Merton College proved particularly arduous and Roberts resigned (in uncontroversial circumstances) from the HWG after the publication of the Interim Report. He was replaced by Professor Peter Marshall, Rhodes Professor at King's College, London, also with a specialism in European history. The second academic originally selected also had impressive academic credentials. Dr Alice Prochaska was Secretary and Librarian of the Institute of Historical Research at the University of London and had been a member of the steering committee of the History at the Universities Defence Group, and thus had had the benefit of working with a wide spectrum in the history profession, including academics and schoolteachers. She had written an authoritative book on the *History of the General Federation of Trade Unions* (Prochaska, 1982). Like Jones (1991) and Guyver (1990), Prochaska also wrote of her experiences on the HWG (Prochaska, 1990). This account revealed that, as with other members of the HWG, she was unsure why she had been selected. Her description of the selection process suggests that Baker did not appoint a series of 'yes-men' (or women) for she had apparently disagreed with Baker and Rumbold's claim that history had 'declined' in recent years, arguing instead that it was in a 'state of constructive ferment' (p.81) and expressing her concerns about the dangers of an overly prescriptive NC.

The most interesting appointment of all, it seems, was the Chair, Commander Michael Saunders-Watson, Chairman of the Heritage Education Trust, formerly President of the Historic Houses Association and a landed castle owner from Northamptonshire. He was hardly a left-wing subversive (but as it turned out, he was not a Thatcherite either). As he was to reveal in an interview after the publication of the Final Report, 'he felt he'd been appointed by Baker because of the need to have somebody outside the academic world' and besides 'Baker had stayed at his house one night' (interview given to the *Independent*, 8 April 1990). Such criteria for selection to the body that was to shape the teaching of history for potentially generations to come was hardly going to fill history teachers with confidence (Blum, 1990).

Like all the respective working groups established to create the NC, the HWG contained an HMI 'observer', in this case Roger Hennessey, staff inspector for history. In fact, this term hides more than it reveals. Hennessey's views on content (Hennessey, 1988 and DES, 1988a: see Chapter 4), particularly the need for specific selection within a chronological framework, were to become highly influential as the work of the HWG progressed. The HWG was headed by a 'management team' comprising Saunders-Watson, Hennessey and a DES secretary, described by HWG members as capable, hard working and highly efficient. Her role was important: not only was she responsible for writing the minutes but also contributed to the formulation of agendas. She was also vital for coordinating the link between the work of the HWG and the DES. Also 'in attendance' at HWG meetings were the DES representatives; their chief role was to advise on various issues of policy and, as can be seen below, their occasional intervention provided the opportunities for the most heated debates, particularly over the assessment of historical knowledge.

Inevitably, members brought their own individual agendas to the group; the HWG in this sense was never a neat homogeneous grouping. The respective biographical backgrounds outlined above provides scope for speculation about these various individual 'interests'. Nevertheless, all the available data generated through interviews, minutes and published personal accounts suggest that a surprising degree of unity and collective identity built up during the HWG's lifetime. Only on a small number of occasions, as we shall see, did HWG members threaten to resign on matters of principle. Of course, group and individual priorities were shaped and influenced by the political, personal and institutional factors which directed the HWG's work. These included the influence of the Secretary of State, the DES and, at times, the Prime Minister herself. As well as the complex situation relating to the teaching of history (see Chapters 1–4), the HWG had to work within a fairly public arena and the glare of the press. These were the kinds of imprecise and subtle influences which it is the major task of this chapter and particularly the next, to evaluate. Of more pressing and more immediate relevance at this stage are the terms of reference within which the HWG had to operate.

Terms of Reference: Possibilities and Constraints

The first meeting of the HWG took place on 24 January 1989 at Elizabeth House, the DES building near Waterloo Station (NC/HWG (89) 1st). Members were formally introduced to the management committee and were then invited to introduce themselves. At the very outset, the HWG was made aware of the potential influence of the media on the work of the group and members were reminded of the importance of confidentiality, particularly in view of intense press interest. They were counselled not to give interviews or reveal anything about the internal workings of the HWG. At this meeting, the HWG was visited by the Secretary of State for the first and only time. He stressed to them that its task would be very difficult because history was a very controversial subject and he urged the HWG to attempt to make history interesting and exciting to pupils (ibid, 1.7).

Most of the time during the first meeting was spent on the immensely important task of outlining the HWG's terms of reference (DES, 1989a, Appendix 1). The group was told that it would have to produce interim recommendations by 30 June 1989 and then provide the Secretary of State with final advice by Christmas 1989. The HWG's initial task was four-fold. First, it had to articulate history's contribution to the school curriculum; secondly, provide provisional thinking about the knowledge, skills and understanding which pupils of different abilities should attain; thirdly, offer advice on suitable attainment targets and programmes of study; finally, the HWG had to identify essential information, bearing in mind the need for a balanced history curriculum in England and Wales and the need for appropriate content for Wales. The HWG was also to consult with other subject groups, take into consideration the degree to which history could contribute to other subjects and liaise with the NC History Committee for Wales (HCW). This would, in effect, throughout the HWG's working life, be done through Gareth Jones.

The 'Supplementary Guidance' provided to the Chairman of the HWG was, in many ways, more important in the way that it revealed, in more precise terms, what was required in the attainment targets and in the programmes of study (DES, 1989a, Appendix 2). Points 3, 4 and 5 of the supplementary guidance were particularly important. Point 3 required that the programmes of study should provide a detailed description of the 'content, skills and processes which all pupils need to be taught'. Point 4 contained the significant phrase which was to influence the future direction of history in the NC:

> The programmes of study should have at the core the history of Britain, the record of its past and, in particular, its political, constitutional and cultural heritage. They should take account of Britain's evolution and its changing role as a European, Commonwealth and world power influencing and being influenced by ideas, movements and events elsewhere in the world. They should also recognize and develop an awareness of the impact of classical civilizations. (ibid)

Point 5 affirmed that:

> The programmes of study should give proper emphasis at each key stage to the content of historical knowledge and lay the foundation for the progressive development of the processes and skills of historical inquiry . . . and assist the progressive acquisition of skills in the collection, objective analysis, interpretation, discriminating use and reporting of evidence from a variety of sources. (ibid)

In addition to the advice on the programmes of study, the supplementary advice to the Chairman stipulated three things which were to be significant for the way in which the HWG approached its job. First, the HWG had to assume that history was to be a compulsory subject across the 5–16 curriculum, including pupils who did not undertake a GCSE in it. Secondly, on the question of time, the HWG was to assume that 3–4 periods in a 40 period timetable, or its equivalent, would be available for history. Thirdly, on assessment, the HWG was told to 'take account of the broad framework for assessment and testing announced by the Government . . . in response to the reports of the Task Group on Assessment and Test'. Finally, the HWG was encouraged to produce a framework which would provide continuity and progression throughout compulsory schooling, 5–16, and which would be broad, balanced and relevant; finally, the history curriculum would have to be sensitive to equal opportunities.

The remainder of the first meeting was devoted to ways of working, including methodology, the timetable and the nature of meetings. In view of the tight timetable (there were only 21 weeks before the Interim Report was due and a further 25 weeks until Christmas) it was important to hold a mixture of day and residential meetings. It was decided to hold most at Elizabeth House, interspersed with residential meetings throughout the country (ibid, 5.1). During the next few months the HWG bandwagon was to meet in places as diverse as Malvern, Great Yarmouth, West Auckland and Crawley; visits were also made by some HWG members to Switzerland and Ireland. The Chairman emphasized that the HWG's immediate task was to produce profile components and attainment targets within them. These and the HWG's initial views on the programmes of study would be published in the Interim Report. In view of the pressure of time, it was impossible to consider all issues in plenary; consequently, the management group proposed to establish three sub-groups, based upon members' expertise and interests. A primary group and a secondary group would be asked to produce appropriate attainment targets; a structure group would be given the important tasks of considering how history could be made enjoyable and exciting, how to structure the range of historical knowledge and provide the justification for the teaching of history in schools. Sub-groups would be asked to submit papers on their work for the rest of the HWG; these papers would be amended in the light of discussion. The Chairman reminded members that because the Interim and Final Reports would be read by professionals and non-professionals alike, their proposals would have to be 'clear, simple and elegant' (ibid, 7.1).

Content Selection, Prescription and the Question of Knowledge

As historians, the realization of the enormity of the task ahead of them in relation to deciding upon the nature of content within the NC was not lost on HWG members. There were three vital issues in relation to content. First, the HWG had to decide what historical content to include within the criteria outlined in the terms of reference and supplementary guidance above. Second, given the need to placate the range of existing parties, as the Chairman had indicated, it was clear that the group would have to justify the actual selection of content in precise, unequivocal ways. Third, the HWG members would have to reconcile themselves in varying degrees to the need to accept the principle of prescription. The three issues were connected and given the scope for professional, ideological and cultural debate which they inevitably implied, discussions on all these issues proved to be vigorous.

The broad philosophy relating to the selection of content which was eventually to manifest itself in the Interim Report (and which was to remain essentially intact in the Final Report) had its origins in a series of papers produced by the 'structure group' at the fourth meeting of HWG at Elizabeth House on 10 March (NC/HWG (89) 4th). One of the papers produced by the group proved particularly influential on HWG's thinking. Entitled 'The distinctive contribution of history to the school curriculum' it was divided into two sections: 'The role of history in the school curriculum' and 'The structure of possible history courses for schools'. The first section began with a justification of the teaching of history: although history was 'valuable for its own sake' (NC/HWG (89) 4th Annex A & D), it had to be something more than that. History, it said, encourages a questioning, curious approach, including making people 'think about questions of right and wrong' and although historical knowledge is useful, a knowledge of the past of one's own nation is likely to be the most useful. After all, it said, 'common citizenship rests on shared assumptions and institutions' (ibid, para.4). The paper thus expressed surprise at the controversy over the view that British history should have a due place in the school curriculum; this did not mean that British history should be taught in exclusion to all others. Rather 'to place British history at the centre of the history curriculum ought not to be contentious. It should be broadly conceived and should provide for the study of Scottish, Irish and Welsh history, as well as that of the various regions of England' (ibid, para.5).

The second section of the paper argued that although British history should be the priority for a national framework, it also called for a history syllabus which drew from as much world history as possible. These examples could be based upon a rich range of evidence, they could stress the different roles of men and women, and provide opportunities for pupils to be aware of cultural variety through history. These topics had to be 'capable of intellectual defence as the foci of ideas without which we cannot really understand where we are today' (ibid, para.7).

HWG members expressed some reservations about aspects of the document. In discussion, members felt that the original selection of the word 'heritage' was too sensitive a word and substituted 'inheritances'; similarly, the words 'national' and 'British' provoked considerable debate because of the changing nature of 'Britishness' over time. These slight reservations apart, it was clear that the HWG had managed to begin to formulate its thoughts upon the criteria by which historical content could be selected. This was based upon the principles that content should be broad, it should reflect a wide range of views and should introduce pupils to a range of 'inheritances', it should pay close attention to British history but also non-British history and in the process it should be an effective vehicle for the development of skills (ibid, 8.5).

Another important question soon raised its head in this connection at the same meeting, namely the extent to which content should be prescribed. The group looked at ten possible models which ranged from a prescriptive chronological list to another at the opposite end of the spectrum which involved no prescribed content at all. It was conceivable that the group could have argued for non-content specific criteria on the lines of GCSE but this proved to be a non-starter. As the minutes indicate this 'free for all' would be unacceptable (ibid, 8.9) given the terms of reference and the comments made by the Secretary of State. Yet the reasons put forward by the HWG for rejecting this model were based on educational, rather than political grounds. Thus 'members accepted the need for prescription' but wanted a structure that would 'allow room for flexibility' (ibid, 8.10). After some discussion, the notion of a 'spiral' model (which remained intact in the Final Report) was thought to be attractive for two main reasons; it allowed flexibility for the 5–7 age range and it was the only model which took into account the relationship between historical content and how children learn history. The model envisaged a 'coherent progression' which could make 'increasing demands on pupils' in terms of 'knowledge, understanding and skills' as they grew older. The main element of content would be British history but important local and world history would also be studied, with the stress on the need for their inter-relationship. The 5–16 curriculum would be 'broadly chronological', with some repetition of topics in primary and secondary schools in order to develop more sophisticated understanding. Finally, in order to balance the requirement for a common structure with the need for schools to teach elements of history which they felt were important to them, the course would be based upon a combination of 'core' and 'optional' units.

However, despite the establishment of a broad working framework on the lines above, subsequent meetings of the HWG showed that three important issues relating to content still had to be resolved, namely the relationship between the programmes of study and the attainment targets, the degree of prescription to be specified in the Final Report (including the amount of compulsory core as against optional units) and the actual selection of units in the programmes of study. By the seventh meeting, at Corby on 8–10 May, the HWG had decided upon separating attainment from the programmes of study, a vital decision which is discussed in detail in the section below. However, the decision had important implications for the selection of content. The management group realized, with advice from the DES officials, that the HWG would have to show that a rigorous amount of historical knowledge was contained in the programmes of study, thus ensuring that the attainment targets were clearly related to knowledge. Core study units, particularly, had to be under-pinned by a specific structure: each history study unit would have a general introduction outlining the main elements to be taught; a statement showing how it linked to attainment targets, how it linked to other subjects, an identification of the specific aspects of the unit which teachers needed to make clear to pupils (political, economic, and social/cultural – the original form of the 'PESC' formula) and suggestions of ways in which teachers could differentiate work (NC/HWG 7th, Annex B). This became known within the HWG as the 'Corby Box'. Again, although the details of this model were amended many times during the HWG's life-time, it provided the essential framework by which selected historical content was organized in the Interim and Final Reports.

Assessment: The Question of Knowledge and Understanding

During only the second meeting, the HWG was given an outline of the DES view on assessment; this was the first of at least four occasions when the DES provided 'advice' on how the HWG should proceed on this important issue. In a formal paper, a DES official made clear that 'the system of assessment and reporting was designed to improve the accountability of schools, particularly to parents' (NC/HWG (89) 2nd, 4.1). The HWG was advised, based on the Secretary of State's comments to other working groups, that attainment targets should be framed in simple language and that they had to be accessible not only to professionals but also to 'laymen'. After detailed discussion on the issue of assessment, an important minute from this meeting articulated the rationale which was also to remain essentially intact in the Interim and Final Reports; it was:

> ... important that the attainment targets should cover knowledge how ... as well as knowledge that ... ie facts and their use ... the attainment targets should allow for some measurement of significance and influences as well as chronology; they should also allow room for 'myths' as well as 'facts'. (ibid, 4.7)

The Malvern meeting (the third) between 20–21 February revealed the first hints of some disagreement amongst the HWG in relation to assessment. One member expressed some concern that too much emphasis upon the skills of analysis early on might hinder the acquisition of knowledge and argued that 'some facts needed to be accepted as given before they could be analysed' (NC/HWG (89) 3rd, 5.5). However, these were disagreements over emphasis rather than principle. It was clear that a consensus had been established early on in the HWG's lifetime (at least expressed through the minutes) that there should be attainment targets devoted to the cultivation of historical skills and concepts: the challenge for the HWG over the weeks ahead would be to show the ways in which they related to the acquisition of historical knowledge.

This began at the fourth meeting, at Elizabeth House on 10 March. Following the influential 'distinctive contribution' paper discussed above (NC/HWG (89) 4th, Annex A & D) the HWG emphasized that pupils should demonstrate 'worthwhile knowledge' of specific aspects of history, including local, national and world history, and also political, social, and technological aspects. It was also agreed that pupils should have an appreciation of those 'concepts by which all history is comprehended' namely continuity and change, cause and effect, chronological awareness and the use of historical conventions. An 'interpretations' attainment target would centre upon the provisional nature of historical judgments, the notion that accounts of the past differ and are influenced by various factors, including the availability of evidence. It was also to touch upon the concepts of objectivity, perspective and anachronism and would introduce pupils to the awareness of 'myths' in history, as well as the uses and abuses of the subject.

The HWG discussed assessment again at the fifth meeting in Portsmouth between 3–5 April (NC/HWG (89) 5th). This meeting was to be crucial in terms of determining the HWG's philosophy on knowledge and, crucially, the way it should be interpreted in the attainment targets and statements of attainment. The central issue here was should and could specific historical knowledge be incorporated within the statements of attainment? If so, how could it be done? If there was to be no specific knowledge attainment target, what was to be the relationship between the statements and the programmes of study? A HWG member tabled a paper concerned with the 'levelling of knowledge' which would provide an important justification for the HWG's views on the assessment of knowledge in the Final Report. The paper argued that if historical progression was entirely dependent upon the acquisition of 'knowledge in an ordered manner', then it was conceivable that 'a 16-year-old who ought to be at level 6/7, but had not progressed beyond level 2, would never have studied anything other than the Romans' (ibid, 8.2).

In the consequent discussion, only one member seemed to question the arguments above pointing out that 'some knowledge was significant for its own sake' (ibid). Yet after the group worked throughout the day on a re-evaluation of the statements of attainment, it was confirmed in discussion that historical knowledge indeed could not be 'levelled' within the model outlined under Task Group on Assessment and Testing (TGAT). Another important minute specified the justification for the group's decision:

> The knowledge component of the attainment target would be better placed within the programmes of study. *They had not wanted knowledge to be simply factual recall; they also wanted to deal with the use to which knowledge was put i.e. understanding* [my emphasis]. They had identified three main areas of understanding: a) chronology; b) cause and effect; and c) continuity and change. (ibid, 9.3)

Furthermore:

> Members agreed that it would be important for pupils to be able to recall salient events and historical facts, but these had to be learned in context. They agreed that recall was necessary to attain a particular demonstration of knowledge. Use of recall would however need to be expressed very clearly, for example as a sensible use of memorized facts rather than rote-learning of facts of information in text-books. (ibid, 9.5)

At the sixth meeting, held at Elizabeth House on 20 April, the HWG's thinking on assessment was put to one of its severest tests by a senior DES official who noted that although the group had decided upon attainment targets which were grounded in skills and understanding, it was important, he reminded them, to show how they would 'enable pupils to learn the basic historical knowledge' (NC/HWG (89) 6th, 6.2). The consequent discussion again revealed only slight differences of emphasis between members of the group. One member pointed out that the historical skills outlined in the attainment targets would be brought to bear on the programmes of study and, following the discussion at the previous meeting, reminded colleagues that there were huge problems associated with connecting historical content directly to levels. On the other hand, another member pointed out that if 'knowledge was not part of the attainment targets, opposition to the Interim Report would be likely' from what he called 'the laity' who would think that the attainment targets were 'entirely skills-based'. Although the minutes revealed that he himself 'accepted that knowledge was implicit in the attainment targets' he emphasized that it was vital that this was spelled out clearly in the Interim Report (ibid, 6.5).

The HWG had reached an important stage here. The decision had been made not to include a separate 'knowledge' attainment target, but mindful of the DES advice on this issue and the sentiments expressed above, it was decided to devote detailed attention to show the clear relationship between the programmes of study and the attainment targets, so as to demonstrate that knowledge permeated them all. The issue was raised again at the Corby meeting (the seventh) where a HWG member warned of the dangers of falling into the trap of the '(non) debate on skills v content'. The HWG then witnessed the strongest example of DES influence to date; a DES official:

> ... warned that the Group would have to bear in mind that if the weight of content was set in the programmes of study, although this was set by statute, it did not guarantee that pupils would have absorbed particular content. The Group would also have to convince the Secretary of State, and the wider audience of parents, employers etc., that its proposed structure complied with the terms of reference and sufficiently emphasized the assimilation of historical knowledge – or there would be a return to the skills v content debate. (NC/ HWG, 7th, 6.15)

Yet one of the HWG members again defended the group's line, stressing that the HWG:

> ... would in fact be emphasizing that there was a body of historical knowledge, arranged chronologically, which all children should learn, apply certain skills to and learn skills through ... In the programmes of study the Group was tying, to a specific body of knowledge, the skills and understanding which a pupil must have acquired, measured against what the teacher must teach. This gave such knowledge greater prominence, not less. (ibid, 6.16)

The result was that the management group produced another significant document entitled 'The logic of the relationship between the programmes of study, profile components, attainment targets and the levels of attainment in history' which sought to 'ensure' that the NC 'delivers the necessary historical knowledge, historical understanding and historical skills – all carefully related' (NC/HWG (89) 7th, Annex D). It summarized the arguments put forward by the HWG above and articulated the complex relationship between knowledge and understanding which was to be expressed in the Interim Report and in important paragraphs in the Final Report. At the same time, in order to guarantee rigour, it was decided to reaffirm the need to apply the 'Corby Box' criteria when planning the programmes of study. Although the minutes reveal that on the next day the senior DES official appeared to probe the HWG's philosophy once more, it was also clear that the HWG, at least for the time being, had won the assessment argument.

Towards the Interim Report

The ninth, tenth and eleventh meetings were devoted to preparing the actual text of the Interim Report. The discussions above had ensured that it would be based upon two fundamental principles. First, it would contain programmes of study which were grounded in detailed historical content based upon the Corby criteria. As the Chairman had indicated, the Report needed to 'provide rigour' in order to 'maintain political credibility' (NC/HWG (89) 9th, 3.2). Second, there was to be no attainment target which specifically 'levelled' knowledge.

By the time the draft of the Interim Report was completed by late June and sent to the Secretary of State for his comments, the press had already started speculating about its contents. On 25 June, *The Observer* reported that although the HWG would request that children learn historical skills, it also emphasized that the group had steered a 'middle line' between 'traditionalists' and 'progressives'. On the other hand, *The Daily Telegraph* claimed that the HWG had supported methods which neglected fact and that it advocated empathy and historical imagination instead. Interestingly, in fact, a close analysis of the minutes suggests that the word empathy was hardly ever mentioned!

The Interim Report was published on 10 August after a short delay, a culmination of months of work since January, the product of eleven meetings, nearly half of them residential of two or more days, hours of discussion and detailed deliberations. In his accompanying letter to Baker and Walker, the respective Secretaries of State, Saunders-Watson emphasized that the HWG's aim had been to 'equip pupils with the historical knowledge, understanding and skills to enable them to play their part as informed citizens of the twenty-first century' (DES, 1989a). Throughout the letter, as in the Report itself, significant statements were directed to a varied audience consisting of, in the earlier words of HWG members, both 'professionals and laymen'. Thus the phrase 'historical knowledge' was repeated in the third paragraph of the letter with the emphasis that the core programmes of study were based upon British history; European and world history had also been included within a chronological framework which would allow schools to draw on their particular expertise. Consequently, the Chairman was convinced that the Report was broad, balanced and coherent. Underlined on the second page of the Report itself was an appeal to read it as a whole and not isolate sections of it.

Chapter 1 dealt directly with the justification for the subject and the rationale underlying the Report itself. Recognizing that there were divergent and strongly held views on the teaching of history, it emphasized that it was impossible to please all. Rather, the Interim Report was based on the terms of reference (ibid, p.4). The important section entitled 'The Fundamental Purposes of School History' contained many of the ideas arising out of the discussions of the 'distinctive contribution' paper (NC/HWG (89) 4th, Annex A & D). History gave individuals a sense of identity, it encouraged a greater understanding of other countries through its breadth, it aroused curiosity, encouraged intellectual sophistication, had a distinct methodology and prepared pupils for adult life (ibid, pp.5–6). The paragraph on the socializing potential of history was phrased carefully; the Report recognized that history was a powerful means of cultural transmission but:

> There can be no standard, uniform culture to be imposed on the young in so culturally

diverse a society as exists in Britain. However, much that is passed on is shared by most of us; school history can put this shared inheritance in its historical context. (ibid, p.5)

Turning to the structure of the curriculum itself, the Report argued that history had a crucial role to play both at primary and secondary levels. It claimed that the standard of history teaching was 'patchy' and this was indefensible. The Report recognized that most history teaching in the primary sector was done through an integrated topic approach, but this did not lead to good history. Rather the 'overall quality of work, as well as the history component, tends to be better when the topic has its foundation in a specific subject (in particular, in history) than where it is but one feature of a more general topic' (ibid, p.7).

The HWG was calling for a radical re-think of the way in which the majority of primary teachers approached the curriculum. This followed from the evidence provided by the HMI report on the teaching of history and geography in primary schools and which had been discussed by the HWG (DES, 1989c). Similarly, at secondary level, history was treated inconsistently within integrated humanities, again confirmed by HMI evidence (DES, 1989d). The Report expressed its concern that more than half of pupils study no history after fourteen; moreover, the number of GCSE courses was 'excessive', with very little rationale provided for their existence (DES, 1989a, p.9: 1.15). The HWG recognized that there was 'growing public concern' about the perceived preponderance of skills-based courses at GCSE at the expense of British history (ibid, p.9: 1.16) but the Report emphasized that the HWG did not 'wish to take sides in these debates which seem to some extent contrived' (ibid, p.9: 1.17). Rather, the main aim of the Report (and which, as we have seen, formed the core of HWG discussions) was to design 'a broad, balanced and coherent course of history for pupils from the age of 5 to 16; a course which will combine rigour, intellectual excitement, and planned programming, and one which respects knowledge and skills equally' (ibid, p.9: 1.18).

Chapter 2 dealt with the vexed question of the selection of historical content. The Report emphasized that historical knowledge was almost 'limitless', resulting in difficulties over selection (ibid, p.10: 2.2). Thus, selection had to be based upon specific criteria; it argued that the content outlined had been selected broadly, to reflect local, national and world history and to encourage an appreciation of different points of view (ibid, pp.10–11: 2.4). Reflecting the 'complex' relationship between content and concepts, it argued that the content was a vehicle also for promoting an understanding of historical method and skills. The chapter contained Hennessey's dual helical cone, representing the progressive attainment of skills, conceptual understanding and historical knowledge (ibid, p.13: 2.12). A section stressed that a 'broadly chronological framework gave coherence to the study of history', however, the group had decided not to impose a rigidly prescriptive chronological line (ibid, p.14: 2.13). The Report welcomed the section in the supplementary guidance to the Chairman that British history should be at the core and (again following the 'distinctive contribution' paper) offered a detailed and varied definition of the term 'British' (ibid, pp.15–17). The political relationships between England and the rest of Britain were complex; moreover, British history should not be solely studied through political or constitutional events (ibid, p.16: 2.23). Migration throughout the ages to Britain had caused rich cultural regional variations (ibid, p.16: 2.24). A 'British' history course should therefore stress the 'richness and variety of British culture and its historical origins' (ibid, p.17:

2.25) described as an 'eclectic view of British history' (ibid, 2,26). It argued that the Report should be viewed as the first stage of a process which moved away from an 'English history-orientated approach' to a 'truly British history syllabus' (ibid, 2.28).

A broad definition and re-interpretation of 'heritage' was discussed (reflecting a number of members' strongly held views on this expressed in the first and fourth meetings). Thus, although the Report recognized that people in Britain have a shared 'inheritance', they also have their own individual or group 'inheritances' (ibid, p.15: 2.19). Similarly, although a broadly defined definition of British history should be at the core of history syllabuses, this did not mean that it had to be 'at the centre of gravity' (ibid, p.18: 2.31). Emphasizing the principle that had been agreed upon early on, the Report stressed that European and world history had to be studied not only in terms of its relationship with Britain but 'from inside' (ibid, p.19: 2.31), thus allowing pupils to see the history of Britain itself in a 'fresh light and a fresh perspective' (ibid, 2.32).

Following the Chairman's advice (NC/HWG 9th, 3.2), the Report described in detail the rationale for the actual choice of content in the programmes of study. It contained an amended version of the 'Corby Box', explaining that programmes of study would follow the same structure in order to encourage coherence and progression in terms of skills, conceptual appreciation and historical knowledge (ibid, pp.21–2). Two paragraphs were dedicated to explaining the complex link between knowledge and understanding and pupils learning and their relationship with the programmes of study (ibid, p.21: 3.3, 3.4), thus preparing the reader for the rationale on attainment targets. The programmes of study would have at the core British and European/world history units, with a choice of thematic units, now with a more rigorously defined rationale from the original HWG list; these would either encourage long-term developments or explore deeper issues (ibid, p.31: 3.22). Likewise (in line with the desire for rigour) the Report explained that school designed themes, although encouraging teachers to utilize local expertise, should be subject to very definite ground rules in order to 'keep them in line with other study units'. On the other hand (reflecting some members' wishes for creative scope) they could enable schools to 'tap their own enterprise and enthusiasm, or in turn to affirm what they feel is important' (ibid, 3.23).

Pages 36 to 44 of the Report specified the programmes of study in terms of British, European and World Thematic history study units and, where appropriate, school-designed themes. KS1 contained the simple approach aimed at introducing younger pupils to the concept of time and people. KS2 required seven core units and a choice of two thematic units from a list of six. Three school-designed units could be selected with a stipulation that at least one had to be based on local history. KS3 contained core units on Medieval Realms, the Making of the UK, Expansion Trade and Industry, the Roman Empire and Islam and the Arabs. Three thematic units could be selected from an eclectic list, including Shogunate Japan and Classical China; there was also a stipulation for one long-term theme to be chosen from either sport or entertainment. Again, three school designed themes had to be chosen, at least one of which had to have a local orientation. KS4 contained four core study units: Modern Britain, the USA, Europe from 1945 to the present and the Modernization of Africa, India or China. There was one thematic study unit to be selected either from the Greek Achievement or Energy. The Report explained that at KS4, an attempt had been made to maintain continuity with existing 'popular GCSE history syllabuses' as much as possible but at the same time they had selected certain units in order to provide coherence between five and sixteen as a whole (ibid, p.43: 3.37, 3.38). Due to the fact that 'hard choices' had to be made at all key stages and for fear of 'overload' or risking 'boring' pupils, certain historical episodes had been left out; three in particular were specified – the Reformation, the Great War and Nazi Germany – but the Report also stressed that these could be included as thematic units if teachers so wished (ibid, p.44: 3.40).

The Report stressed also that the HWG had thought 'long and hard' about the amount of time available for history but based their assumptions on the timings provided in the supplementary guidance. The HWG recognized the practical implications for schools: 'We know that for many schools this will be an increase in time available for history teaching compared with present practice. Nevertheless, we have recommended a coherent course of history which is designed to occupy the time assumed in our guidance' (ibid, p.33: 3.27).

Finally, taking the advice given by DES officials, the Report articulated a lengthy justification of the HWG's recommendations with regard to assessment which had been set out clearly in the 'Logic' paper at the seventh meeting (NC/HWG (89) 7th, Annex D). Attainment targets and programmes of study should not be perceived in isolation but considered together as essential means of cultivating historical knowledge, skills and concepts (ibid, p.22: 3.8). Echoing the discussions at Portsmouth, the Report distinguished between those attainment targets that encouraged pupils to 'know that history is a body of knowledge' and those that encouraged them to know 'how history results from certain defined processes' (ibid, p.24: 3.12). On one point the Report was most unequivocal:

> All our proposed attainment targets relate closely to historical knowledge embodied in the programmes of study and involve its actual recall. The necessary skill of recalling historical knowledge – always in context – is required in order to demonstrate the acquisition of appropriate, and useful, knowledge. By this we mean memorizing facts and not rote-learning for its own sake. (ibid, p.24: 3.13)

This was to be a central argument repeated and given even more precise expression in the Final Report and one which was to cause intense 'readings' in the weeks and months which followed publication. In the Interim Report, the thinking behind each of the attainment targets was explained (ibid, pp.25–6) as were the statements of attainments (ibid, pp.27–8). These statements were given precise elaboration whilst Chapter 6 repeated the HWG's arguments within the context of national assessment arrangements. This gave the HWG the opportunity to hint at the difficulties involved in the application of the TGAT model to history; thus, the learning of history was 'not necessarily linear' (ibid, p.95: 6.5), the construction of assessment tasks was 'complex' and it was imperative that they should not be done in 'isolation' (ibid, 6.4) but should contribute to the 'distinctive' learning of history (ibid, 6.6).

Chapter 6

'Re-Making History?' Towards the Final Report

This chapter examines the creation of the central text of history in the NC, namely the HWG's Final Report (DES, 1990a). It evaluates the ways in which the HWG reacted to the responses to the Interim Report, particularly the request by the Secretary of State to change significant aspects of it. The chapter describes the text of the Final Report in detail and by making reference to interview data, ends with an analytical discussion of the educational politics which created it.

The Response to the Interim Report

Significantly, when the Interim Report was finally published, it contained a letter from the new Secretary of State John MacGregor (who had replaced Baker in July) to Watson, asking the HWG to consider three issues when compiling the Final Report. First, it asked the HWG to pay more attention to chronology; secondly, at KS3 and KS4 the letter noted that less than 50 per cent of time was devoted to British history and the HWG were asked to increase this percentage. Thirdly, the letter doubted whether the recommendations put 'sufficient emphasis on the importance of acquiring historical knowledge and on ensuring that knowledge can be assessed'. The letter made clear that the Secretary of State was not convinced that the case had been made for knowledge remaining only in the programmes of study. The HWG were therefore asked to 'look again at this matter with a view to including essential historical knowledge in the attainment targets' (MacGregor in a letter to the HWG in DES, 1989a). The letter went on to request that HWG produce:

> detailed programmes of study for all the history study units, spelling out the additional or more advanced content of knowledge – including dates, events and people – that must be taught to pupils working towards each successive level of attainment. These programmes of study will also need to make explicit what knowledge is to be taught to pupils of different abilities at different stages. (ibid)

It ended with a request that in the Final Report, statements of attainment should be 'sufficiently precise, specific and well-pitched for assessment purposes' with 'copious examples to illustrate what is wanted'. In particular, the Final Report needed to specify 'how pupils' display of factual knowledge should be treated for assessment purposes' (ibid).

MacGregor's letter was bound to cause controversy as it simply fuelled existing rumours that the Secretary of State, under pressure from the Prime Minister herself and the New Right, was exerting influence upon the HWG. The press had a field day. On the day of publication, the *Evening Standard* headline announced that 'This history is bunk says new Minister' and that the HWG been accused of 'selling Britain's heritage short'. On the next day (11 August 1989), the tabloid press was jubilant. The *Daily Mail* reported 'Get the facts straight, history men are told', while the *Daily Express* claimed that MacGregor had told HWG that 'Children must know dates, events and characters, and not get bogged down with too much theorizing about the nature of history'. The *Daily Telegraph* claimed that MacGregor had sided himself firmly with traditionalists and had 'largely rejected' the Report. This theme was picked up by *Today* which welcomed MacGregor's demands because 'The new curriculum even writes the Nazis out of history with no mention on the compulsory list of the rise and fall of the Third Reich or the First World War. They make way for the study of cowboys and indians and the history of sport, all included in a list of subjects drawn up by a panel of experts'. The *Guardian* was a little more circumspect, choosing to emphasize the Report's claim that the distinction between new and traditionalist history had become exaggerated. However, a leader article offered warnings about MacGregor's intervention which 'has an ominous smack about it, rather as if we were soon to return to the solid, drum banging certainties of H.E. Marshall's *Our Island Story*'. A week later the TES described it as 'deeply repugnant' that a Secretary of State should believe that 'British history belongs to the government of the day' (18 August 1989). It also pointed out that the group had the 'absurd task of deciding what history every English boy or girl should know and be able to do. It seems to have answered that question by putting in far too much', and questioned whether there could be enough time and resources available to implement the new curriculum.

Towards the Final Report

Given these circumstances, the next few weeks and months would be crucial; the fundamental question was whether the HWG would accede to the Secretary of State's demands and change their proposals significantly in the Final Report. At the thirteenth meeting, held at Bournemouth on 29 August, it was decided to establish three 'panels' to look at the programmes of study, responses to the Interim Report and assessment issues. The programmes of study panel would have to review the existing content in the history study units in KS3 and KS4 in particular to see how the proportion of British history could be increased to a minimum of 50 per cent as requested by the Secretary of State; possible 'candidates' for inclusion were The Great War, the Reformation and Nazi Germany which had not featured prominently in the Interim Report. The assessment panel was given the task of reviewing the group's proposals on assessment.

These decisions would partly depend upon the findings of the 'responses' panel. By the end of September, 150 responses had already been received and by mid-October, the responses panel had evaluated nearly 500. Overall, the HWG would receive over a thousand responses to the Interim Report, mainly from teachers (particularly secondary teachers), historians and others, including, of course, various New Right groups. With regard to teachers' responses, the chair of the responses panel reported that there were grumbles about a 'perceived lack of consultation', but overall he could report that the responses were 'sympathetic to the group's philosophy' and 'in favour of the group's proposals' on a ratio of 3:1 (NC/HWG (89) 14th, 4.2). Significantly, many respondents welcomed the decision not to propose a separate knowledge attainment target. There were some concerns about selection of content and in this respect 'KS4 was the most heavily criticized', mainly on the grounds that traditionally popular historical themes (e.g. medicine) taught at this level had been ignored in favour of content which appeared 'dull and boring'. One of the most significant criticisms was that teachers felt that the proposals were too prescriptive. This view was confirmed by regional consultation meetings held throughout the country – organized mainly by the HA – which HWG members attended. One member thus reported that some of these teachers 'felt that they were being viewed as robot deliverers of prescribed content' (ibid, 4.6).

However, given the demands of the Secretary of State and the views of many on the group that prescription was essential to guarantee a rigorous menu of history in primary and secondary schools, it soon became apparent that the amount of prescribed content would not be reduced (NC/HWG (89) 15th). Indeed, again following the Secretary of State, a significant amount of the group's time between the Interim and Final Reports was concerned with making clear 'what each programme of study was expected to achieve in terms of knowledge, skills and understanding' for this was important to demonstrate 'that pupils would know X, Y and Z for assessment purposes' (NC/HWG (89) 12th, 6.19). Many hours of the meetings were also devoted to making the selection of content appear logical, coherent and well balanced within a chronological framework. KS1 and KS2 needed only fairly minor amendments. Most of the debate over content centred upon KS3; discussion in the group revealed that the priority was to ensure that British history was seen to be given a prominent place but that other aspects of history should not be relegated. The pressure of time meant that KS4 was dealt with very quickly by the HWG, the main amendments again involved bolstering the British dimension.

By the end of the fifteenth meeting, three of the major tasks facing the HWG – the proportion of British history, chronology and a rationale for the selection of content – had largely been dealt with. This only left assessment; the discussion, however, centred more on issues of presentation rather than substance, for after lengthy discussion at the thirteenth meeting, the HWG, bolstered by the support for this proposal in responses, confirmed its decision not to include a separate knowledge attainment target. Assessment-related discussion after this decision therefore related to the precise definition of knowledge (NC/HWG (89) 15th, 8.3) a continuation of earlier debates initiated by the Interim Report. The HWG's complex definition of historical knowledge and understanding would be given particular prominence in the Final Report. After hours of discussion of technical issues, the HWG's philosophy on assessment articulated in the Final Report was to remain essentially unchanged from the Interim.

The last minuted meeting, the eighteenth, at Great Yarmouth between 13–15

November, saw the HWG make some finishing touches to the proposals on the programmes of study, with some minor adjustments made to aspects of the key stages. The remaining meetings (five of them) between November and January 29–31, the final meeting of the HWG, were devoted to writing the individual chapters of the Final Report, ready for the Secretary of State's comments and subsequent publication.

The Final Report

The Final Report was due to be published in March but in fact was not published until 3 April. In February, the press had already started to speculate that it was Thatcher's interference which caused the delay, speculation which is discussed in the next chapter. The HWG claimed that the Report was not an attempt to 'please everyone', rather it had been based upon the terms of reference (DES, 1990a, 1.5). It was also an attempt to maintain continuity with the 'best' of existing practices, but that particularly with respect to the selection of content, continuity was not the sole criteria (ibid, 1.11). It stressed that the nature of school history prior to the NC was 'varied in quality, quantity and organization' (ibid, 1.13). It recognized that developments such as the enquiry methods and fieldwork had a positive impact but these had not been 'uniform' (ibid, 1.14). Rather, history had been subsumed into integrated topic work in the primary schools (ibid, 1.16). At secondary school, there was a lack of coherence in the lower school (ibid, 1.20), whilst the lack of history in humanities courses in the lower and upper school were not 'well defined' (ibid, 1.21). More worrying was that history had become optional for more than half of secondary pupils at GCSE (ibid, 1.22) whilst there seemed to be 'no underlying rationale' for the diversity of syllabi at GCSE (ibid, 1.23). The overall picture was therefore of history in a 'tenuous position' in primary schools and 'under threat' in secondary schools (ibid, 1.15) and the Report cited various HMI reports as evidence (ibid, ix). Thus the HWG's aims had been to achieve an entitlement of history for all pupils, fortify history at primary level, improve continuity between primary and secondary, strengthen the position of history in schools, guarantee 'an acceptable minimum' of British history, reduce the discontinuity of pupils moving schools and finally to simplify teacher training, resources and examinations (ibid, 1.27). History was a 'splendid subject for study' (ibid, 1.1) and was 'challenging, relevant and interesting' (ibid, 1.9). Thus in order for history to be 'restored to a central place in the curriculum' the HWG recommended that it be accorded 3–4 periods per week out of a 40 period timetable (ibid, 5.27).

It argued that polarized debates over 'traditional and new forms of history', the teaching of 'skills' and 'empathy' had been exaggerated and distorted, and stressed that HWG had no wish to 'take sides' in such debates which were often 'contrived', resting on 'thin evidence' or the product of 'misapprehension' (ibid, 1.26). Hence an important principle under-pinning the document, the notion of history as an 'organic whole'; thus at the beginning of the document, attention was immediately drawn to the distinction between 'history' and 'the past' (ibid, 1.2) and this provided the opportunity to argue that:

> the study of history must be grounded in a thorough knowledge of the past; must employ rigorous historical method – the way in which historians carry out their task; and must involve a range of interpretations and explanations. **Together, these elements make an**

organic whole; if any one of them is missing the outcome is not history. (ibid, 1.3, document's emphasis)

This was a theme repeated both explicitly and implicitly many times throughout the document. The proposals were thus based upon the 'inter-relationship' between attainment targets and programmes of study, thus ensuring that pupils would not 'develop skills in isolation from a solid foundation of historical information' (ibid, 1.4). Thus the 'attainment targets and the programmes of study are fully complementary; neither can provide a basis for learning and assessment without the other and both have statutory force' (ibid, 3.14). The nine 'purposes of school history' as outlined in the Report (ibid, 1.7) should also not be applied 'individually' but 'taken as a whole' (ibid, 1.8). In describing the structure of the history course proposed in the document, the HWG repeated the attainment target/programmes of study link and thus the delivery of 'historical knowledge, historical understanding and historical skills – all carefully related – necessary for a National Curriculum history course' (ibid, 2.1). The 'helix' combining knowledge, understanding, skills and concepts was illustrated as it was in the Interim Report (2.6). To remind the reader again, the Report stated that the overall objective of the HWG had been to '**give equal weight to knowledge, understanding and skills**' (ibid, 2.10, document's emphasis).

In the same paragraph was the second major principle which had pre-occupied the management team throughout the life-time of the HWG, namely the combination of '**rigour, intellectual excitement and planned programming**' (ibid). Again, the word 'rigour' was given explicit expression, appearing on numerous occasions in the document. More importantly, it appeared implicitly in the combination of knowledge, skills and concepts above, the relationship between knowledge and the attainment targets (Chapter 3), the application of the PESC formula (Chapter 4), the rationale for the selection of content (Chapter 5) and perhaps above all in the allocation of historical information in the programmes of study themselves (Chapter 6). This provided the opportunity to justify the two most contentious decisions taken by the HWG between the Interim Report and the Final Report, namely the assessment of historical knowledge and the selection of historical content.

Chapter 3, *The essence of history,* arguably the most significant chapter in the Report, articulated and summarized the discussions over the assessment of historical knowledge which, as we have seen, had exercised the HWG over the previous months. It drew attention to three types of historical 'knowledge', namely, 'knowledge as information' which the HWG described as the 'basic facts' such as events, dates and names; 'knowledge as understanding' or facts which are studied in relation to other facts and in the process their significance is perceived; 'knowledge as content', the subject matter of history such as a period or theme (ibid, 3.2). As with the relationship between knowledge, skill and concept, these three had to be inter-related to provide the essence of historical study, namely historical understanding:

> In order to know about, or understand, an historical event we need to acquire historical information but the constituents of that information – the names, dates, and places – provide only starting points for understanding. Without understanding, history is reduced to parrot learning and assessment to a parlour memory game. (ibid, 3.4)

The next paragraph went on to justify this rationale in greater depth and in some senses went to the very heart of the debate:

> In the study of history the essential objective must be the acquisition of knowledge as understanding. It is that understanding which provides the frame of reference within which the items of information, the historical facts, find their place and meaning. Knowledge as understanding cannot be achieved without a knowledge of historical information, and the wider base of information the greater the potential for developing understanding through the perception of significant connections and relationships. The learning of facts alone is not in itself sufficient for understanding. (ibid, 3.5)

The HWG explained that it had indeed spent time between the Interim Report and the Final Report considering the Secretary of State's request to examine more closely the relationship between the attainment targets and the programmes of study to ensure that knowledge was both acquired and assessed, and had come to the conclusion again that it was not possible to do this through placing essential knowledge in the attainment targets (ibid, 3.7). Moreover, the 'very few' in the consultation who had offered such proposals had not provided convincing arguments that it could be done (ibid, 3.16). Sections in the chapter outlined the problems relating to chronology, levelling, complexity and rigidity associated with placing specific historical knowledge in the attainment targets (ibid, pp.8–9) and were given even further elaboration in an Annex (ibid, pp.13–14). However, the HWG went to pains to point out that it was keen to ensure that 'historical information will be taught, learned and properly assessed' (ibid, 3.13). The best way of ensuring that historical knowledge was (repeated, significantly, again) 'taught, learned and assessed' was by 'clearly spelling out the essential historical information in the programmes of study' and then assessing through the attainment targets (ibid, 3.8). The Report pointed out that the programmes of study carried the same statutory force as the attainment targets in this respect and thus teachers were 'required to teach the knowledge contained in them' (ibid, 3.9). The HWG explained that this was why in each of the programmes of study the Final Report specified 'the essential knowledge which must be taught' through the objectives set by the attainment targets (ibid, 3.13). Moreover, this approach was 'overwhelmingly welcomed' by respondents to the Interim Report (ibid, 3.16).

Chapter 7 thus stressed that although content was selected on 'historical grounds', attainment targets were chosen on 'educational grounds' (ibid, 7.2). It repeated again the relationship between programmes of study and attainment targets, and emphasized the crucial sections recorded in the minutes which stressed the distinction between the 'know that' and the 'know how' of history (ibid, 7.7) as well as the desire for the 'accurate recall' of essential historical information (ibid, 7.9). This was followed by a brief explanation of the selection of the attainment targets and the nature of the statements of attainment which had to be 'specific enough to give a clear idea of what is expected' and provide 'clear progression' (ibid, 7.19) and 'should be capable of achievement at various levels, so that a pupil's progress against an attainment target can be charted, and the range of performance among pupils within a group can be identified' (ibid, 7.18). The bulk of the chapter (pp.119–66) then went on to describe the statements of attainment. The HWG counselled that 'some care' was needed when using the levels of attainment for 'pupils studying history rarely progress neatly through a series of levels'. Nevertheless they had been based on the available 'research on how children learn in history'. Learning depended upon the teaching context and attainment had to be reinforced in a variety of contexts (ibid). Moreover, assessment tasks should not relate to skills 'in isolation' (ibid, 8.5).

The issue of assessment provided the context in which the rationale for the selection of content and prescription in the programmes of study could be explained. The HWG pointed out the difficulties associated with making selections from the vast content of history (ibid, 4.3) and noted the controversies which had been aroused in this respect by the Interim Report (ibid, 4.4). However, it reaffirmed its commitment to prescription in the NC and thus it had 'grasped the nettle' and made selections (ibid, 4.5). It pointed out in detail the criteria which had evolved: content should pay attention to the various dimensions, interpretations, varieties and inheritances of history, all of which combined to create a balanced approach to content (ibid, pp.15–16). Again, stressing the concept of the 'organic whole', study units were selected according to the same criteria (the HWG's 'Corby Boxes') to ensure that they linked to the attainment targets, followed the PESC formula, showed links within and across key stages and that they provided a broad chronological framework. This would provide coherence (ibid, 4.15).

In relation to the vexed question of British history, the Final Report welcomed paragraph 4 of the supplementary guidance and therefore the HWG's proposals were 'weighted in favour of British history' (ibid, 4.18). However, the Final Report went on to offer a detailed and varied definition of the concept 'British'. First, British history should not be concentrated upon exclusively political history or pre-occupied with English relationships with its neighbours; British history had to emphasize what was distinctive about Wales, Scotland and Ireland (ibid, 4.21). Second, it pointed to the dynamic impact of migration and regional variations which had shaped British culture (ibid, 4.21). Thus, Britain was not 'an undifferentiated mass' and the selection of history study units reflected this variety (ibid, 4.22); they reflected not only English, but Welsh, Scottish and Irish perspectives (ibid, 4.25). A later section in the Report reinforced the point that 'Britain has always been in one way or another a multi-cultural society'; an ethnically diverse population strengthened rather than weakened the argument for an inclusion of British history, nevertheless, it placed 'a high degree of responsibility on the manner in which the material is presented' (ibid, 11.25). However, although British history was at the centre of the proposals it was not 'pivotal' (ibid, 4.26). European and world history were also given prominence in the Final Report on the lines suggested in the supplementary guidance (4.29). This and the commitment to the notion of 'inheritances' (ibid, 3.27) and 'interpretations' (ibid, 3.28) meant that history had a 'great contribution' to multicultural education through 'open-mindedness' and the capacity to 'examine issues critically from a variety of perspectives' which would themselves combat racism and stereotypes (ibid, 11.26). Chapter 5 set out the specific rationale for each key stage within the context of the broad criteria established above. Thus, KS3 encompassed British, European and world history (ibid, 5.15) within a chronological framework (5.10). Specific selections were justified and given further elaboration. Therefore, although 'The Making of the UK' appeared to have a 'strong political emphasis', PESC would ensure that science, the arts and technology could be included (ibid, 5.11). The 'Roman Empire' was included because it continued a 'long and successful tradition of teaching pupils about classical civilizations' (ibid, 5.12). An illuminative paragraph outlined the important inclusions at KS4 as a consequence of consultation after the Interim Report, including the 'Reformation' and the 'Great War' (ibid, 5.13). Moreover, KS4 had been selected bearing in mind the 'special role' history had to play in 'preparing pupils for informed citizenship' (ibid, 5.16). The bulk of the Report (Chapter 6, pp.31–114), in accordance with the philosophy and rationale set out so clearly in the previous sections (the 'Corby Boxes'), outlined in detail each of the study units, including purpose, links, focus, concepts, PESC and, crucially, 'essential information' and 'exemplary information'.

Finally, towards the end of the Report, Chapter 10 was devoted to 'Bringing history to life'. Interestingly, it outlined the ways in which field trips, museum visits, drama, role play and other simulation techniques could 'convey an image of living in the past'; they could show the 'differences between living in the past and living in the present' (ibid, 10.3) and could provide the opportunity to 'explore, and come to imagine aspects of history'; these could even be the 'source of good, imaginative writing, and they help to bring history to life'. However, this went with the pointed warning that they needed to be 'used with care' (ibid, 10.4). Above all, they had to be rooted in '**an uncompromising respect for evidence**', otherwise they would simply be an excuse for 'pretending' (ibid, 10.5). An equally interesting chapter on 'Implementation' (Chapter 9) contained two portentous warnings. First, the HWG had felt obliged to admit that the current level of resources and the limited amount of time meant that many of its recommendations might not be implemented in full. Secondly, with regard to future revisions of the proposals, the HWG warned that they be 'undertaken in such a way as to avoid what appears to be public suspicion that school history may be manipulated for political purposes' (ibid, 9.35).

The History Working Group: 'Captured by the Discourse'?

The Report sought to appeal to a range of diverse views on the teaching of history: it sought in particular to defuse the polarized 'skills versus content' debate by articulating a sophisticated synthesis of historical knowledge and the cultivation of historical skills and methodology within a history course which offered breadth and balance. But what factors – internal and external – accounted for these decisions? What role, for example, did civil servants play? Did government ministers attempt to influence the HWG's work? These questions are addressed by discussing the two issues which pre-occupied the HWG's work, namely the assessment of knowledge and the selection of historical content. In order to shed further light upon the answers to these questions, reference is made below to some of the data generated from interviews conducted with former HWG members and DES officials.

Interviews conducted with HWG members showed a high level of consciousness of the debates over the teaching of history described in Chapters 2–4. This was reflected in their anticipation that the task in hand was going to be difficult, controversial and, at times, likely to lead to animosity from a variety of quarters: teachers, politicians and the general public. The task for one member was thus to 'try and please groupings which were clearly fundamentally opposed to each other'. This reminds us of Roberts' (1990) reference to the 'thankless task' referred to at the beginning of Chapter 5. Hardly surprising, therefore, that a number of members had to contemplate the decision of accepting the invitation to serve on the group carefully. Yet as one interviewee commented 'it was better to have somebody on the HWG who knew what they were doing rather than somebody who didn't . . . I was sure I could do a better job than others who were being contemplated for the job'.

The interviews revealed that 'doing a better job' involved a number of issues relating to their views of the state of history teaching in 1989 and, crucially, their perception of the direction it needed to take in the future. It seemed that the HWG were motivated by three main factors. First, the group believed that the 'skills versus content' debate was contrived and simplistic; however, the majority of members also believed that history teaching had become dominated by skills at the expense of content. Thus, in interview, one member expressed the concern that 'pupils were coming out of an SHP syllabus with sophisticated historical skills but not enough content knowledge'. This would explain why the HWG was prepared to accept the principle of prescription and the selection of content based upon specific (as opposed to general) criteria. Of course, this is what Hennessey had been attempting to argue in the late 1980s (Hennessey, 1988) and in this respect the HWG was merely providing continuity with *Curriculum Matters 5–16: History* (DES, 1988).

Secondly, HWG members were unanimous in their determination to defend history's position as a compulsory foundation subject within the NC. Similarly, no member in interview expressed opposition to the principle or concept of a NC, although there were some relatively minor differences of opinion on the precise form which it should take. The perception that history's place should be defended was an important one for explaining the HWG's work and for appreciating the determination with which members defended the Final Report after it was published. Thus one member described history as a curriculum 'territory' which had to be protected and claimed that no group of committed subject professionals would have tolerated less time for the subject (an observation which, sadly, as we shall see in Chapter 9 accounted for the chronic content overload of the NC as a whole and which culminated in the need for reform). The belief in 'doing our best' for history was a profound unifying factor amongst the HWG. According to Prochaska (1990, p.84) all members of the HWG were 'committed to the proposition that the teaching of history in schools matters very much indeed, and members of the group seemed to take it for granted, without our ever saying so, that we would make this work our priority for the year'.

Third, a number of HWG members expressed the view that they saw the NC as an opportunity for promoting history in primary schools. They believed that the place of history was badly defined in the primary sector by being subsumed into topic work (see Guyver, 1990; Jones, 1991). In addition, some HWG members expressed concern that similar developments were occurring in the secondary sector in the shape of integrated humanities. Here, the HWG was influenced not only by their own experiences but by evidence from the HMI reports (DES, 1989c; DES, 1989d). The minutes reveal that these reports were cited whenever doubts started to appear in members' minds about the need for prescription or when members' morale seemed to be low following some of the negative responses to the Interim Report (NC/HWG (89) 15th). Defence of the subject was often perceived by the HWG as a greater priority than the maintenance of particular pedagogic philosophies such as integration or topic work.

Inevitably, members brought their own individual agendas to the group; the HWG in this sense was never a neat, homogeneous grouping. It was evident, for example, that some were more sympathetic to issues relating to equal opportunities than others, that some were relatively more at ease with the principle of prescription and that at least one member of the group possibly even favoured a separate knowledge attainment target. The respective biographical details provided at the beginning of Chapter 5 provide scope for speculation about these various individual 'interests'. Nevertheless, the triangulated data generated through interviews, minutes and published personal accounts suggest that there was a surprising degree of unity on fundamental issues. Extraordinarily, the minutes reveal only two occasions when, following disagreements, a vote had to be taken, namely over the question of the chronological order of KS2 units of study (NC/HWG (89) 12th) and, more controversially, over the inclusion of Islam within KS3 (NC/HWG (89) 15th). In interview, two members revealed that they had contemplated resigning if this unit was left out.

Given the potential for discussion and controversy over their task, it is surprising that there were not more disagreements of this sort. This unity can only be explained by reference to the group's conviction of the validity of its intellectual case and the difficulty of attempting to placate groups with fundamentally opposed views on key issues such as assessment. Here, it was theoretically possible at least, for the HWG to have rejected the application of the TGAT model to history (Slater, 1991). However, the wording of the Supplementary Guidance made it clear that the group was expected to 'take into account the broad framework for assessment and testing announced by the Government on 7 June, 1988 in response to the reports of the Task Group on Assessment and Testing' (DES, 1989a, Appendix 2, p.107). Interviews conducted with HWG members revealed that the rejection of the application of TGAT to history was not a practical option. The interview data, the minutes and other documentation (see Lomas, 1990, 1991) confirm that although the group recognized that it was difficult to apply history to it, members felt obliged to abide by it, not only because DES 'advised' them to adopt it but that, in the words of one member 'we were worried that if we had not taken on board the TGAT model, then history would be out on a limb. Why should history stick its neck out? This would have marginalized the whole subject' (Interview). On the other hand, as another HWG member revealed to me, this raised fundamental challenges which had to be addressed:

> When we were confronted with the problem of making TGAT work, we had to think carefully. Although we had experience of levelling skills, we felt that we could not level knowledge particularly effectively. The whole notion of levelling knowledge and chronology in this way was absurd and we said so on many occasions. We had to face the civil servants on a number of occasions over this; there were some fierce debates with them over the fact that knowledge could only be assessed as understanding. (Interview)

These 'fierce debates' relating to the decision to separate attainment targets from the programmes of study, as we have seen, took place mainly *early on* in the HWG's lifetime (NC/HWG (89) 2nd). The minutes show, of course, that the HWG used a variety of complex intellectual, educational and philosophical arguments to justify their decision (see back: NC/HWG (89) 6th & 7th). As one HWG member phrased it 'we won the intellectual argument'; moreover, interviews with civil servants and HWG members confirmed that on the surface at least, the group was united on this issue. Thus a civil servant expressed the view that 'there was unanimity in the Group that placing the vital historical knowledge in the Attainment Targets was invalid, illogical and unhistorical' (Correspondence).

Interview data also confirmed the picture conveyed in the minutes that civil servants 'tested out' HWG's arguments in this respect. Thus, one HWG member spoke of attempts by officials to 'try out the alternatives to see the pitfalls'. Yet what is very interesting from the minutes is that although the management group under Saunders-Watson dutifully followed the Secretary of State's instructions following the Interim

Report and 're-visited' the issue, there was no repeat of the intense debate between HWG members and DES officials which had characterized the earlier meetings referred to above. Thus at the thirteenth meeting, the Chairman reported that although he had conveyed the HWG's views on the problems of including a knowledge attainment target to the Secretary of State, MacGregor was yet to be convinced that the HWG could not do as other working groups had done and ensure the assessment of subject knowledge through attainment targets (NC/HWG (89) 13th, 10.1). In the light of this, the Chairman asked the group to look again at the range of options. The minutes reveal that the group looked exhaustively at a range of possible options, none of which were regarded as remotely feasible by the HWG but members felt it was important to show in the Final Report that it had considered them seriously (ibid, 10.3).

The fact that by this stage there was no apparent evidence of DES questioning of the HWG's decision suggests that officials had been convinced by the force of intellectual argument. To his credit, Saunders-Watson on numerous occasions during the HWG's life-time questioned the rigour of the group's rationale on assessment and many other issues which, according to the interviews conducted with them, won him almost universal respect amongst HWG members. As one member revealed to me 'Saunders-Watson obviously had reservations about aspects of what we were proposing but, after asking some pretty tough questions of us, he was also ready to listen. Once he had made up his own mind that what we were arguing made sense, he seemed ready to argue our case' (Interview). When the HWG had been established, teachers such as Blum (1990) had understandable concerns that a person with 'no direct educational experience since he left school' should have responsibility for 'spearheading changes in the way history is taught in an inner London comprehensive' (p.11). Yet, crucially, he was amenable to pedagogical argument. This explains the following extract from the interview with Saunders-Watson:

> I had my eyes opened by the HWG. I had lived with history and had been taught the subject in a very old-fashioned way. Then when I heard the arguments put forward by HWG members it came as something of a culture shock. I became impressed with many of the arguments which I never knew existed. I learnt that history is not just about facts but it is also about acquiring information, processes and learning. History involves a combination of content, understanding and information. (Interview)

Significantly, a civil servant expressed similar sentiments:

> I was soon convinced that the HWG's approach to curriculum and assessment was right, and that specific knowledge belonged in the programmes of study and not in the statements of attainment. (Correspondence)

The minutes and the interviews with HWG members, however, revealed that this had not been the case at the beginning of the HWG's life-time. Yet once the civil servants and the Chairman had been 'captured by the discourse' this was important for the next, even more crucial, stage of persuading Kenneth Baker of the logic of the HWG's case. In interview, Saunders-Watson emphasized that Baker had been broadly sympathetic to the Interim Report but had expressed surprise to him that it had not contained a separate knowledge attainment target and that it had not contained enough emphasis upon British history. These were referred to as 'niggling doubts' at the HWG's twelfth meeting held on 25 July 1989 (NC/HWG (89) 12th). Saunders-Watson revealed that therefore he had to:

... try and convince Baker that the demand for a knowledge attainment target was problematic. I therefore told him, how do you break knowledge down into ten levels? Take the Battle of Waterloo: is level 1 the fact that the pupils know that the battle existed? Is level 2 the fact they know who participated? And so on. How can you develop progression in a scheme of this sort? Do you take a chronological approach to progression? Are you therefore saying that Ancient History (levels 1–3) is easier than modern history? I convinced Baker of our argument. (Interview)

Similarly, the same civil servant who had been 'convinced of the HWG's approach' above, revealed that he had therefore 'used my influence to help the HWG state the case as strongly as possible, and to persuade colleagues and Ministers that they were right' (Correspondence). It seems that Saunders-Watson and the civil servants were partly successful in this respect, at least as far as Kenneth Baker was concerned. In interview, Baker revealed that he believed the Interim Report had been 'broadly right' because it contained reference to 'certain important dates in the constitutional history of the country'; he described it as a 'brave attempt to try and get the balance of what history should be about, namely chronology and the study of how people actually lived' (Interview). However, in his autobiography, echoing what he had told Saunders-Watson himself, Baker confirmed that he had been 'disappointed with the lack of emphasis on the teaching of hard facts and their chronology' (Baker, 1993, p.206).

Faced with such apparently contradictory evidence, the precise nature of Baker's views on the Interim Report has to remain open to speculation; there seems little doubt that he advocated the demand for increased factual knowledge and an increase in the proportion of British history as outlined in MacGregor's letter to Saunders-Watson which accompanied the Report. The letter was written within the context of the Prime Minister's views on the subject. In her autobiography, Thatcher expressed her views on the Interim Report:

> I was appalled. It put the emphasis on interpretation and enquiry as against content and knowledge. There was insufficient weight given to British history. There was not enough emphasis on history as chronological study. Ken Baker wanted to give the report a general welcome while urging its Chairman to make the attainment targets specify more clearly factual knowledge and increasing the British history content. But this in my view did not go far enough. I considered the document comprehensively flawed and told Ken that there must be major, not just minor, changes. In particular, I wanted to see a clearly set out chronological framework for the whole history curriculum. (Thatcher, 1993, p.596)

By the time of the publication of the Interim Report, therefore, it was clear that Thatcher was taking a direct personal interest in the affairs of the HWG. Interviews with civil servants revealed that she was kept informed through Brian Griffiths, head of the No. 10 Policy Unit, who was particularly interested in the history curriculum. Griffiths was a prominent member of the Centre for Policy Studies and at the heart of a wide-ranging New Right network (see Straw's comments on this below). Various New Right groups, including the Campaign for Real Education and the Centre for Policy Studies, had sent responses to the HWG regarding the Interim Report. The Centre for Policy Studies response was written by Sheila Lawlor (Lawlor, 1989). A long, detailed document running to 42 pages, it articulated the familiar themes described in Chapter 4. Thus, Lawlor believed that the Interim Report was a victory for 'new' over 'traditional' history. She claimed that although the Report tried to give the impression that it was committed to the teaching of facts, in effect, this was impossible under the proposals because of the nature of the attainment targets. This was because the authors had been more pre-occupied with 'process' rather than seeing history 'as an end in itself'. The Report had also grossly undervalued the importance of British history and chronology.

Interview data revealed that the HWG had read this particular response to the Interim Report carefully; it was one of the few documents to be selected for particular attention (although this is not mentioned in the minutes). Interview data reveal that the HWG were not at all impressed with the arguments used by Lawlor but members also stressed the importance of the document for their work:

> The Centre for Policy Studies document was important in the sense that we realized we had to marshal our arguments against them and other critics. We had to be ready with a carefully thought out justification for what we were doing. This gave us the opportunity to re-iterate our views on why we disagreed so much with what the Centre for Policy Studies and others like them were saying. (Interview)

This is important for the purposes of this book. I am arguing here that any 'political influence' exerted over the HWG was more indirect than direct, a view confirmed by most of the HWG members. One HWG member commented that it was 'hard to define political'. Here, the interviews revealed that any 'political pressure' as such came from the civil servants rather than ministers direct; none felt that they had been unduly influenced by ministers outside what was specified in the terms of reference and supplementary guidance and as one HWG member commented 'this was the public *interference*: everybody knew what the Secretary of State wanted in this respect'. Baker told me in interview that he had taken a very 'personal interest' in the work of the HWG but when I pressed him more precisely over what this involved he claimed that:

> I didn't intervene in this sense of telling Michael Saunders-Watson what to and what not to include. I let him produce the finer details but certainly he came to talk to me about the proposals and we discussed them.

Yet the context of influence which had been created by the New Right and others prior to the establishment of the NC meant that the HWG realized what it could and could not do. Moreover, inevitably, developments at a macro level did have a bearing upon the HWG's work. One of the most obvious in this respect concerned the debate in the House of Commons on 14 November 1989 after John Marshall MP had made reference to the 'shock and dismay' at the exclusion of the Second World War from the Interim Report. After all, said Marshall, '1940 was our finest hour; why is it too fine for the history mandarins?' (Parliamentary Debates (Hansard), Vol. 161, p.172). Angela Rumbold's response and subsequent clarification was interesting:

> (Mrs Rumbold) I can assure my hon. Friend that the proposals of the interim working group [sic] have been looked at again by the history working group, and that the final proposals will contain full programmes of study on all the units, so that such matters can be taken fully into account.

> (Mr Janner) Will the Minister explain her previous answer? Does this mean that the national curriculum will contain the rise and fall of Nazism and the second world war?

> (Mrs Rumbold) As I understand it, yes. (ibid)

The significance of the statement was clear; this was apparently a direct attempt by the government to dictate what historical content should be included in the Final Report, a point emphasized by Jack Straw, Labour's education spokesman, who claimed that education ministers were 'being rolled over by the Prime Minister and the advisers in the No.10 policy unit who wish to turn the history syllabus into no more than a vehicle for the jingoistic, Right-wing indoctrination of our children' (ibid).

Interviews with HWG members on this matter revealed that the decision not to include the Second World War (see NC/HWG (89) 15th) had been made on the grounds that pupils had abundant opportunities already to study war. Another member commented upon the link between Rumbold's statement and the work of the HWG:

> We did resent this apparent attempt to influence what we were doing. In fact, we had already decided to include World War II partly because we heard through the officials that the government wanted it to be included and because it was left out of the original Interim Report only on the basis of a very slight majority. (Interview)

When asked to comment further upon the extent to which they had been conscious of 'political influence', HWG responses were diverse and complex. Nearly all of them reiterated the role of the DES officials. The same HWG member above who commented that 'political is difficult to define' also commented that:

> Certainly there were influences in the DES who pressed hard on certain points like the proportion of British history and chronology. You know the form of words 'we do not think the Secretary of State is likely to be happy with that'. Certainly hours and days of persuasion were deployed on knowledge; I think HWG felt it had held the fort on that with grudging understanding from senior officials. (Interview)

In this sense the DES officials acted as brokers between ministers and the HWG indicating what was and was not possible. They were prepared, as we have seen, to accept the HWG's rationale on assessment provided it was articulated in an intellectual manner and in a detailed and precise form. This explains so much of the management team's determination for rigour and care in the months following the Interim Report; this was also reflected, as we have seen, in the Final Report itself, particularly with respect to Chapter 3 (see NC/HWG (89) 13th & 14th). This was particularly important if ministers were to have any possibility of persuading Thatcher and the No. 10 Policy Unit of the validity of the case. The following (relatively long) extract from an interview with another HWG member provides invaluable insight into the political possibilities and constraints faced by the group and the complexity of the context of influence described at the beginning of Chapter 5:

> Behind the work of the HWG there was always a political agenda. We knew all the time that the Report could have been rejected by the politicians. Teachers were in some instances naive not to realize this; Chapter three of the Report was produced to convince the wider audience – the politicians – that the teachers were 'with us'. It was obvious that not all teachers would agree with everything in the Report but they wanted some things that would have been impossible for the government to accept. For example, it was no longer possible to avoid the issue of prescription; everybody on the group knew that a GCSE-type vague set of criteria for the selection of content was not on the cards. Within these circumstances, I at least was determined to produce a report that advocated broad, balanced and coherent history teaching. This in our view was 'good' history teaching. This meant at the same time challenging teachers' traditional conceptions about what this actually involved. We wanted to produce a framework which provided scope for different kinds of history (depth, breadth and investigations); we accepted the centrality of British not English history and we wanted to create a diversification of histories – European and non-European. (Interview)

Interview data also revealed that as far as the principle of prescription was concerned, the management team would have been prepared to offer even less scope for teacher autonomy than was actually outlined in the Final Report but a number of members opposed any further erosion of professional creativity; this was reflected, for example, in the detailed debates at the 6th, 8th and 9th meetings of the HWG and again at the 15th. One member informed me that he would have contemplated resignation if there had been any further erosion of school designed units or non-European elements. Similarly, another HWG member believed that the management team was under pressure to ditch the non-Western elements of the proposals, yet the group were determined to maintain them (again confirmed by the minutes: see NC/HWG (89) 14th & 15th).

It was argued earlier that members were relatively unified by a number of factors, particularly their desire to preserve the place and status of history within a prescribed balance of historical content and teaching approaches. In view of this, it would be unwise to over-emphasize the role and influence of particular members. As indicated, Saunders-Watson was described by various HWG members as a 'shrewd', 'brilliant', 'clever' and a 'hard' Chairman, supported by an 'able' and 'very efficient' Secretary. Yet the Final Report clearly reflected the views of HMI Roger Hennessey; in this sense, the Report, with its emphasis upon specific criteria, the selection of prescribed content and its attention to detail had far more in common with the HMI document of 1988 (DES, 1988b) than that of 1985 (DES, 1985a) (see Chapter 5).

But the Final Report was certainly not the product of one person, reminding us that policy texts 'do not have single identifiable authors' (Codd, 1988, p.239). The Final Report was inevitably a 'political compromise' (Dawson, 1990, p.18); a 'powerfully persuading' text, the product not only of a multiplicity of authors but also 'the varieties of advice that was variously sought, gratuitously offered or imposed' (Slater, 1991, p.10). In the words of Jenkins & Brickley (1991) the Final Report was the product of 'much deeper trends in society' (p.8) which encouraged them to argue that although the HWG was 'hand-picked', its recommendations were certainly not Thatcherite. In fact, by stressing 'diverse interpretations, cultural and ideological heterogeneity' (ibid, p.9) the Final Report actually challenged the 'certaintist' Thatcherite view of history. The Report, say Jenkins & Brickley, was a text not only full of 'unintended consequences' for teachers but also 'unintended opportunities'.

Slater (1991) expressed similar views when he observed that the Report recognized (Carr-like?) the 'variety of interpretations of the past, the value-judgments made in selecting, or omitting, content' (p.20). On the other hand, he pointed to a tendency in the Final Report to encourage the (Eltonian?) view that 'there is an objective view of the past waiting to be seized and an historical truth acceptable to all historians' (p.21). This, he said, was the product of a committee keen to provide opportunities for 'contrasted views to fly their conflicting flags'. This reminds us again that policy texts are, after all:

> inevitably addressed to a plurality of readers. Instead of searching for authorial intentions, perhaps the proper task of policy analysis is to examine the differing effects that documents have in the production of meaning by readers. (Codd, 1988, p.239)

This explains why Collicot (1990), in contrast to Jenkins & Brickley (1991) above, viewed the Final Report as 'assimilationist'. The following months would be crucial in the policy process as different 'readings' of the Report were constructed by a 'plurality' of readers – ministers, professionals, academics and the general public – all mediated by the press. It would be particularly important to determine whether the Report, a 'detailed description of content, skills and processes', would 'satisfy some, antagonize others and strait-jacket the rest of the teachers of history' as Truman (1990, p.12: see Chapter 2) had predicted.

Chapter 7

'Contesting History': The Response to the Final Report

The previous chapters have illustrated the work and thought that had gone into the production of the Final Report in order to placate a wide range of interests. Yet speculation had already begun about Thatcher's opposition to it. This chapter examines the response to the Final Report: beginning with the announcement of its publication, it then analyses responses from the press, academics, teachers, the HA and the New Right.

The Publication of the Final Report

On 3 April 1990 the Final Report was finally published and attracted the now customary intense press speculation. The press, in fact, had already started speculating about Thatcher's involvement months before the publication of the Report. An article in the *Independent* of 22 February, for example, had demanded 'Let's not mess with history' and suggested that the delay in publication was caused by governmental disapproval of the Report's contents; it suggested that the government was inevitably going to be accused of 'bias' for its blatant meddling. This speculation seemed to be confirmed in the TES headline of 30 March: 'Thatcher's disapproval holds up history report'. It revealed that the Report had 'failed to win Government support after a top-level meeting between John MacGregor and the Prime Minister'. It was clear that Mrs Thatcher was very 'dissatisfied' with the Report and that the chief stumbling block was the old issue of 'factual information'. Two days before its publication, the *Sunday Telegraph* quoted the question posed by John Stokes in Parliament the previous week (Parliamentary Debates (Hansard), Vol. 170, 29 March). He had asked: 'Instead of teaching what are called themes, why can't we go back to the good old days when we learnt by heart the names of the kings and queens of England, the names of our warriors and battles and the glorious deeds of our past?' Thatcher's response made headline news: 'Children should learn the great land-marks of British history and be taught them at school' (*Sunday Telegraph*, 1 April 1990).

It was in this intense political situation that the Report was finally published. Strident efforts were made by Saunders-Watson to persuade the full range of groups – politicians, teachers, the public and the New Right – to accept the document. In a number of newspapers, he urged people to analyse it objectively and to treat it fairly. The *Sunday Independent* of the same week described him as a man 'with an instinct for what is sensible and liberal and decent'. His press statements, found in most of the quality and tabloid press, smack of a man who was determined to dampen down any notion of 'conspiracy'. Conscious of the detailed debates and sheer hard work over the previous months, Saunders-Watson realized that the carefully balanced arguments articulated in the Report had to be read carefully: 'I am pleading for people to read the Report and read it twice. It is a very complex document and unless people read it they will leap to conclusions about the attainment targets and programmes of study without knowing why we put them there' (Saunders-Watson: reported in *The Times*, 4 April 1990). He also pleaded with people to consider the range of demands facing the group: 'If anyone can do better, I'll take my hat off to them ... I might even eat it!' (TES, 4 April 1990).

Yet despite Saunders-Watson's appeals to the contrary, the press centred particular attention on the issue of 'facts'. *The Times* claimed that 'Thatcher's line on testing of facts rebuffed in report' (4 April 1990). Robert Skidelsky, who had taken a firm interest in school history since the empathy controversy, writing in the same edition, declared that although the Final Report was an 'advance' on the Interim, it was 'still biased against knowledge'. The *Independent* (4 April 1990) reported that the HWG had accepted the government's demand that 'more British history and more dates' should be taught in schools but also claimed that the Report 'strongly rejects ministers' suggestions that dates and facts should be included in attainment targets'. *Today* (4 April 1990) accused the HWG of producing a document which simply asked for pupils to 'use their imagination about 1066 and all that' for which the group had 'run into trouble with Margaret Thatcher'. Press interest centred on the view that Thatcher had involved herself directly in the Report, apparently confirmed by MacGregor's letter announcing that although he welcomed most of the Report, he had also written to the Schools Examinations & Assessment Council (SEAC) asking it to consider whether 'assessment against the attainment targets, as recommended in the report, will reliably reflect a pupil's level of knowledge within each study unit' (DES, 1990b, p.x). On 3 April MacGregor had announced in the House of Commons, that 'because history was such an important and perhaps controversial subject' (ibid, p.iii), he was allowing a period of extra consultation before sending it to the NCC.

Reasons for the Period of 'Extra' Consultation

At the time, the precise reasons for allowing this 'extra' period of consultation were the subject of intense speculation. In her memoirs, Thatcher claims that the impetus for the extra period came from her and that she had been responsible for the delay in publication. She had found the decision not to include a specific knowledge attainment target 'extraordinary' (Thatcher, 1993, p.596) and had also been surprised and disappointed that MacGregor seemed to be 'inclined to welcome the Report', having been convinced of the validity of the HWG's case by Saunders-Watson and by the civil servants. Thatcher's account of the subsequent events is as follows:

It (the Final Report) did not put greater emphasis on British history. But the attainment targets it set out did not specifically include knowledge of historical facts, which seemed to me extraordinary. However, the coverage of some subjects – for example twentieth century history – was too skewed to social, religious, cultural and aesthetic matters rather than political events. The detail of the history curriculum would impose too inflexible a framework on teachers. I raised these points with John on the afternoon of Monday 19 March. He defended the report's proposals. But I insisted that it would not be right to impose the sort of approach which it contained. It should go out to consultation but no guidance should at present be issued. (Thatcher, 1993, p.596)

Thatcher's claim that she was solely responsible for the period of extra consultation is somewhat exaggerated. Data derived from interviews and correspondence suggest that the situation was more complex than that, as this letter received by me from a senior DES official reveals:

I haven't read Mrs Thatcher's memoir, and did not realize that she claimed the credit for the extra period of consultation on history. My recollection is that Ministers collectively found it difficult to make their minds up and wanted a further pause for reflection and a cooling of heated views on the subject of the history curriculum . . . Certainly Mrs Thatcher and her advisers were unconvinced. My impression is that Mr MacGregor was too. I thought the consultation period was his idea, but we would not have been told in detail what passed between him and Mrs Thatcher. (Correspondence)

MacGregor, in fact, through correspondence emphasized to me that it had been his decision (following discussions with Baker) to send the Report out to consultation because of the:

differing points of view amongst historians as to the degree of emphasis to be given to interpretation and to the acquisition of historical knowledge and facts in the way in which history is taught. It was for that reason that I took the Final Report out to more public consultation before the statutory processes under the Act. (Correspondence)

This seems to confirm the DES official's claim that it would provide a period for 'cooling off'. MacGregor himself informed me that the period of extra consultation proved 'most useful', the full meaning and implications of which are outlined in the sections below. Whatever the precise motivation and origins of the decision, it initiated frantic activity from a range of interested parties wishing to influence the policy process.

Enter the Academics

As Coss (1988) has suggested, apart from the formation of the History in the Universities Defence Group and some high profile intervention by Skidelsky and a few others over GCSE, British academics had traditionally shown only token interest in school history. The publication of the Final Report and the national reaction which ensued, however, saw a wide range of academics contributing directly to the debate. On 22 March, the *Teachers' Weekly* could proclaim that 'Academics Enter History Row' and reported the establishment of the History Curriculum Association (HCA), an organization formed by Skidelsky, McGovern and Freeman (the former Lewes teachers) and whose members included a host of prominent historians: Norman Stone, Jonathan Clark, Lords Beloff and Blake, in fact mainly those who had been responsible for the publication of an earlier alternative GCSE syllabus (Beloff *et al.*, 1989). On 11 May the HCA proclaimed in a large, bold advertisement that the HCA had been formed to 'defend the integrity of history as a school subject'; claiming that the HWG in their Final Report had 'not mentioned' knowledge in their proposed attainment targets, the HCA declared that it would 'campaign for a knowledge attainment target' (TES, 11 May 1990).

Although its members denied any political motive or affiliation, nevertheless, due to the HCA's avowed aims, its high profile and its prominent membership, the HCA became associated with the Right. The newspaper pages of this crucial period in the debate were dominated by the writings of Skidelsky, Stone and Clark. Skidelsky claimed that although the Final Report was an improvement on the Interim Report, this was not enough and demanded that pupils be allowed to 'learn the landmarks' of British history. The HWG's decision not to include a specific attainment target for knowledge ruined its whole approach (*The Times*, 4 April 1990). Stone expressed similar sentiments, after all 'facts and dates must be known: they are like mathematical tables' (*The Sunday Times*, 8 April 1990). In a particularly important article which went to the heart of the ideological aspect of the 'great history debate', Jonathan Clark justified the Right's political interference in the history curriculum (echoing many of the themes described in Chapter 3). Clark claimed that it was the state's duty to utilize history in order to defend the concept of 'nationhood'. Thus, although it was possible to 'leave chemistry to the chemists and geography to the geographers', history was different because it was national property and the decisions to be taken on the history curriculum will be ultimately connected with our national self-image, sense of heritage and purpose'. The post-war consensus which Clark described as 'Marxist and Keynesian' had broken up, allowing the Right to confidently assert, once again, notions of Britishness. The chief vehicle in this vision, said Clark, were to be academics, because 'educationists' had corrupted the subject by trying to make it 'more interesting to teach'. This was not surprising as they are 'a producer monopoly. For them the teacher comes first, not the product (history) or the customer (the pupil)'. Thus it was vital that 'professional historians be brought in as a counterbalance to that most peculiar breed, the educationists' (*The Times*, 23 March 1990).

Enter, then, the good knights – Clark, Skidelsky and Stone – to snatch the innocent victims – the pupils – from the wicked clutches of the educationists. In fact, the hostility displayed by Skidelsky and his colleagues towards the Final Report initiated a backlash from within the academic establishment itself and led to one of the most acrimonious furores in the whole debate. The controversy was sparked by the HCA's TES advertisement on 11 May. As we have seen, it had claimed that 'knowledge had not been mentioned in the attainment targets' and that it was going to campaign for this. The advert then contained a list of names of eminent historians who, it was claimed, supported the statement. In fact, the advert provoked a host of letters from many of these historians, disclaiming any association with the HCA. Peter Clarke, from Cambridge, stated that he could not support the advert because it was grossly inaccurate and he went on to quote directly paragraph 7.9 of the Report that specified, quite clearly, that historical knowledge would have to be studied in order to show historical understanding (TES, 8 May 1990). The most damning letter of all came from Derek Beales who stressed that although he had given general support to the HCA because he had agreed that 'the exercise of skills is impossible except on the basis of acquired knowledge' (TES, 25 May 1990), he also disagreed with the HCA's advertisement, claimed that he had not been shown it before it appeared and that therefore he was resigning from the association immediately. These developments gave even more substance to earlier support from academics for the Final Report (see Russell, TES, 20 April 1990; Samuel, *New Statesman*, 6 April 1990). Skidelsky and his colleagues seemed to be on the defensive.

This provided the background to a remarkable debate which took place at Ruskin College Oxford on 19 May 1990, organized by *History Workshop*. Prominent speakers from a range of perspectives were asked to give their views on the Final Report under the title 'History, the Nation and the Schools'. Again, the debate centred upon familiar issues such as skills, knowledge and heritage. In an early morning session, Chris McGovern repeated the familiar claims that if history was defined simply in terms of skills then it was not history, denounced the HWG for refusing to understand this and condemned the HA for supporting the Report. After contributions during the day from prominent academics as ideologically diverse as Jonathan Clark and Stuart Hall, the Conference culminated in a remarkable concluding session. Samuel (1990) and Yeo (1990) offered sympathetic interpretations of the Final Report. Skidelsky (articulating the views of the HCA) repeated the views he had expressed in *The Times*, and particularly attacked the Final Report for its failure to test knowledge (Skidelsky, 1990). Stone declared that teaching was relatively straightforward and that 'all pupils should have the nation's culture rammed down their necks' (reported in TES, 25 May 1990). Ruskin showed the Right to be totally uncompromising; as the same TES article went on to comment, although earlier in the day 'it had seemed possible that a consensus might emerge between the warring factions', later there was still a 'deeply entrenched reluctance on the part of the Right to give any ground at all'. This encouraged those who supported the broad principles of the Final Report to rally support for it both amongst teachers and in the press: few organizations were more important in this respect than the HA.

The Historical Association and the Development of a NC Strategy

As we saw in Chapter 4, the HA had a mixed reputation for representing teachers' views and the announcement of the NC posed new and peculiar problems for it. On the one hand, it clearly welcomed the Secretary of State's decision to embrace history as a NC foundation subject; on the other hand, it could not prevent a repetition of the experiences of the *History for Life* debacle, which, as we have seen, had alienated many teachers and undermined the HA's credibility with the teaching profession, mainly because of its propensity towards accepting the notion of prescribed content. As the responses to the Interim Report had indicated, teachers were as sensitive over this issue as ever.

In order to counter criticisms that it was elitist and out of touch with teachers' views, the Education Committee of the HA had established a schools sub-committee in 1988, consisting predominantly of practising teachers. It was, as its name and membership suggests, an attempt to re-establish the HA's credibility with teachers. Its other major task was to formulate a strategy over the NC, particularly regarding the interpretation of the Final Report. Over the weeks and months which followed, the HA developed a political strategy which, I shall argue, had an important impact upon the ways in which the Report was interpreted.

It was clear that the HA's basic aim over the NC – and before – was to preserve not only the position of history in secondary schools but also to increase the amount of formal history teaching in primary schools, which had been perceived to be inadequate (DES, 1989c). HA members had been particularly alarmed at the apparent demise of history in secondary schools, caused by the growth of new subjects such as economics and the development of established ones such as geography. Even more serious in the HA's eyes was the dilution of history teaching through integrated humanities and other cross-curricular initiatives which had the potential to devalue history as an academic subject (Lewis, 1987; Roberts, 1990). The publication of the Final Report therefore represented a 'big prize' for the HA because it was an opportunity to preserve the place of history in secondary schools and to restore the teaching of more formal history in the primary sector which had been superseded by integrated topic work. As a prominent HA member asserted, topic work had 'failed to deliver the goods as far as history is concerned' (Noble, 1990, p.33).

The problem for the HA was to convince the sceptics – including teachers themselves – about the need to accept the fundamental basis of the Final Report, a task made even more demanding given that the HA itself (reflecting teachers' own views) had been critical of aspects of the Interim Report (HA, 1989). Given the changes in the Final Report and that some former members of the HWG were also HA members, it was even more likely that it would support the Report. Prominent HA members and members of the schools sub-committee were more concerned with the pragmatic strategic goal of establishing history's permanence in the curriculum than, for example, ensuring the survival of the SHP. The HA was therefore prepared to compromise on certain principles provided the 'big prize' – the permanent establishment of history in the primary and secondary sectors – was assured. Hence it was perfectly possible in the eyes of the HA to endorse the Final Report, for it contained little to which the HA could object. It emphasized the need for a history curriculum which had 'breadth' and 'balance'; 50 per cent of the programmes of study prescribed British history, including Welsh, Irish and Scottish perspectives; it was broadly chronological and more importantly (for the HA) it offered a carefully articulated justification for the teaching of history in primary and secondary schools. These were just the kinds of basic principles advocated by the HA in the late 1980s through documents such as *History for Life*.

The period of extra consultation announced by MacGregor provided both opportunities and problems for the HA. It had to take into account a number of factors. It was obviously intensely aware of the political pressure being placed upon the Secretary of State to reject the Final Report on the grounds that it was not sufficiently traditional, particularly in relation to the assessment of knowledge. Thatcher and the HCA have already been mentioned and the Centre for Policy Studies, as we have seen, also campaigned vigorously against the Interim Report (Lawlor, 1989). In addition, Deuchar had put forward his ideas at HA meetings in the late 1980s and was in the process of completing a damning critique of the Final Report for the Campaign for Real Education (Deuchar, 1992). The HA was therefore well aware of the potential political influence which the Right could exert over the Secretary of State, a situation made even more politicized by the high profile of the academics in the debate. In addition, rumours were circulating that history was in danger of being dropped as a foundation subject entirely (see below). Opposition to the Final Report would only give greater weight to the argument that history should be dropped from the NC.

In view of these circumstances, at an early stage (i.e. before the official round of consultation meetings took place in May) senior HA members decided to endorse the findings of the HWG on the grounds that there was sufficient potential that the Secretary of State would reject the HWG's advice and replace the Final Report with something much worse. Therefore, at the Ruskin College Conference on 19 May, Martin Roberts, Chair of the schools' sub-committee, defended the Final Report against the criticisms of Skidelsky and Stone. He had already articulated the HA's views in an article in the TES on 20 April and was to repeat these arguments again on 14 December, and on 22 March 1991. Roberts declared that the Final Report was 'a considerable achievement. Its 205 pages are impressively detailed yet lucidly argued, and it reads as the work of a group which is genuinely unanimous and convinced that it has to a large extent succeeded in fulfilling its brief' and was to be the 'foundation on which durable school history courses are able to be built' in the future (TES, 20 April 1990). Roberts saw his major task as maintaining the mediating role of the HA which had begun in the 1980s in order to achieve consensus or 'synthesis' over the teaching of history (Roberts, 1990). Styles, a teacher from North Yorkshire, explained the compli-cated dilemma facing the HA, caused by the recommendations of the Secretary of State, in an article in *Teaching History*:

> Will the results of this DES consultation period encourage Mr MacGregor and his political mentors to recommend that knowledge should form a separate Attainment Target? Will he recommend an even greater proportion of British history? That is the problem. If we go hammer and tongs at the detail of the Final Report we stand in danger of this being interpreted as wholescale opposition to it: we could then lose that which is good about the Report – the way in which the thorny problem of historical knowledge has been dealt with by integrating it firmly in to the Programmes of Study at every level. Conscience and a love of history, therefore, tell me to give every support to the Working Group's efforts to produce a document which reflects the results of a nigh impossible task. (Styles, 1990, p.13)

Consultation, Conferences and the HA Strategy

The HA, of course, once again ran the risk of alienating teachers who might not fully have appreciated (as Styles did) the logic behind the strategy. Its success depended upon a number of things being achieved. First, it was vital for the HA to provide opportunities for genuine consultation so that it could claim to be representing teachers' views through extensive regional meetings. Thus, according to the HA's own figures, thirteen conferences were held around the country which were attended by a total of 1600 people: 65 per cent were secondary school teachers; 25 per cent came from primary schools; the remainder came 'mainly' from higher education (HA, 1990).

Second, a careful observational analysis of the way in which the conferences were organized suggests that they were centrally influenced by the schools sub-committee. Conferences followed an identical pattern: the opening address was provided by a person or persons of high status – in the case of the Oxford conference, for example, by Roberts and Saunders-Watson. Crucially, some conferences, for example those held in Birmingham, Oxford and London, were addressed directly by former members of the HWG. Each conference then divided into working groups to discuss aspects of the Final Report, on the basis of a specific agenda under the headings: attainment targets, structure, chronology and assessment (ibid). This was crucial for the type of views which came out of the HA meetings and which met the HA's overall pragmatic political objectives, namely to develop consensus behind the broad principles of the Final Report. More fundamental teacher concerns – for example in relation to prescription, workload and autonomy – were not given prominence. A recurring theme from regional conferences was the need to interpret the Final Report in a decidedly positive light; above all, keynote speakers at the conferences stressed that the Final Report was only a broad framework within which teachers could be creative and that it did not represent a threat to teachers' existing working practices.

An examination of these conferences demonstrates the influence of the HA's political strategy upon the way that the discussion subsequently progressed. There was a close correspondence between the aims that were spelt out at the beginning of the conference and the general sentiments that were then expressed by the delegates, as the summaries to the HA's Education Committee make clear (ibid). In his keynote speech to the Oxford conference, Roberts explained the HA's strategy which was echoed around the country by other keynote speakers. He argued that the broad outline of the HWG's report should be accepted on the basis that if teachers were seen to be rejecting it, the government would either introduce something 'worse' or that a negative reaction on the part of teachers might provoke the Secretary of State into ditching history as a foundation subject. The conference at Oxford was crucial for setting the tone in other conferences, amplified as it was by close press coverage (TES, 1 June 1990). It was no coincidence, either, that Oxford was one of the first in the conference round.

Former members of the HWG were invited to lead conference debates. One conference keynote speech described the members of the HWG as 'pragmatists' who had devised a NC that was 'workable'. Concern about some aspects of the Final Report were recognized – such as prescription – but delegates were then asked to take into consideration the political context within which the document had been formulated. The speech amounted to a wholescale defence of the HWG's proposals. Other speakers at HA conferences claimed that the prescriptive nature of the Final Report had been compiled in order to satisfy the DES, the Centre for Policy Studies and the government in terms of providing a comprehensive and detailed outline of what should be taught. A former HWG member at one of the HA conferences urged teachers not to be overly concerned about the amount of prescribed content in the Report because they would be able to select the information that they wanted to teach. Another keynote speaker chose to compare the relatively light demands of the Final Report in terms of statements of attainment with other 'less fortunate' subjects, pointing out, for example, that history had only 51 statements, whilst geography had 248.

At many of the meetings, speakers emphasized that the 'much better' Final Report was always placed in the context of the unpopularity of the Interim Report. A surprising argument used to reinforce the logic of the HA's strategy was to claim that the report was not 'final' and that teachers could be creative in their interpretation of it. Such strategic pragmatism, in fact, contradicted information the HA had received months earlier from Mrs Thatcher's office which confirmed the power of the Secretary of State:

> Neither the working groups nor the NCC can usurp statutory Ministerial responsibilities and decide for themselves the content of the National Curriculum. (Paul Grey, Thatcher's Private Secretary, to Historical Association, 8 September 1989)

The Historical Association's Response to the DES

Given the range and purpose of the selling strategies outlined above, one would have expected overwhelmingly positive responses from the regional conferences. In fact, delegates expressed some major reservations about various aspects of the Final Report. At Liverpool, delegates spoke of the 'great concerns' about the selection of content. At Leeds, concerns were raised that the NC would be 'inadequately taught and unenthusiastically received'. The Midlands conference made reference to a 'number of concerns about limitations on a balanced view of world history'. The Bristol conference could still report that 'there was resentment at the idea of a National Curriculum'. Even at Oxford fifteen 'weaknesses' of the report were identified compared with only ten 'strengths'! (HA, 1990).

Nevertheless, the tone of the HA's consultative summary document submitted to the DES was cautiously positive. The document emphasized that participants had welcomed the broad outline of the HWG's selection of attainment targets, particularly the decision not to include an attainment target that was specifically aimed at assessing historical knowledge, and that they welcomed the broad structure of the history course outlined in the Final Report. The chronological approach, the PESC formula and the balance between British and other types of history were also welcomed. References were made to some of the concerns expressed by delegates, including the lack of time to implement the Report's requirements, the unsuitability of the TGAT model and the lack of resources available. Overall, however, the document seemed to endorse the comment expressed by the Oxford conference that 'the tone of the reply to the DES should be positive and should show broad support for the Report – the reservations should not be left out but emphasis [sic] on how to improve the Report further' (ibid, para.5.2).

The conciliatory and unifying tone of the HA's response was consolidated through press coverage. A TES article noted that 'History report wins support from the ranks' and went on to report that the HA 'which represents most school history teachers' had approved the Final Report following a range of extensive consultation around the country' (TES, 1 June 1990). Nevertheless, the HA's strategy was not unanimously endorsed. The Ethos Group, which contained prominent HA figures, had for some time harboured serious reservations about the Final Report and the HA's strategy. A letter from the Ethos Group on 19 June condemned the way in which teachers had been 'misled' at HA meetings by former HWG members into believing that the Final Report could be 'subverted'. The letter claimed, in fact, that the DES was unequivocal about the fact 'the curriculum is to be taught in toto' and that procedures would be set up to see that this was enforced; it ended with an appeal to teachers to reject the report outright (*The Times*, 19 June 1990).

A Strategy Justified? The Move Towards 'Consensus'

The HA's strategy seemed justified when one considers that even SHP teachers seemed to endorse the Report for, co-incidentally, the annual SHP Conference was being held at the very time that the Final Report was being published (April 4–6). Of all the interested teachers' groups, this one clearly had the potential to be the most vociferous in its opinion and potential opposition. The large numbers that attended the Conference – approximately 300 – demonstrated the intense interest generated by the issue. Organizers of the Conference ensured that key elements of the Final Report were copied and distributed to delegates. Crucially, three former members of the HWG attended the Conference to explain the philosophy and thinking behind the Report. The Conference subsequently welcomed many aspects of the Final Report, particularly the HWG's decision to exclude a specific knowledge attainment target. There were concerns expressed about prescription, content overload, assessment and the over-emphasis upon British history but, again, the feeling at the Conference was that the Report could have been much worse.

The SHP, the Ruskin Conference and the HA meetings conveyed the impression that there was a consensus of support for the fundamentals of the Final Report. By June, this had been given greater impetus after rumours had started circulating in the press and elsewhere that history was to be dropped as a foundation subject from the NC. Consensus even seemed to break out amongst the academics! On 1 June the Cambridge historians wrote to *The Times* highlighting these rumours and demanding that history should retain its place as a crucial foundation subject. They stressed that they were not acting out of 'corporate self-interest'; instead, they emphasized that due to the wide range of political, social and economic changes that the country had experienced over the past 25 years, it was essential that all British pupils should be provided with a sound historical education (*The Times*, 1 June 1990).

Later, the Cambridge historians were supported by an unlikely combination of High Tory and Marxist historians, ranging from Blake and Skidelsky to Samuel and Hobsbawm, who wrote directly to the Secretary of State expressing their alarm at the rumours that history was to be dropped from the foundation list. They stressed that 'despite well-publicized disagreements', all historians agreed that history was a 'knowledge based subject' and that without a study of history, children 'grow up politically disadvantaged, culturally deprived, and ignorant of the society in which they live'. Moreover, the letter went on to stress that there can be no substitute for history 'least of all the mixed grill of now fashionable courses constructed out of the "humanities" courses' (Blake *et al.*, letter to DES, 20 June 1990). As an article in the TES pointed out, 'Historians bury hatchet to safeguard subject' (TES, 22 June 1990).

The rumours about history being dropped as a compulsory subject in the NC had originated from two main sources. First, in a remarkable interview given to the *Sunday Telegraph* (15 April 1990) two months earlier, the Prime Minister had expressed her views about school history in characteristic fashion. Although offering a justification for the teaching of history by claiming that one could not be a 'complete person' without a broad historical education, it became clear as the interview progressed that she was concerned about three main aspects of the Final Report: first, the sheer amount of detail and content over-load; second, the degree of prescription demanded by the HWG; third, most surprisingly, she expressed concern that the Final Report would undermine teacher creativity. At first sight, the interview was remarkable: was Thatcher advocating a return to teacher autonomy?

The comments must be considered within the political context in which they were being given and the nature of New Right ideology itself. Only a few weeks earlier, a Commons select committee had warned of falling teacher numbers caused by low morale, under-pay and over-work. Thatcher's comments were made with this in mind.

The interview also showed a deep concern about the notion of prescription, a degree of centralized dictum which contradicted the Thatcherite neo-liberal principle of free enterprise. Neo-liberal versus neo-conservative tensions within New Right ideology were raising their heads once more. More serious for the HA and academics were her misgivings about the compulsory nature of the present arrangements. Thatcher's worry was that the proposals were prescriptive and detailed for 'once you put out an approved curriculum, if you have got it wrong, the situation is worse afterwards than it was before' (*Sunday Telegraph*, 15 April 1990).

Thatcher clearly recognized history's importance but her concerns about prescription and detail caused her to question its place as a foundation subject; this also confirmed her misgivings regarding the over-elaborate administrative machinery established by Kenneth Baker to monitor the NC. As she indicated in her memoirs:

> By now I had become thoroughly exasperated with the way in which the national curriculum proposals were being diverted from their original purpose. I made my reservations known in an interview I gave to the *Sunday Telegraph* in early April. In this I defended the principles of the national curriculum but criticized the detailed prescription in other than the core subjects which now had become its least agreeable feature. My comments were greeted with consternation by the DES. There was no need for the national curriculum proposals and the testing which accompanied them to have developed as they did. Ken Baker paid too much attention to the DES, the HMI and progressive educational theorists in his appointments and early decisions; and once the bureaucratic momentum had begun it was difficult to stop. (Thatcher, 1993, p.597)

The second source of the rumour that the government was beginning to re-consider history's position as a foundation subject came from the DES, fuelled by further press speculation. It was clear that the DES was becoming concerned at the degree of clutter and over-load caused by Baker's original blue-print, particularly at KS4; the implication, of course, was that various subjects, including history, might be omitted from the foundation list or that pupils could undertake a modular course with geography in the interest of streamlining. Speculation was further generated in the press that the Secretary of State was considering omitting history from the list of compulsory assessed subjects (subsequently raised by the Secretary of State in a speech on 31 July). The implications for the status of the subject were clear; as the TES commented 'history tells us what happens to subjects that are not examined' (TES, 22 June 1990).

The MacGregor Proposals

It was this speculation about the future status of the subject which explains the HA's strategy between April and June and which accounts for the academics' public show of unity, a consensus which had been forced upon them in the interests of the self-preservation of their subject. The views of the academics, as we have seen, had been given particularly high profile in the post-Final Report period and some teachers believed that they had 'hi-jacked' the debate (see letters in the TES, 15 June 1990 and 6 July 1990). The academics had centred upon one specific aspect of the debate and by far the most contentious, namely the assessment of historical knowledge, and it was this which was proving the most demanding issue for MacGregor and his 'history team' at the DES.

Thatcher herself has indicated that MacGregor was 'under constant pressure from me' (Thatcher, 1993, p.597) to ensure that the Final Report was changed, particularly in relation to the assessment of knowledge. He was also under intense pressure from such bodies as the Centre for Policy Studies (Lawlor, 1990) and the Campaign for Real Education: to them, any 'compromise' on this issue would be no compromise at all. This is where the HA's strategy paid dividends: their meetings around the country, as we have seen, had demonstrated public support amongst teachers for the HWG's decision not to include a specific knowledge attainment target. It is worth reiterating that every regional conference had emphasized this. On the other hand, although academics agreed that their subject was knowledge-based, the controversy over the HCA's advertisement had shown that they were less united on the precise manner in which knowledge could be assessed.

All roads for MacGregor and his advisers at the DES seemed to lead back to assessment. Their problem was how to suggest a scheme of assessment that was acceptable to the teaching force but which would not be seen as a 'compromise' in the eyes of the New Right. As we have seen, MacGregor, under pressure from Thatcher, had written to SEAC at the time of the publication of the Final Report concerning the feasibility of the HWG's proposals regarding the assessment of knowledge. If he was looking to SEAC for an opportunity to avoid pronouncing on this politically sensitive issue himself, he was to be disappointed. On 12 June, Philip Halsey, Chairman of SEAC, wrote to the Secretary of State confirming that SEAC was 'convinced that the working group's proposals are both workable and sound for assessment purposes' (DES, 1990b, p.xi). To put it crudely, by 15 June when the period of extra consultation was completed, MacGregor's problem and that of his team was how to produce a compromise, which, in the eyes of the New Right and Thatcher, did not look like a compromise at all!

When the proposals were finally published on 26 July (as usual, widely reported in the press) it seemed that MacGregor had succumbed to political pressure. He proposed that the first attainment target be re-named 'Knowledge and understanding' and that it should be given greater weighting for assessment purposes (DES, 1990b, p.iii, para.9); he also proposed that the fourth attainment target – organization and communication – should be combined within the other attainment targets. In order to encourage simplification on the lines suggested by Thatcher in the *Sunday Telegraph* interview, MacGregor proposed that the examples drawn from the programmes of study should be omitted from the statements of attainment and the NCC was asked to publish exemplary materials for teachers (ibid, p.iv, para.11). As far as the programmes of study were concerned, he proposed a number of significant changes. KS1 was to be left untouched but in view of the desire for more flexibility, MacGregor proposed a reduction in each key stage of one study unit (ibid, p.iv, paras.16, 17, 18). Significantly, at KS3, he proposed to give schools the opportunity to design all four non-core history units if they so wished, either using the ground rules specified by the HWG for school designed study units or to use the optional history study units. But in order to reduce the total study units by one he suggested that two of the option lists recommended by the HWG be amalgamated. This meant that schools would have to choose between either a non-European or a New World culture from its own perspective (ibid, p.iv, paras 18, 19); schools would thus not have to select from the optional history study units suggested by the HWG but because schools were likely to find the advice provided in them useful, the NCC was asked to consider how they could best be used as guidance for teachers (ibid, p.iv, para.20). At KS4, MacGregor asked the NCC to consider how the original HWG proposals could be made broader to provide a synoptic view of British and European history (ibid, p.v, paras 22, 23).

The final aspect of the MacGregor proposals were the most intriguing in many respects given the HWG's pre-occupation with detail and prescription. MacGregor had obviously taken the Prime Minister's advice on the matter, for the proposals stated that 'certain changes in the format of the HSUs [history study units] are needed to reduce the amount of real and apparent prescription'. MacGregor recognized that the exemplary materials provided in the Final Report were useful but that it was inappropriate for the Statutory Orders; he therefore proposed that much of the exemplary information should be done away with. In short, the NCC would be required to produce a much condensed version of the Final Report (ibid, p.v, para.24). In order to reduce the perception of prescription and encourage a more consistent provision of historical information to be taught across history study units, the NCC was asked to indicate prescribed content under the heading of 'Content' rather than 'Essential Information' (ibid, p.v, para.26).

The *Independent* claimed that 'the champions of traditional facts and dates school history triumphed over progressive colleagues yesterday' because MacGregor's proposals 'to make knowledge a distinct area for testing and to give it greater weight than historical skills' which ran contrary to the Final Report. It also claimed that 'supporters of the skills-based new history said they were disappointed by his proposals' (*Independent*, 27 July 1990). By re-naming the first attainment target, MacGregor was merely playing a game of semantics. But by placing greater weighting on it for assessment purposes, the Secretary of State was clearly providing the New Right and Thatcher with what they wanted. Certainly Skidelsky seemed to think so: it was reported in the same *Independent* article that he was 'delighted' with the proposals, claiming that 'the days of the skills-based new history approach were numbered'. A few days later *the Sunday Times* (29 July 1990) ran a profile of Chris McGovern who asserted that 'we have won the intellectual and educational battle' over the teaching of history and that his views on history teaching had finally been vindicated. It seemed that the HA's strategy had failed and that this indeed was at last 'a victory for the New Right'.

An alternative reading of the proposals suggests, however, that not for the first time during the history debate the press, Skidelsky and McGovern had (to use a historical analogy!) misinterpreted the evidence. A close analysis of attainment target 1 revealed, in fact, that the emphasis was not merely on historical knowledge *per se* but on a combination of historical concepts and skills based on change, causation and, above all, the HWG's articulation of historical understanding (Lee, 1991; Husbands, 1992; Husbands & Pendry, 1992). The proposals could therefore be interpreted as a judicious and shrewd compromise, and represented less discontinuity with the HWG's original proposals than was being suggested by Skidelsky, McGovern and others above. This is not surprising given the composition of MacGregor's small 'history team' made up of Hennessey and some of the officials who had worked with the HWG. Through correspondence with me one of them elaborated upon the rationale behind the proposals:

> The MacGregor compromise emerged with a certain inevitability as the obvious political solution to buy off No. 10 and the hard knowledge zealots with a bit of lip-service to their

position while leaving the integrity of the structure intact. If you accept the view we took, and SEAC had so emphatically endorsed, of the interdependence of statements of attainment and the programmes of study, then the question 'where does knowledge fit in?' becomes pretty metaphysical. It did no harm to include knowledge in the title of attainment target 1 so long as we were not required to rewrite the statements of attainment to include the date of the Battle of Hastings . . . In adopting it MacGregor certainly knew what he was doing, and that he was taking a bit of a risk with political colleagues and supporters. But we got away with it, apart from one or two small voices complaining that it was all a con trick. (Correspondence)

Interestingly, MacGregor revealed to me how he had been convinced of the validity of the HWG's case on the assessment of knowledge, an argument which, as we saw in the previous two chapters, they had spent months articulating. Intriguingly, the same DES officials who had been influenced by the force of this intellectual argument, articulated it to MacGregor:

The only real point of argument in the latter stages was about whether there should be substantial reference in the attainment targets to historical knowledge and facts, or whether the specific material in relation to knowledge and facts should be in the programmes of study. Given my initial request, I looked at the arguments put forward in the Final Report by the HWG with particular care, and considered them carefully with my ministerial colleagues and with officials. We all came to the view that it would be too complex to treat this issue in detail in the attainment targets, and that the right place was in the programmes of study. (Correspondence)

MacGregor's clever politics had two crucial effects. First, by demonstrating, through the HA, that there was a degree of 'consensus' behind the proposals, this made it impossible for Thatcher and the No. 10 Policy Unit to reject the substance of the Final Report. As MacGregor told me:

The Policy Unit at No. 10 had been particularly concerned about ensuring a proper emphasis on the importance of historical knowledge (a concern that I shared). The Chairman of the HWG also stressed that there was no difference between us on the importance of historical knowledge. The real issue became one of sheer practicality, and as you will know the Prime Minister accepted and agreed the final outcome which I put forward. (Correspondence)

Secondly, MacGregor's actions and SEAC's crucial advice, as we shall see, provided the NCC at least with the opportunity to produce a set of workable proposals and gave some credence to Roberts' claim that 'synthesis' in history teaching was possible in the 1990s based upon the Final Report (Roberts, 1990).

Chapter 8

'The End of History?' The NCC, Clarke and the Statutory Orders

This chapter considers the role of the next 'text producer' in the policy process relating to NC history, namely the National Curriculum Council (NCC). The chapter concentrates upon the proposals of the NCC's History Task Group (HTG) (NCC, 1990) which formed the basis of the draft Statutory Orders (DES, 1991b). The analysis is placed within the context of the reflections of Duncan Graham, the former Chief Executive of the NCC (Graham with Tytler, 1993). The chapter culminates with a discussion of the extraordinary last minute events surrounding the creation of the Statutory Orders for history (1991a), namely the controversial interventions in the debate by the Secretary of State for Education Kenneth Clarke, who replaced John MacGregor on 2 November 1990.

NCC's Role and the Establishment of the History Task Group

The NCC had been established under the Education Reform Act (Section 14 (3)) to offer the Secretary of State advice on the basis of statutory consultation with teachers and other professional groups. The Council itself was advised by subject 'task groups' which were responsible for formulating detailed advice in relation to specific subjects. Thus the HTG's major role was to consult with teachers over the MacGregor proposals and then make recommendations to the Secretary of State (via Council) in the light of this consultation; these recommendations would then be used as the basis for the Statutory Orders laid before Parliament. The HTG also had responsibility for producing non-statutory guidance for supporting teachers' implementation of the NC.

The first meeting of the HTG was held on 22 February 1990. Unlike the HWG, the HTG was comprised exclusively of professionals actively involved in education. In addition, the HTG meetings were attended by representatives from the DES and HMI, SEAC and CCW (Curriculum Council for Wales), described as 'assessors' and 'observers' respectively. HTG was also attended in person by members of Council.

The professional officer for history was Dr Nick Tate; he was a relative outsider to the education system in England having worked as a history lecturer in Scotland.

Nevertheless, Tate had not been exclusively detached from developments in England: he had written a student support book for GCSE history (Tate, 1986). The NCC recognized itself that history was 'the most contentious' of all NC subjects (NCC, 1990, p.14) and it seemed that Tate was ideally suited to the role. As Graham himself indicated 'not only was Tate an excellent historian, he was politically astute in a way the working group perhaps had not been when there had been an opportunity for compromise' (Graham with Tyler, 1993, p.68). In interview, one of the HTG members remarked that 'Nick's political skills impressed me' claiming also that 'his influence on the work of the group was immense but in a way that was not obvious. What was obvious was the fact that he was always taking into account the views of interested parties from DES to HMI to Council and Duncan Graham himself'. Tate's political talents were obviously formidable as his subsequent rapid rise within the NCC bureaucracy was to testify. Tate was to play a profoundly significant role, and, for reasons which are highlighted later in the book, an intriguing one in shaping history in the NC and therefore he features prominently in the remaining chapters.

The HTG's role in the policy process contrasted in a number of respects from the HWG; whereas the HWG had the opportunity actually to conceive ideas on the history curriculum, the HTG's role, of course, was far more circumscribed. Essentially, the HTG's role was to provide the NCC with a sounding board and a source of ideas. The framework for the work was defined by the NCC and interpreted by professional officers. It was clear that some HTG members had reservations about aspects of the HWG's earlier work, particularly in relation to the Interim Report. The publication of the Final Report and the circumstances following publication encouraged the NCC towards a pragmatic acceptance of the Report's major principles, despite the reservations felt by some teachers. Interviews with HTG members revealed that there was a grudging feeling that the HWG had done a basically sound job and that any thoughts that the HTG might have had about the need for a radical re-write were pushed aside in light of the need to maintain the essential structure of the original proposals. At the same time the HTG was keen to produce a more polished version which could be implemented in schools, supported by non-statutory guidance. The parameters of the work of the HTG had been firmly imposed before it began its work and this even had implications for the importance of the statutory consultation process itself:

> We wanted therefore to stamp our mark on it, to show that we had improved upon what the HWG had done, we did not want to go against what ministers were telling us, thus we had a desire to avoid confrontation. So in a sense what I'm saying is that the outlines of the revision by NCC were decided upon before the results of the consultation were received ... We had our limits, within those broad limits we could play around with things, but essentially we had been given our marching orders. Within that there was a lot of flexibility to slim it down, to make it much more user friendly, to change the content to some extent but that we were going to operate within the structure that we had been given. (Interview)

The implications of the interview data above are clearly significant in two respects. First, the actual work of the HTG must be seen as a ratification process for the essentials of the MacGregor proposals. Secondly, and this is rather contentious, the views of teachers articulated in the consultation process were of secondary importance in comparison to the NCC's political/pragmatic objectives. This relative relegation of the importance of the statutory consultation process to the NCC's work was, of course, compounded by the non-statutory consultation after the publication of the Final Report. Statutory consultation could not begin until the MacGregor proposals were published in late July, again complicated by the onset of the summer vacation. The HTG did have access to the responses to MacGregor's consultation, passed to the NCC by the DES, some of which were used as the basis for the statutory consultation response (NCC/HTG Minutes, 10 July 1990). Clearly, therefore, the recommendations put forward by MacGregor in the proposals published in July provided the framework within which Tate and the HTG had to work.

Towards the Consultation Report: (i) Assessment

The HTG was not able to discuss the Secretary of State's proposals until its third meeting which was held in September. Nevertheless, at only its second meeting it had expressed its concern at the issues which were eventually to be raised by MacGregor. On the attainment targets, the group expressed the view that there was not enough progression between levels and recognized that a balance had to be struck between precision and flexibility. It accepted the principle behind PESC but questioned whether it should apply to all units. Moreover, concern was expressed about the relationship between 'essential' and 'exemplary' information and that the programmes of study needed further work. HTG also shared HWG's concerns about the status of a 'reduced' national curriculum history course at KS4 (NCC/HTG Minutes, 10 April 1990, p.3, para.5 (i) – (iv)). At its third meeting a sub-group of the committee reported that the history study units should be based upon 'focus statements' which emphasized the key features of the unit. Again, the usefulness of PESC was recognized but it was felt to be 'cumbersome in practice at times' (NCC/HTG, 10 July 1990, p.2, para.5 (i)).

By early September, the HTG had started to formulate specific ideas on the issues raised by MacGregor, firstly dealing with the issue of assessment. It was decided early on to leave the issue of the re-naming of attainment target 1 and its greater weighting until responses were received through the consultation process. The proposals relating to dropping attainment target 4 and the amendments to statements of attainment were discussed early on. A working paper prepared by a HTG member for the meeting of 17 September addressed these issues (NCC/HTG 'Issues Paper', 17 September 1990, Annex D). The paper expressed the view that it was theoretically possible for the HTG to advise that this could not be done; however, given the HWG's fairly tenuous justification for its inclusion, elements of this attainment target were better placed within the others. Nevertheless, the paper also stressed that given that the HWG's attainment targets were conceived as a whole, this would involve a 're-examination of the relationships between the remaining three' (ibid, para.3.2). It was decided that attainment target 4 should indeed be 'deconstructed and reassembled within the remaining attainment targets or where appropriate in preambles to the programmes of study' (NCC/HTG Minutes, 12 October 1990, para.4).

The HTG also considered the extent to which statements of attainment should be revised to ensure clarity and progression. Again, the paper referred to above summarized the issues as follows. The HWG had phrased the statements in a general way because not enough precise knowledge was available about the ways in which children's learning progresses, but this meant that they had the disadvantage of lacking obvious progression. On the other hand, the Secretary of State's request that specific examples from the statements of attainment be removed although simplifying matters also opened up the possibility of randomness and ambiguity. The paper argued that 'clarity and simplicity' could only be achieved by reducing the number of statements of attainment within certain strands or providing 'gaps' within the levels. This would mean that 'the statements are descriptors which require interpretation in specific contexts, not a "levels" mark scheme' (NCC/HTG 17 September, Issues Paper, Annex D).

These ideas formed the basis of the HTG's proposals on assessment. As far as the titles of the attainment targets were concerned, two considerations were regarded as important by the HTG. First, the second attainment target 'evaluation and interpretation in history' was regarded as politically significant, particularly as far as equal opportunities were concerned and should remain separate and visible. Second, titles should remain 'pithy' providing clarity for teachers, particularly non-specialists, and in this respect attainment target 3 was regarded as potentially confusing (NCC/HTG, 12 October 1990, para.4). In line with this, the second and third attainment targets were re-named as 'Interpretations of History' and 'The Use of Historical Sources' respectively. At the same meeting, on 12 October, it had been decided that discussion of attainment target 1 could not take place until the results of the consultation were known. A HTG member and an NCC officer worked hard on the responses between this meeting and the next. The responses from the consultation confirmed what the HTG had been working on to date: the majority of respondents favoured removing attainment target 4 as a separate attainment target; 'anxiety' had been expressed about progression in the statements of attainment. Yet the most significant response related to the first attainment target: 'a sizeable proportion of respondents disliked the title of attainment target 1, and opposed the higher weighting for this attainment target' (NCC/HTG, 16 November 1990, para.3). Potentially, this was to provide the NCC and the HTG with its greatest challenge: should it, on the basis of the consultation report, go against the Secretary of State's recommendations on attainment target 1?

In fact, this issue proved to be a non-starter. At the very same meeting, Tate introduced the draft attainment targets which fully endorsed the Secretary of State's recommendations. The minutes reveal that there was no disagreement amongst the HTG on this matter; they only make reference to 'some concern' about progression within attainment target 1 (ibid, para.5). By advising on greater weighting, the NCC was illustrating a difference in emphasis between SEAC and the NCC. Here again, the political/pragmatic dimension of the HTG's work was apparent. Interviews with HTG members revealed that it was made clear to them via DES officials that this was what ministers wanted. Thus, although SEAC had put up a strong intellectual case against greater weighting, in the words of a HTG member: 'although we considered the educational grounds at great length, it was felt that ministers wanted this and this was neither the time nor the issue to be challenging the DES or ministers' (Interview).

Similarly, with respect to the application of the TGAT model, both Tate and other members of the HTG recognized that it was inconceivable that the NCC would advise that it should not be applied to history on educational grounds, despite the difficulties associated with it. Again, the pragmatic/political agenda came to the fore; TGAT was compulsory and in the circumstances, in the words of an interviewee, 'our task was to do the best we could with the structure that we were given, there was no point thinking otherwise. That was the atmosphere at NCC, we had a job to do, we had to produce a politically acceptable compromise and something that was workable for teachers' (Interview).

In the Consultation Report, therefore, NCC confirmed that it supported the title of attainment target 1 and had clarified the title of the other attainment targets to make them 'readily understandable' to teachers, parents and pupils (NCC, 1990, p.14, para.3.9). A separate attainment target 4 was 'not necessary' because communication of information was required in the other three attainment targets. However, it proposed that a requirement that pupils organize and communicate the results of historical study 'including extended writing of different types' should be included in the programmes of study (ibid, p.14, para.3.10). It also reported that it had provided 'greater clarity and precision' to the statements of attainment and clearer progression. It had, as the Secretary of State requested, omitted reference to essential information but provided examples intended to provide greater clarity 'by describing a context in which each might be demonstrated' and that these had been made 'sufficiently specific to assist teachers in relating statements to classroom practice' (ibid, p.15 para.3.14).

The issue of the greater weighting to attainment target 1 had to be phrased very carefully. The report recognized the 'great importance' felt by the Secretary of State towards this attainment target, illustrated by his request that it should be given greater weighting. Although it admitted that consultation had shown opposition to this, it suggested (rather weakly!) that this was because respondents had based their views on the original four attainment targets proposed by the HWG, not the three re-drafted attainment targets suggested by the HTG, and on 'misunderstanding that the changed title of attainment target 1 implied a redirection of its content'. Thus although it recognized both the advice given by SEAC and the views of respondents against greater weighting, it nevertheless believed that attainment target 1 had 'greater substance than the other attainment targets, because of the wider range of elements and larger number of statements' which it now contained. Therefore there should be two profile components for history, one for attainment target 1 and the other for attainment targets 2 and 3, equally weighted (ibid, p.15, para.3.11). The effect was to confirm the impression that 'knowledge and understanding' were given priority in the proposals.

Towards the Consultation Report: (ii) Programmes of Study

The HTG's work on the linked issues of selection of content and the structure of study units was heavily influenced by the proposals of the Secretary of State that the amount of 'real and apparent prescription' should be reduced. Moreover, consultation confirmed the view that teachers 'should have greater discretion' over the selection of the content of history study units and that they wanted a 'reduction in the degree of prescription'. Thus, many respondents called for a reduction in content and welcomed the proposal to omit the detailed information provided under 'Links, Focus, Concepts and Exemplary Information' provided in the Final Report (NCC, 1990, p.9, para.2.6). Respondents also felt that the PESC formula was artificial and should not be statutory (ibid, p.10, para.2.7). At KS2, there was concern about too much content and prescription and the requirement that British history core units should be taught in chronological order (ibid, p.10, para.2.9). There was a 'mixed response' to KS3, a majority agreeing that schools should be free to design all four non-core units, but at the same time there was concern about the removal of the non-European unit (ibid, p.10, para.2.10). KS4 seemed to cause most consternation: respondents disagreed with the selection of content, its prescriptiveness and the sheer amount to be covered (ibid, p.10, para.2.11).

It was clear that the HTG had reservations about the degree of content and prescriptiveness within the NC at an early stage; as one interviewee indicated, 'the feeling was that the HWG had gone too far in its very detailed statements on content and that (a) it had been too prescriptive and that (b) it was attempting to cover too much, and that is why we cut back on the precise references within the study units, so that it was all very much slimmer at the end of the day' (Interview). As with issues relating to assessment, the HTG had decided upon many of its eventual decisions some time before it received the consultation responses. The first meeting had expressed concern about the 'volume and degree of prescription of content' in the primary curriculum (NCC/HTG, 22 February 1990, para.4 (i)) and the 'problems of overload' at KS4 (ibid, para.8). The sub-titles outlined by the HWG in relation to descriptions of content were first discussed at the second meeting (NCC/HTG, 10 April 1990, para.3). At its third meeting it was decided that the key features of study units should be described in 'focus statements' in contrast to the detailed way in which it was described by the HWG (NCC/HTG, 10 July 1990, para.5 (i)). At its fourth meeting, it recommended that there should be no statutory requirement to teach KS2 British core units in chronological order; similarly at KS4, a two history study unit NC course and a four history study unit course would be more appropriate than the proposed three and five study unit courses because this would 'reduce potential overload' (NCC/HTG, 17 September 1990, para.4). At the same meeting the HTG endorsed a template for core study units which provided concise focus statements and the historical information which 'pupils should be taught about' (NCC/HTG, 16 November 1990, para.5).

The Consultation Report therefore showed a genuine attempt by the NCC to make the NC more flexible and less prescriptive on the lines proposed by MacGregor and required by teachers through consultation. Nevertheless, Tate and other NCC officers (like the HWG's management group) were aware of the need to maintain rigour and, to this extent, recognized the need to maintain the principle of prescription. Alongside the requirement for flexibility went the pragmatic/political need to ensure that politically sensitive content was maintained – and seen to be maintained – in the proposals. This was evident in the NCC's decision to abolish school designed history study units in favour of supplementary units at KS2 and more significantly at KS3. The rationale for this decision was explained in the 'issues paper' discussed at the HTG meeting on 17 September: 'the increased emphasis given to school designed history study units in the Secretary of State's proposals for key stage 3 make it even more important that the ground rules for these units be reviewed. School designed history study units are designed to give flexibility to teachers, but need to be unambiguous' (NCC/HTG, 17 September 1990, Issues Paper, p.3, para.5.3). Thus, 'prescribed ground rules' would under-pin thematic units (NCC/HTG, 16 November 1990, para.4 (ii)). In the Consultation Report, the new supplementary units which replaced school designed history study units contained specific and rigorous criteria (NCC, 1990, pp.44–5, 54–5). This also had the advantage of allowing the NCC to ensure that a unit on a non-European society should be included. This provides an important insight into the NCC's views on prescription; the NCC clearly wanted to maintain rigour, breadth and balance which caused some tension within the HTG itself, particularly as the responses in the consultation had overwhelmingly been towards more flexibility. Tensions broke out, for example, over KS2 as the following extract from an interview with a HTG member reveals:

> There was one particularly difficult meeting when some on the group threatened to withdraw their services. It came about over the amount of content which Nick [Tate] wanted to see maintained at KS2. A number of us felt that there were too many units and there were some (for example Tudor and Stuart times) that prescribed far too much detail. Yet it was obvious that we couldn't budge Nick on this one. Again, it was a case of him knowing that this was something that was not open to discussion. (Interview)

Tate was obviously aware through the DES officials and members of Council of the need to ensure rigour at all costs. An interviewee also revealed the need to include 'essential' references:

> We knew that there had to be references to the Battle of Hastings, and to Elizabeth I and to Henry VIII, various things like that, certain icons. This meant that we had to spell out certain things clearly in the preambles to the programmes of study. This caused quite a lot of debate within the HTG as to whether we should do that. But in the end we did it in order that it was seen that ministers were achieving their objectives in ensuring the inclusion of certain 'essential' information. (Interview)

Again, this caused some tension within the HTG when certain anomalous selections of historical content seemed difficult to justify. An example is the discussion over the inclusion of the Roman Empire at KS3. A paper presented by a HTG member dated 11 September 1990 claimed that the unit did 'not sit well with the other three core units' for it introduced 'a non-British component into the core, but a somewhat arbitrary and inflexible one'. Its removal 'from the core could increase the flexibility enjoyed by schools in planning KS3 as a whole', for example giving them the opportunity to study a local history unit. Yet Tate opposed this, no doubt not just because of his own fondness for classical civilization but also because he knew of ministers' enthusiasm for it.

There were similar tensions over KS4, the issue which perhaps caused both the NCC and the HWG most difficulty. The consultation process had indicated widespread dissatisfaction with the amount and the actual selection of content in the KS4 proposals. Yet the Secretary of State had demanded that the units be broader. In the end, the Consultation Report claimed that the KS4 course had 'been written in a way as to ensure rigour and challenge, but to reduce the content to manageable proportions' (NCC, 1990, p.18, para.3.25). In fact, the sixth meeting of the HTG had indicated that 'there was still concern about the amount of content in the NC course' (NCC/HTG, 16 November, 1990, para.4 (iv)). These tensions over certain issues of content and prescriptiveness illustrate yet again the political/pragmatic agenda which the HTG (and the HWG before it) had to take into account at all times.

When the Consultation Report was finally published in December 1990 it was, like the Final Report, a carefully crafted political document. It was influenced by two major (yet possibly contradictory) influences, namely a desire to be seen to accede to the Secretary of State's major proposals, particularly over the issue of prescription, whilst at the same time being seen also to base its proposals on the consultation process.

Mixed in with this was the NCC's own strategy of ensuring rigour and balance. The HTG's work was also inevitably influenced by the relationship between the NCC and the DES. In his book, Graham (1993) reflects upon attempts by DES officials to interfere in the NCC's work, particularly in relation to its proposals on the whole curriculum. I found no evidence of similar interference by the DES in the work of the HTG; nevertheless, the presence of a DES assessor inevitably established what was politically and pragmatically feasible. In other words, if the HTG had wanted to embark upon a radical overhaul of the Final Report (again, there is no evidence that they did), the continued presence of DES officials (and their links with ministers) meant that this was simply not a viable alternative. Thus although Graham and the NCC were prepared to argue against the ministerial will on the issue of cross curricularity (see Maw, 1993), it was clear that he perceived that history was not a subject upon which an independent line could be forged.

The Response to the Consultation Report

As ever, the press response was important for the ways in which the proposals would be interpreted. Most of the newspapers had no doubt about the inclination of the NCC's proposals. *The Times* (29 December 1990) declared that as a result of the recommendations the 'Knowledge of facts will be the basis for history lessons'; the same edition of the *Guardian* agreed that 'Facts hold key to history teaching'. Reports gave prominence to the fact that the NCC had agreed with MacGregor's proposal to re-name the first attainment and that it should be given greater weighting; in the words of *The Times* it was 'twice the value of each of the other two targets' (ibid). The *Independent* (28 December 1990) therefore stressed that the NCC had ratified the government's proposals; characteristically the *Daily Mail* (29 December 1990) put it more forcefully, claiming that 'Ministers win the battle for history'. This was given confirmation when Duncan Graham was reported as saying that 'attainment will be firmly based on learning historical information. Pupils will need to acquire precise knowledge about key events, people and dates from each of the periods studied' (reported in *The Times*, 29 December 1990).

Nevertheless, reports also stressed that the proposals emphasized a balance between British and European and world history and that it had called for adequate resources for the proposals to be implemented effectively. Indeed, a TES article of 4 January 1991 was accurate in its claim that it was a Fleet Street 'misreading' to claim that the NCC had succumbed to traditionalists. Only the *Daily Telegraph* (29 December 1990) reported that although the proposals ostensibly elevated the learning of knowledge, 'it upholds the original working group's view that pupils should not be assessed on specific items of historical knowledge'. The TES article pointed to the greater flexibility and choice given to teachers at key stages 2 and 3 and 'the moves against the general direction of prescription and learning of facts'. The same article reported cautious support for the proposals from a range of different sources, including Robert Skidelsky, the HA and a former member of the HWG. It seemed, therefore, that Tate and his colleagues had achieved what they wanted: consensus had been seen to break out once more. On reflection, Graham claimed that the HTG had 'embarked on some high-speed work to meet all the demands ... There was a feeling on all sides that a reasonable balance had been achieved, and that honour had been satisfied' (Graham with Tytler, 1993, p.69). The Consultation Report had managed to encourage the view that all sides had won the debate. Yet whilst the Report sat on the Secretary of State's desk, few could have predicted what would happen next.

Clarke's Intervention: 'Opting-out' and 'Cutting-off'

According to press speculation, Kenneth Clarke had been appointed Secretary of State for Education in the November cabinet re-shuffle with instructions to wage 'class war' with teachers (see *The Financial Times*, 11 January 1991). This would be in contrast to his predecessor who had appeared too weak, particularly in the eyes of the No. 10 Policy Unit. Clarke soon made his mark; with the Prime Minister's views in mind, he announced in a speech at the North of England Education Conference that the original concept of a ten subject 'entitlement' curriculum would be changed (DES Press Release, 2/91, 4 January 1991). Significantly, he confirmed that history and geography would no longer be compulsory at KS4: pupils could do either history or geography or a combination of both. This, of course, had huge implications for the history and geography proposals which had been designed on the assumption that both subjects would be compulsory.

At a stroke, Clarke seemed to be undermining the careful planning undertaken in the previous eighteen months regarding KS4 and his decision went against all the advice provided by the NCC after consultation (Graham with Tytler, 1993). As an editorial in the TES pointed out, this decision showed that the curriculum had become 'beyond question a political plaything, which politicians can tinker with to suit their own ideas and ideologies'. The article went on to point out, however, that this sort of political interference was particularly significant for schools that had based all their planning 'on the principle, enshrined in the Act, that all pupils would study all subjects in the NC until they were sixteen. The subject working groups planned their recommendations on this basis. Schools have been planning on this basis' but now it was 'back to the drawing board' (TES, 8 February 1991). The article ended with the demand for a one-year moratorium on the NC to sort out the confusion that had been created by Clarke's speech.

Clarke's announcement, of course, seemed to leave the HA's strategy of defending the compulsory teaching of history up to age sixteen in tatters. It lobbied MPs to call for a debate on KS4 on the grounds that any pupils opting out of history at fourteen would have studied no history after that age. Martin Roberts declared that 'it is only in the last two compulsory years of state schooling that young people have the maturity to understand the complexity of the modern world. Without this essential historical knowledge of twentieth-century developments, how else could they understand the recent changes in East Europe or the crisis in the Middle East or Britain's role in Europe and the world?' (quoted in the TES, 11 January 1991). Roberts went on to accuse Clarke of incompetence for the way in which he had interfered. For the HA, the relegation of history from compulsory status was a disaster for the future of the subject: '. . . the fact that we now have only the core and extended core, will put in the minds of heads and governors the idea that these are somehow more important subjects than history and geography' (ibid).

If this was bad enough, the news which broke on 14 January 1991 was even more controversial and added to the woes of the HA. Clarke announced the publication of the Draft Orders for history, which would now go out for further consultation until 15 February; he confirmed that he had endorsed the amendments made by the NCC in response to the MacGregor proposals, including the amendments made at KS4, but the sting in the tail came on the second page of the press release: 'I have made certain further changes, as explained in the letter to those being consulted, to make it clear that the focus of study of this unit should be the first half of the twentieth century. I believe that it is right to draw some distinction between the study of history and the study of current affairs' (DES News 7/91: 14 January 1991). The news took everybody by surprise, especially the NCC. As Duncan Graham indicated, 'NCC made the grave mistake of relaxing and thinking that now history was at last in the bag, the National Curriculum was unlikely to face any other major traumas. Clarke, it appeared, was quite convinced that teachers could not be trusted to teach modern history in an even-handed way' (Graham with Tytler, 1993, p.69).

There was almost unanimous opposition to the decision, some coming from the most surprising quarters. Jonathan Clark decided to enter the debate once more by declaring that 'History has come to an end' in an article which outlined some of the difficulties and dangers of attempting to prescribe a cut-off point for history (*The Times*, 16 January 1991). Skidelsky was reported as stating that although he recognized the distinction between current affairs and history he also regretted that history syllabuses would not make reference to some of the most important changes that have shaped the modern world (*The Times*, 16 January 1991). Lord Briggs declared that 'history cannot just stop' and Lord Blake called the decision 'ridiculous' (*Independent*, 17 March 1991). These comments were quoted by Jack Straw in the House of Commons (Parliamentary Debates (Hansard), Vol. 190, 29 April 1991, p.120). Clarke's decision encouraged the Labour Party to press for a Commons debate on the issue. Jack Straw declared that the decision was an 'arrogant and doctrinaire' attempt to interfere in a political way in the history curriculum (*The Times*, 16 January 1991). In the subsequent Commons Debate he accused the Secretary of State of interfering in the NC for 'partisan ends' and described his actions as 'dangerous' and 'silly'. Above all, 'in the absence of any evidence to justify his decision, the Secretary of State must recognize that he has gratuitously attacked the skill and professional integrity of history teachers' (Parliamentary Debates (Hansard), Vol. 190, 29 April 1991, p.120). Predictably, the HA was incensed by Clarke's actions; Martin Roberts called the decision 'incomprehensible' and also demanded a Commons debate, claiming that the events of the late 1960s through to the 1980s were not current affairs but were crucial for understanding the present: 'The Gulf Crisis, the Common Market, changes in the Welfare State and the coming general election all depend on a good understanding of the recent past for people to make sense of them' (TES: 18 January 1991). The same article summarized the absurdity of the decision: 'The building of the Berlin Wall is history; its destruction is not'.

One of the most potent attacks on Clarke's decision came from John Slater, the former HMI who had been mainly responsible for the 1985 HMI recommendations on history teaching (DES, 1985a). Slater argued that it was vital for teachers to deal with issues such as the Gulf War, not because pupils did not have enough information but because they were actually exposed to too much of it through the media: thus 'teachers can help their pupils reflect on and use their knowledge and experience, through analysis and critical evaluation' which represent 'skills of coping not solving', for at the heart of history, said Slater, was the drive towards 'informed scepticism, of responsible doubt, hostile to the stereotypes and bamboozlers. History is, to pillage a phrase of Hemingway's, a "crap detecting" subject. Is this what lies at the heart of Mr Clarke's anxiety that warns historians off the events of the past 30 years?' (TES, 1 February 1991).

Reasons for Clarke's Decision

Clarke was ambitious (at that time a serious candidate for future Prime Minister) and was determined to stamp his own authority at the earliest stage on education and the NC in particular. There was a feeling that MacGregor had been too soft; this and the fact that Thatcher had shown such personal interest in the subject gave Clarke an excellent opportunity to intervene in a high profile manner. There was evidence that he had already become irritated with the work of the NCC which was advocating, in Clarke's eyes, too much of an inflexible structure (see Graham with Tytler, Chapters 8 and 9). The press was convinced at the time that Clarke was determined to ignore any advice offered by the NCC and to formulate his own ideas based upon advice provided by some DES officials and other political advisers (see three articles in the TES, 8 February 1991). On the other hand, Graham believed that the decision was entirely his own: 'there is no evidence to show that this had anything to do with anybody other than Clarke' (Graham with Tytler, 1993, p.70). In an extraordinary statement in his book, Graham claimed that Clarke had no discussion with the NCC about history between the publication of the consultation document and the Statutory Orders which were to be published in March 1991! (Graham with Tytler, 1993, p.70). This was as a result of Clarke's distrust of 'experts' (TES, 29 March 1991). An article in *The Financial Times* (11 January 1991) was probably accurate also in the belief that Clarke had a natural distrust of teachers, as his apparent contempt for the NCC showed.

The sensitive political circumstances surrounding the publication of the NCC's proposals (namely the Gulf War) may also have played a part in Clarke's thinking. In response to the question posed by Jack Straw in the Commons on 12 February, Clarke indicated that it would be wrong for history lessons to make reference to the latest news from the Gulf; rather, history lessons could include the circumstances which had led to it: 'That is the proper subject of the history curriculum; this morning's news on the radio, and current events in the Gulf War, are not. A proper history curriculum with perspective, enabling pupils to view the past and form judgments on it, is the best way for schools to prepare people for making continuing judgments on current events' (Parliamentary Debates (Hansard), Vol. 185, 12 February 1991, p.722).

In the subsequent Commons Debate on the issue, Clarke gave other reasons for his decision; he cited the decline in history and geography in schools, the HMI reports which indicated that they were being subsumed by integrated humanities, the need to restore the teaching of 'our knowledge, culture and history' and the imperative for history lessons to concentrate upon 'historical perspective'. He also pointed out that the study of current affairs was not being banned, merely that they were not included in the Statutory Orders. Consequently, the Orders had been 'misunderstood' (ibid, Vol. 190, 29 April 1991, pp.118–28).

The Publication of the Statutory Orders

Clarke's decisions were attacked in an extensive contribution by Straw in *The Times* on 13 March. This, and the criticisms from the HA, academics and teachers in the press amounted to a widespread vocal opposition which put pressure upon Clarke to reconsider his decision by the time the period of consultation on the Draft Order (DES, 1991b) was completed (15 February). Critical responses to his proposals even came from the Centre for Policy Studies (Lawlor, 1991) and the Secondary Heads Association (*The Times*, 18 February 1991). According to Graham, the most effective pressure came from Clarke's own officials; he claims that Clarke's original intention had been to impose a 1945 deadline but that as a consequence of a 'Dutch auction' between the Secretary of State and DES officials he had agreed on a rolling review date (Graham with Tytler, 1993, p.70) which was subsequently decided as twenty years. This was confirmed through my own correspondence with a DES official:

> Clarke's decision took us off-balance because it had never been identified as an issue in the HWG or in discussion of their report. Ministers **made it** an issue. We tried to persuade them that it was a phoney one, because the National Curriculum could not actually prevent any content from being taught in school lessons; if recent events were not treated under some other heading, without the safeguards of balance and objectivity which the NC history study units were thought to provide. All to no avail. Ministers were not to be budged, and the only discussion was **how** the date-cap was to be defined. The rolling boundary – twenty years ago – had the advantage of not requiring an annual Order to amend the curriculum. (Correspondence)

Fittingly, when Clarke announced the publication of the Statutory Orders for history on 25 March 1991 (Parliamentary Debates (Hansard), Vol. 188, 25 March 1991, p.275) they attracted the typical press headlines and controversy which had characterized the history debate throughout the long labyrinth-like policy making process which had been initiated over two years earlier. Thus, in the *Guardian* (26 March 1991), attention was focused upon the fact that Clarke, under the pressure indicated above, had trimmed his 'exclusion zone' even further by announcing a twenty year rolling deadline decided every five years; this was clearly a compromise but Clarke was reported as saying that 'my view remains that pupils should not be legally required to study contemporary events . . . because of the difficulty of treating such matters with historical perspective'. He also emphasized that 'the National Curriculum is placing history and geography firmly in the syllabus for all pupils and rescuing them from near extinction as valid subjects in some schools'.

If this was an attempt to placate teachers and the HA in particular, it was unsuccessful. Martin Roberts described the changes as an 'improvement' but still regarded the twenty year rule as ridiculous: 'Mr Clarke accepts that history should be taught to help pupils understand how the world in which they live has been shaped by events in the twentieth century. But how can they make sense of, say, the Middle East if their studies end before the Yom Kippur War?' (*Daily Telegraph*, 26 March 1991). He also declared that Clarke had in fact insulted the professionalism of teachers for 'there is no logical reason to impose the 1970 ceiling on study. The decision shows that Mr Clarke does not believe we teach in a balanced way. It demonstrates a complete misunderstanding of teachers and teaching. Most of the history teachers I know are sensitive not to express their own opinions in class' (*Independent*, 26 March 1991).

A significant decision made in the proposals was that to include a unit on the Second World War at KS3. This was to prevent the possibility of the situation arising (as the HA had warned) of pupils who dropped history at fourteen not studying any modern history. My own research revealed that this had been the last minute work of Tate and Peter Watkins (deputy Chief Executive of the NCC) and two other members of the HTG. Tate and his colleagues had realized that the ministerial decisions meant that they had to take into consideration how this would influence the overall structure of history at the 11–14 level. They therefore decided to include the Second World War in KS3 (rather than KS4) so that those pupils who stopped studying history at fourteen under the new proposals would know something of twentieth century history. At the last minute, then, here was pragmatic/political consideration joining force with educational logic.

As we have seen, the Statutory Orders were the product of intense debate and subject to the politicization which had been so characteristic of the NC history debate in the previous two years. A former HWG member, Henry Hobhouse, reflected in the TES (26 March 1991) that since January 1989 over 100 people had contributed in some way to the policy process relating to history and questioned whether all the effort had been worthwhile; in addition to being inconsistent, Hobhouse claimed that the history NC was now 'bland, innocuous, an evident political compromise; it inevitably lacks cohesion, consistent quality, bite, flavour and authority' and was a great disappointment in comparison to the way in which the original NC proposals had been conceived by the HWG. This was, of course, a matter of debate and Hobhouse was inevitably being proprietorial about his own group's proposals. Yet the frantic, last minute circumstances in which the NC had been completed did indeed make a mockery of the earlier intensive attention to detail outlined in Chapters 5 and 6. As a leader in the TES suggested, it seemed that all the exciting pedagogical developments in history and in geography had been discarded. But on the eve of the next important phase of the policy making process – the implementation stage – it had this word of advice for teachers who 'should take heart . . . remember that a Statutory Order simply lays down the minimum . . . history teachers can ignore the Education Secretary's rather eccentric definition of "current affairs" as any event which took place in the past twenty years. Such very recent history is not forbidden – it is simply not compulsory' (TES, 29 March 1991). Much, then would depend upon the ways in which history teachers interpreted the legislation within the *context of practice*.

Chapter 9

'Slimming History': Implementation, Dearing and Reform

This chapter does three things: first, it evaluates the ways in which history teachers responded to the 1991 Statutory Order within the *context of practice*; in doing so, it makes reference to research work conducted on the implementation of history in the NC, including my own analysis of its implementation in secondary schools (see below). Secondly, in doing so, it considers some of the problems facing teachers both in secondary and primary schools during this period which eventually led to the reform of the NC under Sir Ron Dearing (Dearing, 1993a; 1993b). Thirdly, the chapter ends by describing the politics surrounding the work of the Schools Curriculum and Assessment Authority (SCAA) review group established under Dearing to reform history in the NC and whose work formed the basis of the final NC history text published in January 1995 (DFE, 1995).

The first few sections below are based mainly upon my own research work on history teachers' views of the NC and the implementation of KS3 history during the period 1990–94, much of which has been published (Phillips, 1991, 1992a, 1993a, 1993b). The research was concerned with evaluating teachers' perceptions of the NC texts, specifically to determine whether they perceived congruence between their own pedagogical discourse as discussed in Chapters 2 and 4 (see Evans, 1994; Haydn, 1992a, 1992b, 1993, 1994; John, 1991) and those presented in the NC texts.

Research data were obtained in three main ways. First, I attended many of the major consultation meetings during the period noting, for example, the ways in which teachers responded to speakers involved in the policy process (such as NCC and SEAC representatives). Secondly, I was given access to some of the submissions to the HWG regarding the Interim Report; these, of course, are referred to below anonymously. Thirdly, the bulk of the research data was derived from questionnaires completed by a large (N = 85) representative sample of heads of history departments in five English local education authorities, in 1990, 1991 and 1993 during the crucial period of implementation; these were followed up with in-depth structured interviews with a smaller sample group. In addition, these data were cross-referenced to my own studies on implementation in Wales (Phillips, 1992c; 1992d; 1993c) and to other surveys which, although smaller in scale compared to my own study, nevertheless provided an invaluable source of evidence for triangulation purposes (Gwent History Teachers Working Group (GHTWG), 1991; Hawkey, 1993; O'Neill, 1994; University of Birmingham History Education Group (UBHEG), 1993; Watts, 1993). In addition, I was also able to refer to official reports and texts (NCC, 1992; OFSTED, 1993).

Autonomy or Control? Teachers Initial Perceptions of History in the National Curriculum

The challenge, of course, for both the HWG and the HTG had been to produce proposals which were broadly acceptable to teachers but which also had to take into consideration the views of the New Right, academics and the government. Yet the successful implementation of history in the NC ultimately depended upon two inter-related factors, namely the extent to which teachers perceived that the NC was in congruence with their own pedagogical practices and whether they believed that the Statutory Orders were practicable and workable. We saw in Chapter 7 the ways in which attempts were made by teacher organizations – primarily the HA – to mobilize teacher support behind the Final Report, not only to preserve the position of history in schools but also to ensure that the proposals were not replaced by those favoured by the New Right. I want to argue that although there were laudable and genuine reasons behind this strategy to achieve a 'consensus' over the teaching of history (Roberts, 1990), ultimately they masked fundamental structural, epistemological and technical weaknesses which, it could be argued, flawed the NC from the outset.

Evidence of these problems first emerged, for example, at the HWG meeting on 9–11 October, 1989 (NC/HWG (89) 15th) when it was reported by the chair of the 'responses' panel that although there was support for aspects of the Interim Report, there was also real concern about various aspects of it. An analysis of the submissions indicated a clear contrast between support for the *general* aims, philosophy and proposals on assessment in the Interim Report, and the articulation of a range of complex and varied concerns about *specific* aspects of the document, particularly in relation to the selection of prescribed content and its implications for professional autonomy.

Submissions thus expressed support for the stated aims of the Report; one submission claimed that it was a 'worthy document which has taken note of the best developments in the teaching of history in recent years'; another noted that the HWG had 'attempted successfully to balance knowledge and skills' which was 'sound methodology building on the best of current practice'. Given that the vast majority of respondents were secondary teachers, it was not surprising that submissions gave endorsement to the HWG's forceful justification of the place of history as a compulsory element in the curriculum. There was also very strong support for the group's proposed attainment targets, particularly the decision not to include a separate attainment target for knowledge because, in the words of one submission 'accurate and precise factual knowledge is basic to all history, and the proper use of factual evidence should be an important criterion in all attainment targets'. On the other hand, the submission claimed that a 'knowledge attainment target might lead to the rote learning which the Working Group rightly deplores'.

A significant number of submissions specifically made reference to the Secretary of

State's letter which was described as 'regrettable' because the Report did 'recognize that knowledge has a fundamental part in the teaching of history' and that it had proposed a 'good balance between knowledge and interpretational skills'. Another pointed out that 'the provision you are proposing for the place of knowledge in the programmes of study is correct and must be retained'. Such strong sentiments of support, of course, explain why the HWG resisted attempts to change their view on this issue in the Final Report.

In contrast to the above, concerns about the selection, nature and amount of prescribed content in the Interim Report dominated the majority of submissions. The first concern was that there was a mismatch between the Report's aims of providing a broad and flexible choice of history and the actual content selected, thus in the words of one submission 'the detail of the study units seems to contradict the group's rationale'. The second major concern relating to the Interim Report was that the content was 'overloaded' or 'excessive' (particularly at key stages 2 and 3) and 'overly prescriptive', the selection of content summed up by one representative comment as being 'content-laden, obscure and disparate'. A range of reasons – practical, philosophical and professional – were given by respondents for opposition to such detailed prescription. There was the belief that the selection of content at KS3 and KS4 particularly was 'incoherent and out of line with what is currently represented in the stock cupboards of the nation's history departments'. The 'esoteric' choice of certain units such as Shogun Japan (in contrast to the omission of the World Wars and Nazi Germany) meant that the HWG had ignored 'continuity with good practice'. Concern about content and resources was closely associated with the belief that this would have a negative impact upon the way in which the subject would be perceived by pupils. Thus, there were common references to the fact that content was 'uninspired', that it would be 'boring' to teach and that the Report had paid little attention to pupils' conceptual abilities.

Concerns relating to the selection, prescription and scale of historical content were often expressed within the context of the belief that the Report did not provide enough scope for professional judgement. Thus, submissions spoke of the 'enthusiasm of teachers' or 'teacher expertise' having been 'ignored' or 'discarded'. The following extract illustrates the tension which went to the very heart of the 'great history debate' (and this book), between recognizing the potential advantages of a state-initiated compulsory prescriptive NC and the negative implications for professional autonomy:

> There has been vast variation in the standard and quality of some history which is taught in schools today, and it is necessary to bring the quality of history into line for different ages and abilities ... The problems arise, however, because you state what is to be taught and where, rather than leaving that up to the individual schools and departments to decide what is taught as has been done in the past ... What you are actually proposing is cutting down on individuality and the expertise of professionally trained historians in the class-room.

Nowhere were pedagogical concerns relating to excessive prescription, content over-load, inappropriate selection and lack of due regard for variety and teacher expertise better illustrated than in comments relating to KS2 and KS4. The relatively small number of submissions from primary teachers expressed 'dismay', 'concern' and 'bewilderment' at the 'lack of sensitivity' to integrated topic work in primary schools. Rather, the prescribed subject-specific content had been included without reference to the 'teacher expertise and interest, current resources and local/topical relevance' of primary culture. This was hardly surprising given the commitment of the HWG to the teaching of history in a discrete fashion and to the antipathy of some of its members towards integrated topic approaches. What is interesting about primary teachers' responses to the Interim Report, of course, was that they were describing some of the structural weakness of the NC overall (Kelly, 1990).

Some of the most heartfelt and anguished sentiments related to KS4. Submissions spoke of the 'unanimous dismay' relating to the 'excessively prescribed and dull content' in the KS4 proposals which failed to meet the purported aim of giving pupils an understanding of the modern world. The selection of content at KS4 was very unpopular and was regarded by many as 'irrelevant' to 14–16 year olds. Above all, submissions thus referred to a 'complete mismatch with current GCSE courses' such as SHP which had the effect of 'de-skilling' teachers. Again, this aspect of the submissions went to the core of the debate. Thus although 'good teaching stems from a personal commitment to the curriculum being taught' too much prescription prevented teachers 'making judgments about course content based upon the pupils they teach'. Many teachers who responded were sensitive here to the political dangers of prescribing historical knowledge in such a detailed fashion. Thus, one submission pointed out that a measure of a democratic society was the 'degree of political control that the government has on the teaching of history within its schooling system'. Far from criticizing the diversity of GCSE courses in schools, the Interim Report should praise them because they reflected the 'diversity and richness of our schools today'.

Although, as the HA had emphasized (HA, 1990), teachers perceived that the Final Report was an improvement on the Interim in a number of respects, nevertheless my own study of the perceptions of heads of history departments revealed that important reservations remained (Phillips, 1991, 1993a). Thus, respondents to my 1990 survey expressed general support for the compulsory nature of history in the NC and held the view that it provided potential for coherence and higher standards. Respondents were particularly supportive of the 'clever', 'balanced' and 'shrewd' justifications for the teaching of the subject set out in the Report, described by one as a convincing argument for a 'combinations of skills and evidence' and another as a 'breath of fresh air given what I was hearing in the press'. The research also showed that the teachers were conscious of the pressure upon the group with regard to the selection of historical content; as one indicated, 'would we ever be able to agree over the selection of historical content? We will never be able to agree on everything'. Another described the selection of content as 'a fair compromise given the pressures on the group'.

As with the Interim, however, the main source of concern related to the amount of prescribed content. Respondents repeated some of the comments above in connection with the Interim; content was often referred to as 'dull', 'boring', 'stuffy' or 'inflexible'. Thus one commented that he had never heard of any schools covering some of the topics in the Report; it was therefore 'the Year 0 Syndrome. Heaven knows how we will teach it properly'. Another comment was particularly significant: 'I accept that history teachers will never agree on selection of content but I resent the lack of school designed units, the emphasis on political history and the sheer waste at KS4 with the abandonment of SHP'.

With regard to assessment, the research showed an interesting dichotomy: although respondents showed a degree of satisfaction with the selection of attainment targets (again, particularly with regard to the HWG's stance on knowledge) there was considerable dissatisfaction with the statements of attainment. Thus, some comments referred to concerns that the levels either had the potential to hinder effective teaching or that they were different to the assessment procedures which had been developed for GCSE. Thus, one respondent claimed that 'intellectual acrobatics have been performed here to create something wholly artificial to comply with the TGAT formula. There is great confusion over levels – how practical will assessment be? I would rather teach the subject!' Finally, other concerns related to the lack of time available to teach the content, lack of suitable resources and the general view that the Report would lead to a decline in creative approaches in favour of didactic teaching methods.

An interesting aspect of the research was that many of these perceptions remained relatively unchanged with regard to the 1991 Statutory Order. On assessment, only a minority of respondents expressed concern about the greater weighting given to attainment target 1 and its re-naming. Thus, one respondent commented that attainment target 1 looked 'a little daunting because it's supposed to assess historical knowledge but the strands really include things like chronology, change over time and causation which makes greater weighting quite sensible'. Although respondents felt that the statements of attainment were an improvement from those in the Final Report, there were feelings that 'historical understanding does not move in a smooth ten step fashion so while I feel the attainment targets are OK, the levels are contrived'. Likewise, although teachers perceived that there had been a reduction in the amount of prescribed content, thus welcoming the greater flexibility that this afforded, there was still significant evidence that there was 'not enough time to enjoy the subject matter' and that certain units (such as the Romans at KS3) seemed out of place.

Unsurprisingly, however, the most dominant concern amongst teachers in relation to the Statutory Order concerned the proposals at KS4. The decision to make KS4 no longer compulsory was regarded by a significant proportion as a betrayal of the original concept of entitlement within the NC, that the last minute changes had disrupted the balance and structure of KS3 and KS4 and again, views were expressed that the actual selection of content at KS4 was 'dry', 'boring' and 'irrelevant'. Significantly, there was a perceived mis-match between the NC proposals and existing GCSE courses. Thus, one teacher spoke of feelings of dread at the idea of 'ditching our existing course which has been so successful and popular. The NC destroys over night the amount of effort and dedication we've put into this area of our work'. Others spoke of the 'outrageous' decision to 'date-cap' history which demonstrated the 'contempt with which the teaching profession is held by this government' and which made a 'mockery of any so called "consultation process". Everyone else's opinions – particularly those of teachers – are ignored'. Again, therefore, these comments went to the very heart of the debate; as one particularly angry (but equally representative) respondent exclaimed:

> My biggest regret is that all the hard work which went into setting up our Modern World GCSE course stands to be wasted and replaced by a load of Thatcherite cant about the development of pseudo democracy in the UK. Hopefully, the battle for KS4 is yet to be won and the groundswell in favour of a less British history dominated course will finally prevail.

'Rushing through the ages': Implementing the NC in Schools

When it came to actually implementing history in the NC in September 1991, teachers were provided with an abundance of advice and supporting documentation, the most important of course being the non-statutory guidance produced by the NCC which was sent to schools with the Statutory Orders in the late spring/summer 1991 (NCC, 1991a). As the implementation period progressed, the NCC published further guidance material (e.g. NCC, 1991b, 1993). Other sources of information during this period included the publication of a wide variety of NC history textbooks (see SCAA, 1994a) and texts produced specifically to 'advise' teachers on how to 'deliver' (Watts, 1992) or develop a 'clearly defined' interpretation of the NC (White, 1992). One particular text set out with the intention, no less, of showing teachers 'how to plan, teach and assess' history in the NC (Teaching History Research Group, 1991). At a local level, the period saw intense activity at INSET meetings to interpret the requirements of the Statutory Order (OFSTED, 1993). At a national level, the HA and SHP held conferences which were dominated by implementation issues and these also provided opportunities for teachers to hear the views of NCC and SEAC professional officers (HA, 1991). Finally, as ever, the press remained a constant source of news for teachers wishing to keep up with developments at the macro level. My own research revealed that implementation was dominated by two inter-connected issues which had preoccupied debates over history in the NC since its inception (and which had been identified by history teachers as causes of concern at an early stage: see above): namely, how to implement the prescribed historical content in the limited amount of time available, and how to respond to the technical demands of assessment.

The information derived in the non-statutory guidance illustrated the dilemmas facing history teachers. On the one hand, the documentation emphasized that 'all content is statutory and provides a framework for detailed planning' but, on the other hand, it was up to teachers to 'decide how much detailed factual content is required by each topic or theme. Some parts may be taught in depth, others in outline' (NCC, 1991a, B10). The challenge for the teachers in my surveys was how to teach the prescribed historical content within the limited time available. Thus one respondent emphasized that 'there is so much prescribed content to cover, especially in the core units. What to leave in and what to leave out is a tricky question. At the moment it feels like a rush through the ages'. This was a picture confirmed by the other studies of KS3 history implementation. Concerns that there was not enough time for 'in-depth' treatment of historical content proved to be one of the most recurring themes and again, this was closely connected to the issue of assessment. Thus Watts' (1993) 'major reservation' about effective implementation was the 'amount of time available'; the problem for her department was how to 'cover rather more in less time, giving deeper attention to historical skills and coping simultaneously with new ways of assessment' (p.13); consequently, she seemed to be 'galloping through the material' at a 'breathless pace' and 'insufficient work in depth had been done in the lesson' (p.14). Hawkey (1993) also emphasized that the 'overriding constraint' of her interpretation of the NC was lack of time (p.140). Similarly, a study of KS3 implementation in Midlands schools found that 'one of the most pressing problems is that of time with every department acutely worried about how they could cover the content let alone meet the statutory requirements of the Order' (UBHEG, 1993, pp.49–50). The study found too that 'again and again teachers pleaded for the prescribed content to be reduced' (ibid, p.50). O'Neill (1994) found similar sentiments amongst teachers in the North West. Even the NCC monitoring conference report (NCC, 1992) confirmed that teachers believed there was 'too great an emphasis on content' while OFSTED (1993) also stressed that in their planning of schemes of work teachers were often preoccupied with the specific content demands of the NC.

It was clear that one of the major reasons for teacher concerns about content related to their worries and uncertainty about the 'long dark shadow of assessment' (Bowe & Ball with Gold, 1992) in the shape of the Standard Assessment Task (SAT) scheduled for the end of KS3. A respondent to my 1992 survey revealed the inevitable connection between planning, content selection and assessment: 'All issues relating to the planning of content are dependent upon the issue of assessment. Teachers are trying to pack in as much as possible at the moment because they don't know yet what's going to be in the SAT. Until they know, they'll continue to use the "headless chicken" approach to curriculum planning'. Another stressed that teachers were 'so unsure about the SAT that they had to crash through the modules to make sure we are prepared for it'. Again, this was confirmed in other studies; it was reported that history teachers were 'working in the dark' as far as planning was concerned (TES, 11 December 1992). The UBHEG (1993) study found that teachers were reducing the amount of time given to supplementary units because they would not feature in the SAT, while the NCC conference monitoring report stated that 'the pressure of tests has helped to promote a content-led approach' (NCC, 1992, 2.1).

Concerns were exacerbated by the technical consideration of assessment, particularly with regard to the ways in which the attainment targets and the statements of attainment should relate to teaching and learning. Great efforts were made by SEAC to emphasize the links between the NC procedures and current practice in schools. Thus, there was 'nothing new' about NC methods of assessment and teachers 'had always assessed their pupils as part of their teaching', the only difference being that 'assessment must take place within a new framework of objectives' namely the attainment targets, the statements of attainment and the ten level scale and it was therefore important that teachers 'review the ways in which they currently assess, and to adapt these where necessary to National Curriculum requirements' (SEAC, 1992, p.1). Despite this document and efforts made by SEAC officers at INSET and consultation meetings during the period, my research showed that there was profound uncertainty and concern about assessment. Teachers complained that the NC was 'assessment led'. This preoccupation involved, for example, devising individualized, specific, statement-related tasks to ensure that pupils had 'reached' certain levels. Frustration with this approach was evident, particularly as teachers in my survey frequently complained that the statements were not (and, given the nature of history, could not be) hierarchical or progressive.

A worrying aspect of history's implementation at an early stage for the NCC was that 'teachers see the attainment targets as purely assessment objectives and do not relate them to teaching activities. This tends to divorce assessment from normal classroom activities' (NCC, 1992, 3.2), a view also confirmed through evidence found by OFSTED (1993). My own research demonstrated that after approximately eighteen months of implementation teachers were becoming more familiar with the NC's assessment procedures and were developing ways of integrating them into prevailing practices;

thus one respondent to the 1992 survey claimed that after attempting to 'test everything that moved', she reported that her department had 'wised up and put enjoyment of work as our main priority ... we now slip in assessment tasks in a more common sense way without urgency or pressure'. Another commented that although initially assessment was 'a nightmare', he reported that the department were 'now doing occasional tests geared to levels of attainment and in a way that we used previously'. Yet significantly, the research also revealed that some teachers had become so frustrated with the complexities and uncertainty of assessment that they had attempted to ignore the NC altogether! (See the following for further discussion on assessment: Booth & Husbands, 1993; Lomas, 1995; Medley & White, 1992; Tyldesley, 1993.)

In many ways of course, the picture in history was being replicated in many other subject areas too. This, combined with the chronic overload in the primary sector, meant that the NC was under severe strain – and that history became dependent once more upon educational politics at the macro level.

Planning a Hi-jack? The Right, Dearing and Reform

The period of implementation saw no reduction in the degree of political speculation surrounding the NC and history in particular. As Ball (1993) has demonstrated, Thatcher's replacement by Major witnessed, if anything, a significant move to the Right as far as education policy was concerned, represented by a number of important appointments. Whereas New Right activists prior to 1991 had operated largely outside the policy making machinery, after 1991 they were given responsibility within the *context of text production* itself. In July 1991, Philip Halsey, Chairman and Chief Executive of SCAA, and Duncan Graham, Chairman of NCC, were replaced by Lord Griffiths and David Pascall respectively. Griffiths was Chairman of the Centre for Policy Studies and, as a key member of the No. 10 Policy Unit, had undoubtedly influenced Thatcher over the Final Report. Pascall had also been an adviser in Thatcher's No. 10 Policy Unit. Furthermore, almost a year later, John Marks was appointed at NCC and John Marenbon joined SEAC. Marks had a long New Right pedigree, whilst Marenbon, a Cambridge don, was the husband of Sheila Lawlor of the Centre for Policy Studies. Ironically, it seemed that, under Major, the New Right had at last obtained what it had earlier been denied by Baker and Thatcher! No wonder that former Chief Inspector Eric Bolton expressed his 'fury over Right influence' (TES, 24 July 1992; see Bolton, 1993). Finally, John Patten replaced Kenneth Clarke as Secretary of State for Education on 11 April 1992 following the General Election. His period in office saw the relationship between the teaching profession and the government plummet new depths of antagonism and distrust, culminating of course in the infamous boycott of NC testing arrangements in 1993.

The period saw direct interventions by Major himself in the history debate when he claimed that the government had been engaged in a 'struggle to resist the insidious attacks on literature and history in our schools' and praised the History Curriculum and the work of Freeman and McGovern (the former Lewes teachers) who had 'amply documented challenges to the traditional core of this crucial subject' (Jarvis, 1993, p.3). They were rewarded for their work when Skidelsky and Freeman were appointed to the history committee at SEAC. The *Sunday Telegraph* (13 September 1992) could therefore confidently report that 'traditionalists in the education battle, fresh from their successes in overhauling the teaching of English, are ready to march on history and take the subject back to basics' in line, of course, with Major's infamous slogan. Later in the week the TES (18 September 1992) reported that 'right wing educationalists' were 'laying plans for a hijack' and that history was going to be 'The Next Battlefield'.

This seemed to be confirmed when the second former Lewes Priory teacher Chris McGovern was appointed to SEAC in October 1992. Before the year was out, Deuchar (1992) had denounced, in a typically forthright manner, the lack of emphasis in the NC upon the testing and acquisition of knowledge, and called upon the Secretary of State to abolish the present system, including dislocating history from the TGAT framework (see Husbands & Pendry, 1992, for a critique of Deuchar's views). Given these circumstances, the appointment of Skidelsky and Freeman at SEAC suggested that it would recommend a more traditional form of assessment, particularly in relation to the testing of historical knowledge. Speculation inevitably focused upon the likely form which the history SAT (due to be set in the summer of 1994) would take. SEAC established a consortium to design the SAT according to specifications which were announced in January 1992: the SAT would consist of two written papers, provide opportunities for extended writing, cover all the attainment targets and the programmes of study at KS3. Yet speculation continued throughout 1992 as to the precise form which the SAT would take; teachers were given further information throughout the early part of 1993 by the SAT consortium representatives at, for example, the SHP Conference between 2–4 April.

It was evident that there were severe pressures being exerted on SEAC to reform assessment on more traditional lines. In February, the *Sunday Telegraph* reported that Lord Griffiths was to write to John Patten to demand a review of the whole subject, as Griffiths believed that 'children should be tested on facts and dates rather than on theoretical skills' (*Sunday Telegraph*, 21 February 1993). The early part of 1993 witnessed an internal struggle within SEAC between Skidelsky and his supporters, and the rest of SEAC's history committee. It was evident that Skidelsky shared Griffiths' discontent with fundamental aspects of NC assessment, particularly the application of the TGAT model which he claimed distorted the subject (Skidelsky, 1993b; 1993c). On 17 March he described the assessment and testing arrangements as 'half-baked', of 'Byzantine complexity' (*Daily Telegraph*, 18 March 1993). And a few days later the TES (26 March 1993) reported that the piloting of the SAT, due to be conducted in the summer, could be delayed as a consequence of the concern by Skidelsky and Griffiths that knowledge could be assessed effectively. In the meantime, SEAC published some long awaited support materials for assessment at KS3 in the spring of 1993. The booklet provided thirteen 'case studies' of pupils' work drawn from nine schools in England and Wales with suggestions for recognizing attainment (SEAC, 1993). Significantly, the advice recommended extended writing tasks which were known to be dear to Skidelsky's heart. Yet, frustrated with not being able fully to achieve his aims of overhauling the assessment system relating to history, he resigned from his post in May 1993.

Meanwhile, chaotic events at a more general level started to eclipse what was happening in history. Since 1991, frustration and anger had been building especially amongst primary teachers about various aspects of the NC, particularly in relation to content overload and assessment. A NCC report claimed that overload in the primary sector was causing 'superficial teaching' and that key stage 2 particularly was 'unmanageable', 'too complex' and 'over prescriptive'. After pressure exerted by teacher and parent organizations, including the prospect of a general boycott of testing arrangements, John Patten was forced on 7 April to write to Sir Ron Dearing, the new Chairman of the Schools Curriculum & Assessment Authority (SCAA) (which was due to replace SEAC and NCC in the summer) to conduct a complete review of the NC. Dearing was asked to look at four key issues which, in fact, had plagued the NC since its inception, namely: What was the scope for slimming down the curriculum? What was the future of the TGAT ten level scale? How could the testing arrangements be simplified? And finally, how could the central administration of the NC be improved?

Given the difficulties and pressures faced by teachers in the previous few years, the Dearing Review was warmly and genuinely welcomed by the teaching profession. Dearing provided at least an opportunity for peace to break out after the nadir in teacher–government relationships by 1993. The Review provided an opportunity for the government to 'consult rather than insult', learn from the mistakes of previous years and listen to the views of teachers (TES, 4 June 1993). It was evident from the beginning that Dearing was genuinely committed to consultation and openness as his frequent dialogues with teachers in the press testified and the formal consultation process created by Dearing was one of the most extensive and far reaching in the history of education.

For history teachers, however, the Dearing Review again provided opportunities and dangers (see George, 1994); on the one hand, teachers were relieved that the uncertainty over the SAT was removed and they welcomed the opportunity of teaching a more manageable diet of historical content. Yet this would depend on how it was done; a 'slimmed down' version of the NC could conceivably involve a narrow list of historical names and dates; as an article in the *Guardian* (29 June 1993) stressed, the 'reduction to a basic set of historical facts is a worrying prospect'. These concerns were given potency by reports that the Centre for Policy Studies was reiterating its demands for a minimalist core curriculum which could exclude history (see Lawlor, 1995), Skidelsky's demand that the Dearing Report should simply recommend that schools 'test knowledge' (TES, 30 July 1993) and Deuchar emphasizing that 'the case against the assessment of historical knowledge has collapsed' (TES, 3 September 1993). All this gave substance to the view of Clare (TES, 16 April 1993) that it was a mistake to think that 'the battle is won', for the Dearing Review provided a 'door to a right-wing, and much more unacceptable history curriculum'.

Ironically, therefore, the HA found itself in a similar situation to that faced over the Final Report. The HA's concern about the fragile state of history in schools was strengthened when, at its autumn conference, the new HMI for history, John Hamer, reported that not enough time was being devoted to history. Faced yet again with the need to defend the fragile status of the subject in schools, recognize the concerns of history teachers, as well as preventing the New Right capturing the initiative, the HA's submission to Dearing (following consultation) was characteristically cautious (HA, 1993). It expressed the view that the current Statutory Order was workable and provided the basis for good and effective history teaching. It also defended the balance between local, national, European and world history, as well as the attainment targets which, it maintained, not only reflected the central elements of the discipline but also ensured that historical knowledge and understanding were assessed. The submission recognized, however, the need for some reduction in content and prescriptiveness, although in order to maintain balance it recommended that the amount of prescriptive content within the units should be reduced rather than a reduction in the number of study units themselves.

It was evident from Dearing's Interim Report (Dearing, 1993a), published in July, that he had a sound grasp of the fundamental problems facing the NC since its inception. Although the Report stressed that most teachers supported the concept of a NC, it argued that the problem of content overload stemmed from the fact that the various Working Groups, which had been made up of 'subject specialists who were keen to see that their subject was well covered' (p.27), had been unable to judge the collective weight of the curriculum as a whole and that the consequent prescriptiveness was 'unacceptably constricting' (p.5) to teachers. There was thus a need to review what was defined nationally and what was to be left to the professional judgement of teachers. With regard to assessment, the Report emphasized some of the difficulties of coherence and progression associated with the TGAT model. The Report specifically mentioned the problems in history where it was 'impossible to divorce the development of historical skills from the acquisition' (p.39). Whilst recognizing these and other problems associated with the TGAT model, the Report stressed that given the amount of work invested by teachers in attempting to make it operational, the recommendation was that it should be reformed rather than abolished altogether.

The Final Report (Dearing, 1993b) recommended the establishment of a series of review groups, under the authority of SCAA, to offer proposals for reform, specifically to recommend how the programmes of study of each subject could be simplified and made less prescriptive and to suggest ways in which the number of attainment targets and statements of attainment could be reduced, all changes which would give greater scope for professional judgement. To avoid the mistakes made under the original policy making structure, review groups were under strict instructions to work simultaneously and within specific criteria over-arching 'key stage' groups. The Report's confirmation that history, geography, art and music would become optional after the age of fourteen seemed to put the final nail in the coffin of Baker's original entitlement NC.

The Final Battle? The SCAA History Review Group

SCAA established a range of subject and key stage committees to undertake the review, all of which, following Dearing's recommendation, contained a heavy component of teachers. Unlike the long period of time given to the HWG, the SCAA committees would only be given three weeks to identify the compulsory core of their subject, three to draft the new programmes of study and a further three to simplify the application of the ten level scale in the subject, all of which would be coordinated by the key stage group. In addition, to maintain the sense of coherence across the review as a whole, all committees were given coordinating information in a review handbook. The recommendations produced by the review groups would eventually go to the Secretary of State in late March and to another period of consultation shortly afterwards.

A TES article (14 January 1994) suggested that history was 'likely to be the most hotly debated' of the review groups because although it comprised mainly history teachers and advisers (described in the article as 'progressives'), the group also contained 'GCSE rebel Chris McGovern and right-wing philosopher Anthony O'Hear' (described as 'traditionalists'). The article emphasized that with the content of the history order having to be slashed almost in half at KS1 and KS2 and cut significantly at KS3, 'old rows' about 'facts versus skills' and 'quarrels about the centrality of British history' would re-emerge. This seemed to be confirmed when McGovern reiterated his by now familiar demand that the new proposals should contain merely a core of British history. McGovern's and O'Hear's success in this endeavour would depend heavily upon the work of the SCAA officers appointed to the group and the chair, who was again to be Nick Tate, the newly promoted assistant chief executive of SCAA. Yet, in contrast to the degree of collective unity achieved by the HTG under Tate's astute chairmanship, the SCAA's history review group was characterized by profound controversy, recrimination and conflict.

Again, I was given access to the official working documentation of the group; however, compared to the HWG and even the HTG, this was fairly limited and, as indicated above, the history review group was heavily circumscribed by the criteria set out in the review as a whole and the limited amount of time available. The group met for three two-day meetings, one in January and two in February, 1994. An early briefing document produced by senior SCAA officials entitled the 'key subject principles to be followed in revising the Order' (following the 'review handbook') specified that it was the task of the group to clarify the knowledge, understanding and skills to be taught, identify the depth and breadth of content to be taught without making it unduly prescriptive, make progression more explicit and establish a clearer relationship between the programmes of study and the attainment targets.

In addition, in conducting the review, the group was asked to take into consideration the amount of time teachers had invested in implementing the existing Order and the resource implications of any proposed changes. In their attempts to slim the amount of historical content, the paper asked that the group's proposals ensure that 'by the age of fourteen pupils will have developed a clear understanding of the major themes of British history and the key people and events related to these themes' as well as maintaining the balance between local, British, European and world history. Finally, the group was asked to consider whether the attainment targets adequately described the key areas for teaching, learning and assessment in history.

Other sections of the papers given to members of the group also set out, in a less explicit manner, the broad parameters for the direction of its work. Thus, one section stressed the key principles under-pinning the HWG's Final Report; although the present Order differed markedly from the original HWG proposals, 'the essential structure reflects the remit and their original proposals'. The document went on to outline some of the problems associated with the implementation of the Order (see above) yet the emphasis was very much on the need for continuity within the existing structure. As one of the review group members informed me in an interview: 'Our brief was very much to slim not to go back to first principles!'

Given the composition of the group, any disagreements over 'first principles' was likely to emerge between 'the traditionalists' (O'Hear and McGovern) and some of the teacher representatives. Yet it emerged that any unity between McGovern and O'Hear was more apparent than real, for the TES (18 March 1994) was soon sensationally reporting that these two 'Men of the Right scrap over history'. The disagreement had come about because McGovern was apparently angered by the fact that there was to be only 36 per cent 'uniquely British' history in the revised proposals and had expressed this anger in a five page letter to Ron Dearing. He was also angry that 'well-known' events in British history such as the Great Fire of London and the Gunpowder Plot had been left out of the proposals and that SCAA had therefore been guilty of doing a 'botched job'. Even more surprising, perhaps, was that O'Hear supported the SCAA proposals; in the *Daily Mail* on 15 March 1994 he criticized McGovern by stressing that although it was true that the Plague of 1665 and the Great Fire of London were not specifically mentioned in the proposals, this did 'not mean that they cannot be taught'; he also posed the question 'can it really be pretended that the Plague and the Fire are key political events, on a level with the Civil War, the Interregnum and the Restoration, all of which are mentioned?'

The situation had come about as a result of McGovern becoming profoundly dissatisfied with the work of the review group, so much so that he published his own 'minority report' through the Campaign for Real Education (McGovern, 1994). McGovern had two main criticisms of the proposals. First, he claimed that SCAA and its officers – whom he claimed had dominated the work of the group – were more concerned with slimming the NC than with providing a rationale for the new proposals. There had not been enough time to conduct the work effectively which was a 'frivolous' way of revising the original Order which 'for all its inadequacies, had at least been carefully put together over a period of two years'. By contrast, SCAA had been 'more concerned with the manageability of change than with protecting the integrity of the subject' (p.2). Second, although the proposals did put 'a predominant emphasis on British history' and thus in theory the group had agreed to the Secretary of State's demands articulated in his speech on 18 March, the proposals had not included what McGovern called 'distinctive' British history. This was because political history was given the same emphasis as other aspects such as cultural or social. Thus the Secretary of State would have to 'search in vain for any requirement to teach about a named British monarch or a specific Parliament' (p.3). The paper then went on to claim what was and what was not prescribed in the proposals, including the references, amongst many others, to the Gunpowder Plot and the Great Fire of London (mentioned above). Other 'omissions', claimed McGovern, included 'great figures' such as Nelson, Florence Nightingale, Queen Victoria and Winston Churchill, and the 'great landmarks' such as Agincourt, the Wars of the Roses, the Napoleonic Wars and the development of British democracy since 1900.

One of the important aims of this book throughout has been to show, following Wallace (1993), the role played by the press in the debate over history. The portrayal of the SCAA proposals in the press on 5 May (they were not actually published until a week later) provides the clearest examples of framing, polarization and derision described in Chapter 1. Most of the tabloid and broadsheet newspapers ran stories based almost entirely upon McGovern's report which had been released to the press the day before. The *Daily Express* announced that there were 'Fireworks over plot to ditch Guy Fawkes'. The proposals would 'allow "trendy" staff to teach social history instead of great events'; they included topics like Islamic Civilizations and Black Peoples of the Americas, while subjects such as the Battle of Agincourt, Nelson and the Gunpowder Plot were optional. Similarly, in what it described as the 'Battle of Britons', *Today* claimed that the 'great events and figures from British history could disappear from school timetables' in favour of topics such as 'everyday life in Benin – an ancient African society'. According to the *Daily Star* 'British heroes were set to become history'. MPs were 'dumbfounded to learn' that there was to be 'no mention of national heroes' and that exam advisors 'even want to give King Harold the arrow and axe King Charles'. Apparently, 'All battles, including Waterloo, Trafalgar and Agincourt and EVERY British King and Queen, go'. On the same sensational theme, the *Sun* declared that 'Britain's glorious past banished from lessons'. Thus 'OUT' go Henry VIII, Churchill, Guy Fawkes and Nelson but 'IN' comes 'struggles of Namibian women'. The *Daily Telegraph*, in a series of reports devoted to history, even reproduced the annex to McGovern's report in full, indicating in detail the 'prescribed' and 'optional' content.

The publication of the draft proposals on 9 May revealed that the portrayal above had been, unsurprisingly, a gross simplification of what SCAA had been proposing and explains O'Hear's reaction to McGovern's claims. The TES (18 March 1994) even reported that professional officers at SCAA were actually considering legal action against McGovern! The proposals showed that the review group had complied with Dearing's request for slimming and simplification, for the new Draft Orders consisted of only thirteen pages. The introduction explained how and in what ways content had been slimmed across all three key stages by reducing the number of core units (for example at KS3 making the Roman Empire optional), making the focus statements which described the major themes of each unit more precise and specific, and by increasing the clarity about what should be covered in outline and what should be treated in depth. However, the document also stressed that there was a 'predominant emphasis on British history' (SCAA, 1994, iii) as well as the criteria outlined in the 'key principles' paper mentioned above. The proposals also explained why the group had decided to replace the statements of attainment with level descriptions based upon only one attainment target. This had been done to 'reduce complexity' arising from teachers planning work around 'the plethora of detailed statements of attainment'. By contrast, one attainment target based on level descriptions would allow teachers to 'judge which level descriptions "best fits" that pupil's performance', thus using their own 'professional judgment' (ibid, i).

An analysis of what was actually being proposed in the 'key elements' and in the programmes of study revealed the inadequacy of McGovern's interpretation of the proposals described in the press. Thus although the key elements specifically stated that pupils should be taught the 'main events, personalities and developments studied' and although Florence Nightingale at KS2 and Nelson at KS3 appeared in optional sections, the impression conveyed in the press that they had been deliberately left 'OUT' was a distortion. Likewise, the fact that at KS3 the Wars of the Roses appeared as an illustrative example of the relationships between monarchy, Church, barons and people made a mockery of the absurd claim that 'EVERY' British King and Queen was left out. Similarly, other 'great figures' and 'key events' such as Nelson and Churchill and the French and American Revolutions were specifically mentioned in other parts of the proposals.

There was, however, one significant omission: McGovern's 'British democracy since 1900' was not included. As we have seen, this had originally been suggested under the HWG's KS4 proposals (following the requirement in the original terms of reference for how a 'free and democratic society has developed over centuries') and had been particularly unpopular with teachers, not only on the grounds that it was, in the words of one of the teachers in my own survey 'absurdly Whiggish' in emphasis but also that it was 'uninteresting' and out of line with existing GCSE syllabuses. This unpopularity had been confirmed by SCAA's own surveys and conveyed to the review group in the early documentation. The problem for the group, following the decision not to make history compulsory at KS4, was how to include this potentially unpopular theme into the KS3 programme of study. The documentation demonstrated that the group had considered this issue seriously but had decided not to impose it at KS3 because this key stage was already overloaded, that it imposed too much of a political and constitutional focus which would be conceptually demanding for pupils and that it would require new resources. In addition, this would involve an additional demand at KS3 which would have been out of line with the overall thrust of the Dearing Review which was to slim within the existing structure.

It was hardly surprising that McGovern's claims received severe rebuttal from a range of sources. O'Hear repeated that McGovern had 'failed to appreciate the exercise being undertaken', that the SCAA were not writing a new set of proposals but slimming the original and in so doing it had ensured that 'there is now far more emphasis than previously on the vital importance of historical knowledge' as well as the centrality of British history and that pupils were required to 'demonstrate factual knowledge of the relevant people, events, developments' (*Daily Telegraph*, 5 May 1994). Indeed, Martin Roberts of the HA accused SCAA of succumbing to pressure from Patten and pointed out that under the original Order the percentage of British to European/world history was about 50:50, under the new Order the proportion was nearer 75:25 (TES, 24 June 1994). Ironically, one of the most fierce criticisms of McGovern came from Patten himself who, the day after the proposals were published, claimed that it was 'bunkum and balderdash to suggest that British history is not going to be taught properly, that we are going to see the death of British history' (*Daily Telegraph*, 10 May 1995). The same report went on to quote SCAA's claim that the percentage was nearer 75 per cent. Even more significant was the admission in the same paper (contradicting its own reports during the previous week) that 'yesterday's proposals show that almost all children will be taught about key figures such as Queen Victoria, the Tudor monarchs, Florence Nightingale, King Alfred, Sir Francis Drake, Nelson and Wellington'! Similarly, the *Sun* confirmed that the proposals 'remove fears that British history will not be taught properly' (10 May 1994).

The proposals now went out for yet more statutory consultation; SCAA held a total of 120 meetings throughout the country to evaluate the response to history and the other NC subjects. The initial response to the proposals was positive; in a summary of some of the responses in the TES (17 June 1994), it was reported that history teachers felt that the chronological thread running through the Draft Order was much clearer and that in the words of one history teacher, 'this was vital for knowledge. Skill is now the servant, not the master of history – as it should be'. There was also praise for the level descriptions. The HA also gave the Order cautious support, although as Roberts's earlier comments revealed, there was some concern that in the proposals the original balance between national, European and world history had been diluted in favour of British history. McGovern, however, continued to denounce the Order, criticizing the HA for 'rushing in to support proposals which enshrine teachers' loss of control over what they teach'. He denounced the 'acquiescence' amongst the teaching profession, for the consultation meetings were merely 'gatherings of the faithful' to 'celebrate the miraculous achievements of SCAA in slimming down' the NC. SCAA officials at the meetings were 'cheerleaders, as the multitudes of teachers cast palms of acceptance before the feet of a messiah riding his curriculum donkey from SCAA headquarters in Notting Hill Gate' (17 June 1994).

SCAA officials were again clearly incensed by these claims and a number of articles and letters appeared in the educational press in the following weeks written by members of the advisory group defending their work. The first of these pointed out that the group had done the opposite of what had been claimed in the original press reports of 5 May: the group had not only enhanced the role of knowledge and actually increased the proportion of British history; in addition, they had attempted to 'bring skill, knowledge and understanding closer together' without ditching the 'original principles of the original' NC. Although McGovern was right to point to 'the state's interest in history' his accusations about their proposals were 'politically biased and pedagogically absurd' (TES, 1 July 1994). A letter from another former advisory group member refuted McGovern's claims that SCAA officers had ignored his views; in fact, they had 'bent over backwards' to listen to him; moreover, the letter pointed out that 'the fact that study of a personality or event is not required by law does not mean that it is forbidden by law to teach it' (TES, 15 July 1994).

The most significant defence of the SCAA proposals on history and the NC, however, came from Nick Tate himself. Far from leaving out such things as the central role of British history, SCAA had 'come off the fence' through its proposals which were designed to 'reinforce a common culture' (TES, 29 July 1994). This also provided an intriguing insight into Tate's views for, as we shall see in the concluding chapter, Tate was soon to come 'off the fence' himself by articulating his own discourse in relation to the future direction of history teaching in schools.

Chapter 10

Conclusion: Contesting the Past in the Future: History, Nationhood and the State in the Twenty-First Century

This book was ambitious in that it sought to do three things. First, it tried to illustrate why history teaching was contested in the late twentieth century. Second, it sought, within limitations, to 'get inside' the policy process in relation to history in the NC as well as the educational politics of the period. Third, closely connected with the first aim, it attempted to show that the 'great history debate' was inevitably bound up with issues relating to nationhood, cultural politics and identity. In this final chapter, then, I want to reflect upon the state of history teaching at the turn of the century and illustrate why history may remain a source of contestation for some time to come. I then want to consider what can be learned from the history debate about educational policy making and educational politics in the 1980s and 1990s. Finally, in a book devoted primarily to the study of the past, like Furedi (1992) and Heilbroner (1995), I want to turn to the future by speculating about issues concerning the relationship between history teaching, nationhood and identity in the twenty-first century.

Contesting History in the Late Twentieth Century: Heroes, Heroines and Villains

The history NC text which finally emerged in January 1995 (DFE, 1995) had been, as we have seen, one of the most fiercely contested documents in what had been an extraordinarily turbulent period in the history of education–state relations. An ironic observer may, in fact, reflect upon what all the fuss had been about for, in essence, the NC history Order was remarkably similar in style, structure and substance to the HMI document produced nearly a decade earlier (DES, 1988), particularly in terms of the criteria for the selection of content set out in sections 10 and 11 of the earlier document. In addition, despite the many changes to it since, the Order also reflected the broad substance of the HWG's Final Report. The content thus reflected a sense of historical breadth, encompassing not only political but social, economic, religious, cultural, scientific and technological aspects of history. It advocated the utilization of both general organizational historical concepts like cause and effect, as well as specific ones such as feudalism and revolution. At the heart of the document's definition of what constituted historical knowledge was still the HWG's idea of historical understanding. It also specified the need to cultivate historical skills as an essential means of understanding the past. It re-affirmed that broad-based definition of British history and a commitment to plurality and diversity which had been at the core of the Final Report, and by making elements of non-European history compulsory it also confirmed the need for pupils to gain a better understanding of 'the other'.

Although the Order was similar in fundamental terms to the draft version (SCAA, 1994), this final element of the document reflected some of the concerns raised during the summer consultation. As Bracey (1995a) points out, the Draft Order assumed that more time would be spent on the core units at KS2 and KS3 which increased the emphasis on British as opposed to European or world history. By treating all the study units equally, however, the final Order shifted the balance. More importantly, the final Order established, as Bracey has also emphasized, an important guiding principle for the future direction of the history curriculum and history teaching, the notion that British history should, where appropriate, be set within a European and world context. Compared, as we have seen, to the veritable storm of interest shown by the media and the public at large in the numerous history NC texts published since 1989, the final Order, ironically, slipped into professional usage quietly and unceremoniously in September 1995. It seemed that peace had at last broken out in the history debate.

Major efforts were made throughout this book, following Ball (1990a, 1994a), to demonstrate the serendipity, ad hocery and sheer messiness of the educational policy making process in the 1980s and 1990s. The story of history in the NC provided perhaps the very best example of this vision of policy as rough and cyclical rather than smooth and linear. Thus, attempts were made throughout the book to place emphasis upon the unpredictable and surprising elements of the debate such as the interventions by Clarke and the apparent 'U turn' by Thatcher on the NC described in Chapters 7 and 8. It is therefore rather fitting that in this final chapter we need to devote attention to one of the most interesting twists in the whole debate, namely Nick Tate's decision to 'come off the fence' on history from his position, following promotions within the policy making process itself, first as Deputy Chief Executive, then as Chief Executive of SCAA.

The metaphor of the fence used by Tate himself (Tate, 1994) was an entirely appropriate one. Tate until this point had been careful to disassociate himself from the public controversies of the debate; his work on the HTG and on SCAA's review group meant that he had to demonstrate his neutrality. Graham (1993), as we have seen, made reference to his political skills at the NCC. Similarly, my own interviews with people who worked on these groups with Tate commented upon his ability to gauge what was and what was not possible (the ultimate in political skill) but at the same time he managed (in line with the earlier metaphor) not to reveal too much about his own views on the politics of history. Tate therefore earned himself great credit and the grudging respect from professional circles for preserving some of the best elements of the Final Report in the 1991 Statutory Order, particularly the 'victory' of preventing a discrete knowledge attainment target but also for endorsing attainment 2 interpretations of history which, of course, emphasized the contested, provisional (even relativist?) nature of history and historical activity which was loathed by the New Right. He had subsequently also steered SCAA through the troubled waters following the media's handling of McGovern's minority report.

Given this fairly 'neutral' stance, it was interesting to note Tate's subsequent contributions to the history debate, starting with his 'off the fence' TES article in 1994. I want to spend some time discussing this and some of his other contributions because they represent a continuation of many of the themes articulated in this book. Much of what I say below is based upon my own evaluation of Tate's views (Phillips, 1997b).

Tate emphasized in the TES article (Tate, 1994) a theme which was given much attention throughout Chapter 3, namely that the curriculum should be a vehicle for the transmission of a common cultural heritage. He also expressed profound irritation with the 'evasive' English tendency to avoid issues relating to what constituted an English national identity. In the following year, he elaborated upon this central theme in a range of ways and (significantly) through a variety of media. At a Council of Europe Conference exploring the relationship between history teaching and national identity, Tate thus mourned the loss of the first person plural in school history textbooks. He also claimed that there was an over-emphasis in schools upon historical methodology as opposed to 'historical content' and 'historical narrative'. He also lamented the tendency to ignore the teaching of famous individuals (citing our old friends Florence Nightingale, Lord Nelson and Alfred the Great) which combined to undermine 'history's traditional role in sustaining and developing a sense of national identity'. Tate (1995b) then blamed the onset of rapid social, economic and technological change, as well as individualism and globalization, for making the English uncertain about their identity. Hence the need for a common, collective culture, with the assurance also that it was possible to preserve dual identities – a view which was reiterated in the *Sun* (Tate, 1995c) and in other works (Tate, 1996a; 1996b, 1996c).

He thus referred to what he called his 'big ideas' on the connection between curriculum, culture and nationhood (Tate, 1996a). The first was the reiteration that the curriculum should be a means by which we 'transmit an appreciation of and commitment to the best of the culture we have inherited'. The second was that the 'best' constituted a 'cultural heritage that has its roots in Greece and Rome' and in Christianity for these were 'at the heart of the common culture of this country'. The third 'big idea' did not, at least in Tate's views, contradict his first two, namely that the recognition of 'other cultures and other traditions' could be only be achieved by ensuring a 'strong majority culture which values itself'. The fourth and final of Tate's 'big ideas' was that the curriculum should enable children to recognize and appreciate a canon of literature, music and art, known as 'high culture'. Tate ended the speech by emphasizing that education should in the future have at its heart 'the centrality of the written word and the book'. Moreover, because English was an internationally spoken language and thus subject to many variants, it was vital that 'the distinctive features of English be maintained'. Tate later emphasized that he did not have in mind here a static view of English culture, heritage and national identity, even though they were 'handed down ... given and inherited' (Tate, 1996b). Learning about these issues was essential (Tate, 1996c).

The subsequent reporting of Tate's views followed the familiar pattern. *The Sunday Times* (17 September 1995) on the day after Tate's Council of Europe speech, declared that the heroes of British history had been 'killed off' by new textbooks. Making direct reference to the speech, it reported that in the schools of the 1990s the Battle of Trafalgar was merely 'illustrated by pictures and maps' but that 'the bravery of Nelson, who had a tremendous impact on our history, is barely mentioned'. Similarly, Florence

Nightingale 'used to be described as one of the "noblest women"' but now, school textbooks referred to her 'merely as the source of statistics about hospital death rates'. Similarly, textbooks used to 'regale children with the 900 year old story of King Alfred letting the cakes burn' but now he was no longer referred to as 'Alfred the Great', textbooks merely made reference to 'the basic facts of his victory'. A few days later, the *Sun* congratulated Tate for trying to prevent teachers turning 'our heroes into zeroes'. Thanks to Nelson, 'Britannia ruled the waves for almost 100 years' for he had 'trashed the combined fleets of France and Spain' at his 'final and most famous victory' at Trafalgar. This 'glorious triumph saved Britain from invasion and ended Napoleon's challenge to seapower'. However, far from learning about this, pupils were more likely to learn about conditions on board ship. The article asked readers to imagine if schools taught the history of the Falklands War in the same way as they taught 'more distant glories'.

Certain Past, Uncertain Future: Discourse, History Teaching and Restorationism

The debate over what constituted the 'heroic' in the late twentieth century encapsulated what this book has been about. In a sense, of course, the 'great history debate' was not about the past but the present; its dynamism stemmed from the tension between contrasting discourses on the nature, aims and purposes of history teaching, linked to correspondingly different conceptions of nationhood, culture and identity. One vision of history and history teaching envisaged certainty, closure and stricture; the other uncertainty, openness and fluidity. Thus whereas one ideology seemed determined to maintain the iconoclastic reputation of the heritage of 'the nation', the other reflected a propensity to search for new or undiscovered heroes and heroines as different representations of nationhood at the end of the twentieth century emerged and presented themselves. This only makes sense to us when we are reminded of Furedi's (1992) observation (cited in Chapter 1) that these sorts of debates and reinventions stem from an 'anxiety about the future' which in turn stimulate 'a scramble to appropriate the past'. It is worth reminding ourselves here also that the 'great history debate' was concerned with 'that elusive, displaced notion of Englishness' (Schwarz, 1996). It stemmed from an identity crisis, a sort of national schizophrenia borne from intense ideological, cultural and social change. Interestingly, the shifts and turns in Tate's own outlook mirrored this national uncertainty. Whatever the precise reasons for Tate's move from peace-maker to defender of the national soul, a closer examination of this discourse within the context of the themes raised throughout this book might shed further analytical light on the nature of 'the politics of history teaching' at this time.

Tate's intellectual impetus derived itself from those views described in Chapter 3, particularly those of Scruton, for like many of the others described earlier, Tate combined thesis and antithesis. The thesis tried to set out his view of what constituted citizenship, culture, nationhood and a sense of identity, whereas the antithesis of his arguments identified those intellectual developments, ideas and trends which apparently undermined this vision. The distinction made between 'national identity', 'nationalism' and patriotism' (Tate, 1996c) and the desire to define 'patriotism' around the theme of collective pride in one's 'own' cultural traditions and ways of life, as well as deeply held 'feelings of affinity to the immediate group which are the source of a sense of duty and civic responsibility' derived intellectual inspiration from Scruton's (1980) 'self-conscious' sense of nation. Similarly, Tate's desire to link history teaching with the creation of a 'common' identity derived from Scruton's (1986) notion of a 'sense of belonging'. Again, like Scruton, Tate's views on culture and knowledge were based upon post-enlightenment certainty.

Both Tate and Scruton, like Norris (1996), were profoundly concerned with the apparent flight towards relativism in intellectual life and the post-modern critique of knowledge. Similarly, like Bloom (1987) who in the 1980s was concerned about the levelling cultural and intellectual impact of multiculturalism and anti-racism on the minds of American undergraduates, Tate was anxious that British schoolchildren were being educated in ways which were somehow uncivilized. He thus craved for the 'development of the "cultured" person', whom he defined as someone who combined 'civility, aesthetic sensibility, a commitment to truth' (Tate, 1996c). As he made clear, his commitment to 'the best that has been known and thought' and his belief in a certain notion of what constituted 'the best' led him to the fairly unproblematic acceptance of the need to educate children in the traditions of a 'high culture' which had its roots in Greece and Rome.

Whereas Tate derived much of his thesis from the Scrutonite tradition of New Right thought, the antithesis and objects of his derision were similar to those articulated by the populist strand. He was particularly influenced by a more recent work in this vein by the columnist Melanie Phillips (1996). Two themes in particular which had been given particular attention by Phillips were close to Tate's heart, namely the ways in which the cult of liberal individualism had permeated the educational system to such an extent that it had presided over both the 'destruction of morality' and the 'deconstruction of the past', and that the country's identity had therefore dissolved 'into a rainbow of pluralistic fragments' (ibid, p.317), all the work of a 'self-hating English intellegentsia'. Similarly, in speech after speech (frequently reported in the press), Tate identified the enemies: 'core values' had been undermined by globalization and an 'individualistic, relativistic and hedonistic view of morality' (Tate, 1995b), while deconstruction and demythology had undermined narrative history (Tate, 1995a) – all the result of the work of academics who should know better. In summary, as others had stressed in the 1980s (see Quicke, 1988), Tate was claiming that the crisis in the late twentieth century threatened the very fabric of nation, state and society.

As we have seen, the core of the New Right view of history was what Slater (1991) has perceptively called 'the common sense view that there is an objective view of the past waiting to be seized and communicated, and a truth acceptable to all historians' (p.21). As we have seen, pedagogical innovations in the last quarter of the twentieth century re-evaluated and questioned traditional forms of historical knowledge and utilized new methodological and conceptual tools to study it. In short, these changes reflected wider intellectual developments and the various 'claims' on the past described by Jenkins (1991). This vision of history teaching as open, subject to change, responding to societal, cultural and ideological factors is not unique in the twentieth century as this fascinatingly appropriate comment from the past illustrates:

> History should not be regarded as a stationary subject, it can only progress by refining its methods and accumulating, criticizing, and assimilating new material . . . it is bound to alter

its ideals and aims with the general progress of society and of the social sciences, and it should ultimately play an infinitely more important role in our intellectual life than it has hitherto done. (Robinson, 1912, p.25)

Robinson could easily have been describing the motivation behind the new history 60 years later. Similarly, his view of history as an open, not a closed text, ultimately explained the dilemmas faced by the HWG, as well as the themes of contestation, conflict and compromise running throughout this book. For neo-conservative, popular-authoritarian discourse, however, historiographical fluidity, as well as the ways in which history was presented, posed problems. Yet shifting interpretations of the past and how it is constructed, as we know, have a vital impact upon the way it is perceived. Let me make reference to three of Tate's 'icons' above to make my point, namely Nelson, Florence Nightingale and Alfred the Great.

The reference to Nelson permits me in this final chapter to point to work of the late Raphael Samuel who died before this book was published. Samuel's inspiration to involve himself so passionately in the great history debate stemmed from his early realization of its important hegemonic implications (Samuel, 1990). He contributed to the debate in various ways, either through scholarly papers or, of course, through Ruskin workshops (Samuel & Thompson, 1990). Yet some of his most important contributions, in my view, were those in the press, for Samuel, unlike other left-wing intellectuals realized the importance of combatting the Right at their own game. At the height of the debate over the Interim Report, Robert Skidelsky had attacked Samuel in the *Independent* (22 August 1989) for his apparent over-zealous advocacy of the need to teach 'history from below' (particularly the history of gender) as opposed to 'history from above' (such as Nelson and the Battle of Trafalgar). Samuel's defence of his position was interesting (*Independent*, 31 August 1989). Far from being a turning point (or the long lasting 'glorious triumph' as imagined by the *Sun* above), Samuel reminded us that Trafalgar was followed a year later by the most crushing of Napoleon's victories at Austerlitz and by the subsequent collapse of the Third Coalition. As Samuel pointed out 'were it not for the heroic circumstances of Nelson's death and perhaps (a subject worth more inquiry) the nineteenth-century romanticization of war, it is possible that we would know no more of it than we do the battle of Copenhagen or the battle of Teneriffe'. On the other hand, the Married Women's Property Act of 1882 (which Skidelsky had taken particular issue over) was 'a landmark in the history of women's rights' yet hardly received a mention either in university or school history courses.

Samuel was pointing attention here, of course, to the ways in which history is created for particular purposes; his energy and commitment during the 'great history debate' originated from his frustration with the realization that the Right had created its own version of patriotism based upon Scruton's concept of the 'self-conscious' unproblematic commitment to the institutions and customs of the nation-state. Whereas this vision of patriotism envisaged faith in traditional icons, events and traditions, Samuel's view of popular-memory patriotism was defined in more radical traditions (the Levellers, Robert Owen and Tom Paine: see also the *Guardian*, 19 September 1995). This re-definition or 'imagining' of radical–popular patriotism was later given lengthy articulation (Samuel, 1994) in the first of what would have been a trilogy before his untimely death. Samuel would be pleased to see this concept of democratic radical patriotism kept alive, however, in the work of the most recent radical scholars such as Giroux (1996).

Similarly, historiographical developments which have concentrated on the ideological factors which create history may explain why the two other icons mentioned by Tate have been reappraised in recent years. Insley (1997) has demonstrated the ways in which the image of Alfred 'the Great' was created. Similarly, other work such as Davies' (1996) account of the origins of Anglocentric medieval historiography have encouraged us to 'be aware of the historiographical mythologies within which we organize our studies of the past' (p.23). Thus, the move towards Celtic re-invention – which has thrown up its own heroes to rival those such as Alfred – has only been matched by the growth of post-colonial history that places emphasis upon 'difference, not homogeneity' (Hall, 1996, p.76). Both of these discourses may have reason to find the careers of Mary Seacole and Elizabeth Davies (two lesser known 'Balaclava nurses') of more interest and significance than Florence Nightingale. Following Samuel, the study of why Mary Seacole became 'lost' from national history is of as much significance as the story of this remarkable woman herself (see Claire, 1996).

State, Nation and Policy: The Future Politics of History Teaching

One of the advantages of seeking to write this account from the perspective of 'history as policy' (Silver, 1990) was that it enabled me to place the 'great history debate' within the wider context of educational politics and policy making in the last quarter of the twentieth century. Inevitably, given the close association between history, history teaching and nationhood, combined with the cultural and ideological intentions behind the ERA, the role of the policy making apparatuses within the state featured prominently within the book. Of course, theoretical work on the state and its relationship with education has concentrated upon complexity (Ball, 1990a; Dale, 1992). The book was influenced by Ball's view of policy as being cyclical, unpredictable and shaped more by 'ad hocery' and serendipity than certain intent. The book not only confirmed this view of policy making but if anything added to the vision of complexity of the process (Ham & Hill, 1992), as well as the various conflicts and tensions between individuals, groups and institutions over policy within the state itself. In this sense, the book gave some substance to Bowe & Ball with Gold's (1992) assertion that the state control model of educational policy making is analytically very limited.

An important issue here is the extent to which politicians in the 1980s and 1990s were able, referring to the phrase used in Chapter 1, to 'reverse the ratchet' with regard to the history curriculum. This implies, of course, that the chief political players in the debate had uniform views upon the shape which history curricula in schools should take. Here, the book confirmed that there were well publicized tensions between, for example, Baker and Thatcher, over the substance of the history curriculum, and differences of emphasis over how reform was to be achieved. The period therefore saw the most blatant attempts by the central state to control the history curriculum – for example Clarke's attempt at date capping – and at other times, clear attempts – most notably by MacGregor – to achieve a degree of consensus between government and teachers. At the same time, frantic attempts were made by a range of extra-parliamentary groups such as the HA and the New Right to influence both politicians themselves and the 'text production bodies' responsible for producing history in the NC between 1989 and 1995.

The result, as we have seen, was a history NC text loaded with ideological and political compromise aimed of course, like other education policy texts, at a plurality of readers (Codd, 1988). I mentioned earlier that it resembled the earlier 1988 HMI text (DES, 1988); interestingly, it also reflected Baker's aims both of demonstrating to pupils how 'the full rounded nature of how our country got from there to here' as well as showing them that they are 'part of a great tradition and a great flow of events' (see Chapter 3). Which version of national history is actually portrayed in school depends in large measure upon the response of teachers now and in the future.

I indicated earlier that the ERA and the NC in particular drew strongly from an ideology which held much of the professional work of teachers in contempt. Part of the research for this book, as we have seen, drew upon my own empirical work which traced history teachers' reactions and perceptions of the policy making process (see Chapter 9). Lack of time and space did not permit me to comment at length about the mixture of anger, bitterness, incredulity, frustration and sheer disbelief with the policy making process relating to history felt by the history teachers in my study, feelings of despair which were exacerbated, of course, by the polarizing influence of the press and Wallace's (1993) 'myth making' which appeared constantly throughout this book. The general feelings of alienation felt by the teaching profession during the last quarter of the twentieth century, particularly with the state's attempt to regulate and constrain their work, has been one reason amongst others why writers have made reference to the undemocratic nature of educational politics during this period (Carr & Hartnett, 1996; Kelly, 1995).

On the other hand, my own research also revealed determined efforts by teachers, for example, to 'make the NC history curriculum their own' (see Phillips, 1991, 1993; also Hawkey, 1993). This reminds us of Ball *et al.*'s other comment that such evidence forces us to question whether the NC represented 'state control over school knowledge'. My own view of this relationship between teachers and the state is to conceive it in terms of being a shift from what Dale (1989) calls 'licensed' autonomy – to 'regulated' autonomy within the state. Yet even within this more regulatory framework, history teachers have been encouraged to read the NC history text creatively (Jenkins & Brickley, 1991; Bracey, 1995a; Pankhania, 1994). This is what may be called 'creative conformity' (Hawkey, 1993). The concept of what Giroux (1992) calls a 'border pedagogy' which 'extends the meaning and importance of dymistification as a central pedagogical task' (p.30) may be useful here. This view of history in the NC as an open as opposed to a closed text, subject by the reader to interpretation, even contestation, may irritate those committed to closure and certainty who see the NC moving in ways which perhaps had not originally been intended.

The commitment in the NC history text to the idea that historical truth, knowledge and certainty can be subject to rigorous analysis does not imply – as its critics claim – the rejection of historical knowledge *per se* but implies instead a reconceptualized, more complex view of what historical knowledge is. I have argued elsewhere (1998b) that I share some of Himmelfarb's (1992) concerns about the 'flight from fact' and the trend towards unfettered relativism. Claims that the profession has placed too much emphasis upon methodology and the nature of evidence as opposed to the knowledge base of the subject deserves, it seems to me, serious discussion both now and in the future, confirming Robinson's (1912) view, cited earlier, that history is not a 'stationary' subject. The tragedy of the 'great history debate', however, was that in the process of raising serious issues about the nature of the subject, those who derided school history teaching in the 1980s and 1990s ensured that history teachers became defensive and proprietorial about their subject. Yet in order to rebuild a degree of consensus between teachers and the state, history teachers, politicians and government advisers in England would be wise to note the views of Partington who, at the beginning of the 1980s, wrote the following before he himself was 'captured' by an alternative discourse:

> In its moderate and limited form of contingent relativism, cultural relativism can be a valuable methodological device which reminds us that all ideas arose in specific circumstances and which counteract ethnocentricism and cultural absolutism. In its extreme and more popular unconditional and *a priori* form cultural relativism presents dangers as grave as those of cultural absolutism. (Partington, 1980b, p.68)

History in the NC should continue to reflect the cultural values of what England is really like at the end of the twentieth century, rather than the England that others would wish it to be. There is no reason why the English or British history taught in schools should be isolationist, parochial or inward looking (Bracey, 1995b; Dawson, 1995). Inevitably, this envisages a history syllabus that continues to stress the pluralism of Britishness within a European and global context along the lines of the present Statutory Orders in England and Wales. This type of approach may enable pupils to make sense of their experience of living in an historical environment, as well as increase their understanding of themselves and others, and thus empower them to have some control over the formation of their own identities (Baldwin, 1996). This in turn may lead to a more inclusive and democratic imagining of 'the nation' in the twenty-first century.

Postscript

This book was completed before the announcement, early in 1998 by the new Labour government, that it was to require primary schools to concentrate more time and attention upon numeracy and literacy. The implication, of course, is that history will no longer be a compulsory foundation subject in the primary sector. This, and the increasingly fragile position of the subject in secondary schools, suggests that history is once more 'in danger'.

References

Aldrich, R. (1984) 'New History: an historical perspective' in A. Dickinson, P. Lee & P. Rogers (eds) *Learning History*. London, Heinemann.

Aldrich, R. (1990a) History Working Group: Final Report. *History of Education Society Bulletin*, 46, 12–15.

Aldrich, R. (1990b) 'The National Curriculum: an historical perspective' in D. Lawton, & C. Chitty (eds) *The National Curriculum*. University of London, Institute of Education, Bedford Way Series, Kogan Page.

Aldrich, R. (ed.) (1991) *History in the National Curriculum*. University of London, Institute of Education, Bedford Way Series, Kogan Page.

Aldrich, R. (1992) Educational legislation of the 1980s in England: an historical analysis. *History of Education*, 21 (1), 57–69.

Aldrich, R. & Dean, D. (1991) 'The Historical Dimension' in R. Aldrich (ed.), *History in the National Curriculum*. University of London, Institute of Education, Bedford Way Series, Kogan Page.

Alter, P. (1989) *Nationalism*. London, Edward Arnold.

Anderson, B. (1991) *Imagined Communities*. London, Verso (revised & extended version).

Andersson, H. (1991) The struggle over history in Finland's schools, 1843–1917. *History of Education*, 20 (1), 5–15.

Apple, M. (1989) 'Critical Introduction' in R. Dale *The State and Education Policy*. Milton Keynes, Open University Press.

Apple, M. (1993) *Official Knowledge: Democratic Education in a Conservative Age*. London, Routledge.

Apple, M. & Teitelbaum, K. (1986) Are teachers losing control of their skills and curriculum? *Journal of Curriculum Studies*, 18 (2), 177–84.

Aranowitz, S. (1992) *The Politics of Identity: Class, Culture, Social Movements*. London, Routledge.

Aranowitz, S. & Giroux, H. (1986) *Education Under Siege: the Conservative, Liberal and Radical Debate Over Schooling*. London, Routledge & Kegan Paul.

Baker, B. (1981) History abandoned? *Teaching History*, 30, 13–14.

Baker, K. (ed.) (1988) *The Faber Book of English History in Verse*. London, Faber & Faber.

Baker, K. (1993) *The Turbulent Years: My Life in Politics*. London, Faber & Faber.

Baker, M. (1994) Media coverage of education. *British Journal of Educational Studies*, 42 (3), 286–97.

Baldwin, G. (1996) 'In the Heart or on the Margins: A Personal View of NC History and Issues of Identity' in R. Andrews (ed.) *Interpreting the New National Curriculum*. London, Middlesex University Press.

Ball, S. (1990a) *Politics and Policy Making in Education: Explorations in Policy Sociology*. London, Routledge.

Ball, S. (ed.) (1990b) *Foucault and Education: Discipline and Knowledge*. London, Routledge.

Ball, S. (1993) Education, Majorism and the curriculum of the dead. *Curriculum Studies*, 1 (2), 195–214.

Ball, S. (1994a) *Education Reform: A Critical and Post-Structural Approach*. Buckingham, Open University Press.

Ball, S. (1994b) Some reflections on policy theory: a brief response to Hatcher & Troyna. *British Journal of Education Policy*, 9 (2), 171–82.

Ball, S. & Bowe, R. (1992) Subject departments and the 'implementation' of National Curriculum policy: an overview of the issues. *Journal of Curriculum Studies*, 24 (2), 97–115.

Ballard, M. (ed.) (1970) *New Movements in the Study and Teaching of History*. London, Temple Smith.
Beattie, A. (1987) *History in Peril: May Parents Preserve It*. London, Centre for Policy Studies.
Beloff, M. *et al.* (1989) GCSE: An Alternative Approach – The Making of the United Kingdom. Unpublished Paper.
Belsey, A. (1986) 'The New Right, Social Order and Civil Liberties' in R. Levitas (ed.) *The Ideology of the New Right*. Cambridge, Polity Press.
Berghahn, V. & Schissler, H. (eds) (1987) *Perceptions of History – An Analysis of School Textbooks*. Oxford, Berg.
Bernbaum, G. (ed.) (1979) *Schooling in Decline*. London, Macmillan.
Bernstein, B. (1986) 'On Pedagogic Discourse' in J. Richardson (ed.) *Handbook of Theory and Research for the Sociology of Education*. New York, Greenwood.
Betts, R. (1990) A campaign for patriotism on the elementary school curriculum: Lord Meath, 1892–1916. *History of Education Society Bulletin*, 46, 38–45.
Billig, M. (1995) *Banal Nationalism*. London, Sage.
Blake, R. *et al.* (1990) History Curriculum Association Letter to Academics. *History Workshop: History, the Nation and the Schools Recall Conference*. Ruskin College: Conference Papers.
Blenkin, G., Edwards, G. & Kelly, A. (1992) *Change and the Curriculum*. London, Paul Chapman.
Bloom, A. (1987) *The Closing of the American Mind: how higher education has failed democracy and impoverished the souls of today's students*. London, Penguin.
Bloom, R. (1956) *Taxonomy of Educational Objectives*. London, Longman.
Blum, P. (1990) Past perfect and present imperfect. *Report (AMMA)*, 12 (3), 10–11.
Blyth, A. *et al.* (1976) *Curriculum Planning in History, Geography and Social Science*. Bristol, Collins.
Bolton, E. (1993) 'Imaginary Garden with Real Toads'. Address given to the Council of Local Education Authorities, 20 July, Liverpool, in C. Chitty & B. Simon (eds) *Education Answers Back: Critical Responses to Government Policy*. London, Lawrence & Wishart.
Booth, M. (1969) *History Betrayed?* London, Longman.
Booth, M. (1980) A modern world history course and the thinking of adolescent pupils. *Educational Review*, 32 (3), 245–57.
Booth, M. *et al.* (1986) *Empathy in History: From Definition to Assessment*. Eastleigh, Southern Regional Examinations Board.
Booth, M. & Husbands, C. (1993) The history National Curriculum in England and Wales: assessment at Key Stage 3. *Curriculum Journal*, 4 (1), 21–36.
Bosanquet, N. (1983) *After the New Right*. London, Heinemann.
Bowe, R. & Ball, S. with Gold, A. (1992) *Reforming Education & Changing Schools: Case Studies in Policy Sociology*. London, Routledge.
Bracey, P. (1995a) Developing a multicultural perspective within Key Stage 3 National Curriculum history. *Teaching History*, 78, 8–10.
Bracey, P. (1995b) 'Ensuring Continuity and Understanding Through the Teaching of British History' in R. Watts & I. Grosvenor (eds) *Crossing the Key Stages of History*. London, David Fulton.
Brown, R. (1988) The new demonology. *Teaching History*, 53, 41–2.
Brown, R. (1989) Teacher perceptions of GCSE – responses to a Historical Association survey. *Teaching History*, 55, 30–5.
Bruner, J. (1960) *The Process of Education*. Harvard, Vintage Books.
Cannadine, D. (1987) British history: past, present – and future? *Past & Present*, 116 (6), 169–91.
Cannadine, D. (1995) 'British History as a "New Subject": Politics, perspectives and prospects' in A. Grant & K. Stringer (eds) *Uniting the Kingdom? The Making of British History*. London, Routledge.
Carr, E. H. (1961) *What Is History?* London, Macmillan.
Carr, W. & Hartnett, A. (1996) *Education and the Struggle for Democracy*. Buckingham, Open University Press.
Carrington, B. & Short, G. (1995) What makes a person British? Children's conceptions of their national culture and identity. *Educational Studies*, 21 (2), 217–38.

Casey, J. (1982) One nation: the politics of race. *The Salisbury Review*, 1, 23–8.

Chaffer, J. (1973) 'What History Should We Teach?' in R. B. Jones (ed.) *Practical Approaches to the New History*. London, Hutchinson.

Chaffer, J. & Taylor, L. (1975) *History and the History Teacher*. London, Allen & Unwin.

Chitty, C. (1988) Central control of the school curriculum, 1944–1987. *History of Education*, 17 (3), 321–34.

Chitty, C. (1989) *Towards a New Education System: the Victory of the New Right?* London, Falmer Press.

Chitty, C. (1992a) *The Education System Transformed*. Manchester, Baseline Books.

Chitty, C. (1992b) The changing role of the state in education provision. *History of Education*, 21 (1), 1–13.

Chitty, C., Dale, R. & Broadfoot, P. (1991) Review symposium: politics and policy making in education: 'Explorations in policy sociology' by Stephen Ball. *British Journal of Sociology of Education*, 12 (2), 243–54.

Claire, H. (1996) *Reclaiming Our Pasts: equality and diversity in the primary history curriculum*. Stoke-on-Trent, Trentham.

Clark, J. (1990) National identity, state formation and patriotism: the role of history in the public mind. *History Workshop Journal*, 29, Spring, 95–102.

Codd, J. (1988) The construction and deconstruction of educational policy documents. *Journal of Education Policy*, 3 (5), 235–48.

Colley, L. (1992) *Britons: Forging the Nation 1707–1837*. London, Pimlico.

Collicott, S. (1990) Who is the National History Curriculum for? *Teaching History*, 61, 8–12.

Collingwood, R. (1946) *The Idea of History*. Oxford, Oxford University Press.

Coltham, J. & Fines, J. (1971) *Educational Objectives for the Study of History: a suggested framework*. London, Historical Association.

Convery, A., Evans, M., Green, S., Macaro, E. & Mellor, J. (1997) *Pupils' Perceptions of Europe: Identity and Education*. London, Cassell.

Cornbleth, C. (1995) Controlling curriculum knowledge: multicultural politics and policy making. *Journal of Curriculum Studies*, 27 (2), 165–85.

Corner, J. & Harvey, S. (eds) (1991) *Enterprise and Heritage: Crosscurrents on National Culture*. London, Routledge.

Coss, P. (1988) British history: past, present – and future? *Past & Present*, 119, 171–83.

Coulby, D. & Jones, C. (1995) *Postmodernity and European Education Systems: Cultural Diversity and Centralist Knowledge*. Stoke-on-Trent, Trentham.

Cowling, M. (ed.) (1978) *Conservative Essays*. London, Cassell.

Cox, B. (1995) *Cox on the Battle for the English Curriculum*. London, Hodder & Stoughton.

Cox, C. & Dyson, A. (1969a) *Fight for Education: A Black Paper*. London, Critical Quarterly Society.

Cox, C. & Dyson, A. (1969b) *Black Paper Two: The Crisis in Education*. London, Critical Quarterly Society.

Crawford, K. (1995) A history of the Right: the battle for control of National Curriculum history 1989–1994. *British Journal of Educational Studies*, 43 (4), 433–56.

Cunningham, P. (1992) Teachers' professional image and the press 1950–1990. *History of Education*, 21 (1), 37–56.

Dale, R. (1989) *The State & Education Policy*. Milton Keynes, Open University Press.

Dale, R. (1992) Whither the state and education policy? Recent work in Australia and New Zealand. *British Journal of Sociology of Education*, 13 (3), 387–95.

Daugherty, R., Thomas, B., Jones, G. E. & Davies, S. (1991) *GCSE in Wales: A Study of the Impact of the General Certificate of Secondary Education on the Teaching of History, Geography and Welsh*. Glamorgan Press, Welsh Office

Davies, B. & Pritchard, P. (1975) History still in danger? *Teaching History*, 14, 113–16.

Davies, J. (1994) 'The History Coordinator's Tale' in M. Harrison (ed.) *Beyond the Core Curriculum: Co-ordinating the other foundation subjects in primary schools*. Plymouth, Northcote House Publishers.

Davies, R. (1996) *The Matter of Britain and the Matter of England*, Inaugural Professorial Lecture, 29 February. Oxford, Clarendon Press.

Davis, R. (1983) History at the Universities Defence Group. *The Historian,* 1, 27.

Dawson, I. (1990) Why does it matter? A personal response to the Final Report. *Teaching History,* 61, 17–21.

Dawson, I. (1995) The re-appearance of a Cheshire cat – teaching the history of Britain at Key Stage 3. *Teaching History,* 80, 14–17.

Dearing, R. (1993a) *The National Curriculum and its Assessment: Interim Report.* London, NCC/ SCAA.

Dearing, R. (1993b) *The National Curriculum and its Assessment: Final Report.* London, SCAA.

Demaine, J. (1988) Teachers' work, curriculum and the New Right. *British Journal of Sociology of Education,* 9 (3), 247–64.

DES (1977) *Curriculum 11–16.* London, HMSO.

DES (1985a) *History in the Primary and Secondary Years: An HMI View.* London, HMSO.

DES (1985b) *GCSE: The National Criteria: History.* London, HMSO.

DES (1987) *The National Curriculum 5–6: a consultation document.* London, HMSO.

DES (1987a) 'Kenneth Baker looks at future of education system', 9 January. Press Release 11/87. London, HMSO.

DES (1987b) Kenneth Baker calls for curriculum for pupils of all abilities', 23 January. Press Release 22/87. London, HMSO.

DES (1988) *Curriculum Matters 5–16: History.* London, HMSO.

DES (1989a) *National Curriculum History Working Group: Interim Report.* London, HMSO.

DES (1989b) 'Kenneth Baker announces progress towards the complete national curriculum', 13 January. Press Release 13/89. London, HMSO.

DES (1989c) *Aspects of Primary Education: The Teaching and Learning of History and Geography.* London, HMSO.

DES (1989d) *Report by HM Inspectors on An Inspection of GCSE Humanities Courses in 20 Secondary Schools.* London, HMSO.

DES (1990a) *National Curriculum History Working Group: Final Report.* London, HMSO.

DES (1990b) *History for ages 5–16: Proposals of the Secretary of State for Education and Science.* London, HMSO.

DES (1991a) *History in the National Curriculum (England).* London, HMSO.

DES (1991b) *National Curriculum Draft Order for History.* London, HMSO.

DFE (1995) *History in the National Curriculum: England.* London, HMSO.

Deuchar, S. (1987) *History & GCSE History.* London, Centre for Policy Studies.

Deuchar, S. (1988) Comments on Peter Lee's review of *History and GCSE History. Teaching History,* 50, 35–6.

Deuchar, S. (1989) *The New History: A Critique.* York, Campaign for Real Education.

Deuchar, S. (1992) *History on the Brink.* Milton Keynes, Campaign for Real Education.

Dickenson, M. (1988) 'The History Man' revisited. *Teaching History,* 50, 30–4.

Dickinson, A. & Lee, P. (eds) (1978) *History Teaching and Historical Understanding.* London, Heinemann.

Dickinson, A., Lee, P. & Rogers, P. (eds) (1984) *Learning History.* London, Heinemann.

Dickinson, A., Gordon, P., Lee, P. & Slater, J. (eds) (1995) *International Yearbook of History Education Volume 1.* London, The Woburn Press.

Eatwell, R. & O'Sullivan, O. (eds) (1989) *The Nature of the Right: American and European Politics and Political Thought Since 1789.* London, Pinter Publishers.

Edwards, A. (1995) 'Changing Pedagogic Discourse' in P. Atkinson, B. Davies & S. Delamont (eds) *Discourse and Reproduction: Essays in Honour of Basil Bernstein.* Cresskill, New Jersey, Hampton Press.

Elliott, B. (1980) An early failure of curriculum reform: history teaching in England, 1918–1940. *Journal of Educational Administration & History,* 12 (2), 39–46.

Elliott, B. (1992a) History examinations at sixteen and eighteen years in England and Wales between 1918 and 1939. *History of Education,* 20 (2), 119–29.

Elliott, B. (1992b) Early examination reform in Scotland and the crisis in history 1888–1939. *Journal of Educational Administration and History* 24 (1), 47–57.

Elton, G. (1967) *The Practice of History.* London, Collins/Fontana.

Elton, G. (1970) 'What History should we Teach?' in M. Ballard (ed.) *New Movements in the Study and Teaching of History*. London, Temple Smith.

Evans, J. & Penney, D. (1995) The politics of pedagogy: making a National Curriculum Physical Education. *Journal of Education Policy*, 10 (1), 27–44.

Evans, R. (1994) 'Educational Ideologies and the Teaching of History' in G. Leienhardt, I. Beck & C. Stainton (eds) T*eaching and Learning in History*. Hillsdale, New Jersey, Lawrence Erlbaum Associates.

Fines, J. (1988) The search for content in a National Curriculum. *Welsh Historian*, 9, 7–8.

Fisher, T. (1982) Can history survive? *Teaching History*, 32, 8–10.

Fitz, J. & Halpin, D. (1994) 'Ministers and Mandarins: Educational Research in Elite Settings' in G. Walford (ed.) *Researching the Powerful in Education*. London, University College London Press.

Foster, E. (1989) 'History' in P. Wiegand & M. Rayner (eds) *Curriculum Progress 5 to 16: School Subjects and the National Curriculum Debate*. London, Falmer Press.

Fowler, R. (1991) *Language in the News: Discourse and Ideology in the Press*. London, Routledge.

Fukuyama, F. (1992) *The End of History and the Last Man*. London, Hamish Hamilton.

Furedi, F. (1992) *Mythical Past, Elusive Future: History and Society in an Anxious Age*. London, Pluto Press.

Gagnon, P. & the Bradley Commission on History in the Schools (1989) *Historical Literacy: The Case for History in American Education*. Boston, Houghton Mifflin Company.

Gammage, D. (1978) *The Teaching of History*. London, Croom Helm.

Gardiner, J. (ed.) (1990) *The History Debate*. London, Collins & Brown.

Garvey, B. & Krug, M. (1977) *Models of History Teaching in the Secondary School*. Oxford, Oxford University Press.

Gathercole, P. & Lowenthal, D. (eds) (1990) *The Politics of the Past*. London, Routledge.

George, P. (1994) History in danger. *Welsh Historian*, 21, 7–10.

Gilbert, R. (1984) *The Impotent Image: Reflections on Ideology in the Secondary School Curriculum*. London, Falmer Press.

Gilroy, P. (1990) Nationalism, history and ethnic absolutism. *History Workshop Journal*, 30, 114–20.

Giroux, H. (1992) *Border Crossings: Cultural Workers and the Politics of Education*. London, Routledge.

Giroux, H. (1996) *Fugitive Culture: Race, Violence & Youth*. London, Routledge.

Goodson, I. (1987) *School Subjects and Curriculum Change: Studies in Curriculum History – A Revised & Extended Version*. London, Falmer Press.

Goodson, I. (1988) *The Making of Curriculum: Collected Essays*. London, Falmer Press.

Gordon, P. & Lawton, D. (1978) *Curriculum Change in the Nineteenth and Twentieth Centuries*. London, Hodder & Stoughton.

Graham, D. with Tytler, D. (1993) *A Lesson for Us All: The Making of the National Curriculum*. London, Routledge.

Grainger, J. (1986) *Patriotisms: Britain 1900–1939*. London, Routledge & Kegan Paul.

Gramsci, A. (1971) *Selections from the Prison Notebooks*. Edited & translated by Q. Hoare, & G. Smith, London, Lawrence & Wisehart.

Grant, A. & Stringer, K. (eds) (1995) *Uniting the Kingdom? The Making of British History*. London, Routledge.

Griggs, C. (1989) 'The New Right and English Secondary Education' in R. Lowe (ed.) *The Changing Secondary School*. London, Falmer Press.

Guyver, R. (1990) History's Domesday Book. *History Workshop Journal*, 30, Autumn, 100–8.

Gwent History Teachers Working Group (1991) Issues of National Curriculum History Assessment. *Welsh Historian*, 16, 9–12.

Gunning, D. (1978) *The Teaching of History*. London, Croom Helm.

Hake, C. & Haydn, T. (1995) Stories or Sources? *Teaching History*, 78, 20–2.

Hall, C. (1996) 'Histories, Empires and the Post-colonial Moment' in I. Chambers & L. Curti (eds) *The Post-Colonial Question*. London, Routledge.

Hall, S. (1979) The great moving Right show. *Marxism Today*, January, 14–20.

Hall, S. (1985) Authoritarian populism: a reply to Jessop et al. *New Left Review*, 151, 115–24.

Hall, S. (1988) *The Hard Road to Renewal: Thatcherism and the Crisis of the Left*. London, Verso.

Hall, S. & Jacques, M. (eds) (1983) *The Politics of Thatcherism*. London, Lawrence & Wisehart.

Hallam, R. (1970) 'Piaget and Thinking in History' in M. Ballard (ed.) *New Movements in the Study and Teaching of History*. London, Temple Smith.

Halpin, D. & Troyna, B. (eds) (1994) *Researching Education Policy: Ethical and Methodological Issues*. London, Falmer Press.

Ham, C. & Hill, M. (1992) *The Policy Process in the Modern Capitalist State*. London, Harvester Wheatsheaf, Second Edition.

Happold, F. (1928) *The Approach to History*. London, Christophers.

Hargreaves, A. (1989) *Curriculum and Assessment Reform*. Milton Keynes, Open University Press.

Harries, E. (1975) Teachers' conceptions of history teaching. *Teaching History*, 14, 151–3.

Hastrup, K. (ed.) (1992) *Other Histories*. London, Routledge.

Hatcher, R. & Troyna, B. (1994) The 'policy cycle': a ball by ball account. *Journal of Education Policy*, 9 (2), 155–70.

Haviland, J. (ed.) (1988) *'Take Care Mr Baker': A selection from the evidence on the Government's Education Reform Bill which the Secretary of State for Education invited but decided not to publish*. London, Fourth Estate.

Hawkey, K. (1993) Implementation of National Curriculum History and Geography at Key Stage Three: a case study. *Curriculum*, 14, 14–145.

Haydn, T. (1992a) History reprieved? *Teaching History*, 66, 17–20.

Haydn, T. (1992b) History for ordinary children. *Teaching History*, 67, 8–11.

Haydn, T. (1993) The chemistry of history lessons, teacher autonomy and the reform of National Curriculum History. *Welsh Historian*, 22, 7–10.

Haydn, T. (1994) Uses and abuses of the TGAT assesssment model: the case of history and the 45 boxes. *The Curriculum Journal*, 5 (2), 215–33.

Haydn, T. (1995) Nationalism begins at home: the influence of National Curriculum History on perceptions of national identity in Britain, 1987–1995. *History of Education Society Bulletin*, 57, 51–61.

Hayek, F. (1944) *The Road to Serfdom*. London, Routledge & Kegan Paul.

Hayek, F. (ed.) (1954) *Capitalism and the Historians*. London, Routledge & Kegan Paul.

Heater, D. (1990) *Citizenship: The Civil Ideal in World History, Politics and Education*. Harlow, Longman.

Heilbroner, R. (1995) *Visions of the Future: The Distant Past, Yesterday, Today and Tomorrow*. Oxford, Oxford University Press.

Hennessey, R. (1988) The content question: an agenda. *Welsh Historian*, Spring, 3–6.

Hillgate Group (1986) *Whose Schools? A Radical Manifesto*. London, Hillgate Group.

Hillgate Group (1987) *The Reform of British Education*. London, Hillgate Group.

Himmelfarb, G. (1992) Telling it as you like it: Post-modernism and the flight from fact. *Times Literary Supplement*, 16 October.

HA (1957) *The Historical Association, 1906–1956*. London, Historical Association.

HA (1986) *History for Life*. London, Historical Association.

HA (1987) *Proposals for a Core Curriculum in History*. London, Historical Association.

HA (1989) A Summary of Conference Reports Relating to the Interim Report of the History Working Group. Unpublished.

HA (1990) The Final Report of the History Working Group: A Submission from the Historical Association to the Department of Education and Science June, 1990. Unpublished.

HA (1991) *Implementing the National Curriculum: Manchester Education Conference Papers, 13–14 September*. London, Historical Association.

HA (1993) Submission to Dearing Review. Unpublished.

Hiskett, M. (1988) *Choice in Rotten Apples: Bias in GCSE and Examining Groups*. London, Centre for Policy Studies.

History Workshop (1990) *History, the Nation & the Schools: Conference Papers*. Oxford, Ruskin College, History Workshop.

Hobhouse, H. (1989) *The Forces of Change: Why we are the way we are now*. London, Sidgwick & Jackson.

Hobsbawm, E. & Ranger, T. (eds) (1983) *The Invention of Tradition*. Cambridge, Cambridge University Press.

Holmes, B. (1986) History within a locality. *Teaching History*, 46, 17–19.

Honeyford, G. (1984) 'Education and Race' in R. Scruton (ed.) *Conservative Thoughts: Essays from the Salisbury Review*. London, Claridge Press, 1988.

Husbands, C. (1992) 'Facing the Facts? History in Schools and the National Curriculum' in Various Authors: *Education: Putting the Record Straight*. Stafford, Network Educational Press.

Husbands, C. & Pendry, A. (1992) *Whose History? School History and the National Curriculum*. Norwich, UEA.

Insley, C. (1997) 'Alfred the Great'. Paper given at the *Heroes, Heroines & Villains and the Shaping of National Identities* Conference, University of Wales Gregynog, 21 July.

Jarvis, F. (1993) *Education and Mr Major: Correspondence between the Prime Minister and Fred Jarvis with a Commentary and Postscript*. London, Tufnell Press.

Jeffreys, M. (1939) *History in Schools: The Study of Development*. London, Pitman.

Jenkins, K. (1991) *Re-Thinking History*. London, Routledge.

Jenkins, K. & Brickley, P. (1991) Always historicise: unintended opportunities in National Curriculum History. *Teaching History*, 62, 8–14.

Jenkins, S. (1995) *Accountable to None: The Tory Nationalization of Britain*. London, Hamish Hamilton.

Jessop, B. *et al.* (1984) Authoritarian populism, two nations and Thatcherism. *New Left Review*, 147, 32–60.

John, P. (1991) The professional craft knowledge of the history teacher. *Teaching History*, 64, 8–12.

Johnson, R. (1991a) 'A New Road to Serfdom? A Critical History of the 1988 Act' in Education Group II Department of Cultural Studies University of Birmingham: *Education Limited – Schooling and Training and the New Right Since 1979*. London, Unwin Hyman.

Johnson, R. (1991b) 'My New Right Education' in Education Group II Department of Cultural Studies University of Birmingham: *Education Limited – Schooling and Training and the New Right Since 1979*. London, Unwin Hyman.

Jones, G. E. (1978) 'Traditional and New History Teaching: Towards a Synthesis' in G. E. Jones, & L. Ward (eds) *New History Old Problems: Studies in History Teaching*. Swansea, University College of Swansea.

Jones, G. E. (1991) Making history: a personal view of History in the National Curriculum. *Welsh Journal of Education*, 3 (1), 3–9.

Jones, R. B. (ed.) (1973) *Practical Approaches to the New History*. London, Hutchinson.

Jones, K. (1989) *Right Turn: the Conservative Revolution in Education*. London, Hutchinson Radius.

Joseph, K. (1984) Why teach history in school? Address by Sir Keith Joseph to the Historical Association Conference, 10 February. *The Historian*, 2, 10–12.

Kaye, H. (1991) *The Powers of the Past: Reflections on the Crisis and the Promise of History*. London, Harvester Wheatsheaf.

Kaye, H. (1996) *Why do Ruling Classes Fear History? And Other Questions*. London, Macmillan.

Kearney, A. (1991) English versus History: the battle for identity and status, 1850–1920. *History of Education Society Bulletin*, 48, 22–9.

Kearney, H. (1989) *The British Isles: A History of Four Nations*. Cambridge, Cambridge University Press.

Keatinge, M. (1910) *Studies in the Teaching of History*. London, Black.

Kedourie, H. (1988) *The Errors and Evils of the New History*. London, Centre for Policy Studies.

Kelly, A. (1990) *The National Curriculum: A Critical Review*. London, Paul Chapman.

Kelly, A. (1995) *Education and Democracy: Principles and Practices*. London, Paul Chapman Publishing.

Kenway, J. (1990) 'Education and the Right's Discursive Politics. Private versus State Schooling' in S. Ball (ed.) *Foucault and Education*. London, Routledge.

Kingdon, M. & Stobart, G. (1988) *GCSE Examined*. London, Falmer Press.

Knight, P. (1989) Empathy: concept, confusion and consequences in a National Curriculum. *Oxford Review of Education*, 15 (1), 41–53.

Knight, C. (1990) *The Making of Tory Education Policy in Post-War Britain, 1950–1986*. London, Falmer Press.

Kogan, M. (1994) 'Researching the Powerful in Education and Elsewhere' in G. Walford (ed.) *Researching the Powerful in Education*. London, University College London Press.

Lamont, W. (1988) British history: past, present – and future? *Past & Present*, 119, 183–93.

Lawlor, S. (1988) *Correct Core: Simple Curricula for English, Maths and Science*. London, Centre for Policy Studies.

Lawlor, S. (1989) *Proposals for the National Curriculum in History: A Report*. London, Centre for Policy Studies.

Lawlor, S. (1990) 'Response to the Final Report: But What Must Children Know?' in S. Lawlor (ed.) *An Education Choice: Pamphlets From the Centre, 1987–1994*. London, Centre for Policy Studies, 1995.

Lawlor, S. (1991) 'Response to the Proposed Draft Order: February, 1991' in S. Lawlor (ed.) *An Education Choice: Pamphlets From the Centre, 1987–1994*. London, Centre for Policy Studies, 1995.

Lawlor, S. (ed.) (1993) *The Dearing Debate: Assessment and the National Curriculum*. London, Centre for Policy Studies.

Lawlor, S. (1995) 'The History Debate' in S. Lawlor (ed.) *An Education Choice: Pamphlets from the Centre, 1987–1994*. London, Centre for Policy Studies.

Lawton, D. (1980) *The Politics of the School Curriculum*. London, Routledge & Kegan Paul.

Lawton, D. (1986) 'The Department of Education and Science: Policy Making at the Centre' in A. Hartnett & M. Naish (eds) *Education and Society Today*. London, Falmer Press.

Lawton, D. (1989a) *Education, Culture and the National Curriculum*. London, Hodder & Stoughton.

Lawton, D. (ed.) (1989b) *The Education Reform Act: Choice and Control*. London, Hodder & Stoughton.

Lawton, D. (1992) *Education and Politics in the 1990s: Conflict or Consensus?* London, Falmer Press.

Lawton, D. (1994) *The Tory Mind on Education, 1979–1994*. London and Lewes, Falmer Press.

Lawton, D. & Chitty, C. (eds) (1988) *The National Curriculum*. Institute of Education, University of London, Bedford Way Series, Kogan Page.

Lee, P. (1984) 'Historical Imagination' in A. Dickinson, P. Lee & P. Rogers (eds) *Learning History*. London, Heinemann.

Lee, P. (1991) 'Historical Knowledge and the National Curriculum' in Aldrich, R. (ed.) *History in the National Curriculum*. University of London, Institute of Education, Bedford Way Series, Kogan Page.

Letwin, S. (1992) *The Anatomy of Thatcherism*. London, Fontana.

Levitas, R. (ed.) (1986) *The Ideology of the New Right*. Oxford, Polity Press.

Lewis, T. (1987) 'The National Curriculum and History. Consensus or Prescription?' in V. Berghahan & H. Schissler (eds) *Perceptions of History: An Analysis of School Textbooks*. London, Berg.

Little, V. (1990) A National Curriculum in History: a very contentious issue. *British Journal of Educational Studies*, 38 (4).

Lomas, T. (1990) How Appropriate is the Model Proposed by the Task Group on Assessment & Testing (TGAT) for History? Unpublished Paper.

Lomas, T. (1991) National Curriculum History: some teaching and assessment issues. *British Journal of Curriculum & Assessment*, 1 (3), 13–14.

Lomas, T. (1995) Good practice in Key Stage 3 History (has the National Curriculum changed our view?). *Discoveries*, 6, 13–15.

Low-Beer, A. (1988) Examining feelings. *History Resource* 2 (1), 4–6.

Low-Beer, A. (1989) Empathy and history. *Teaching History* 55, 8–12.

Lowe, R. (1995) 'Further than ever before …' New Right ideology and education. *Historical Studies in Education*, 7 (2), 177–91.

Lyotard, J. (1984) *The Postmodern Condition*. Manchester, Manchester University Press.

MacLure, S. (1989) *Education Re-formed*. London, Hodder & Stoughton, Second Edition.

Marks, S. (1990) History, the nation and empire: sniping from the periphery. *History Workshop Journal*, 29, Spring, 111–19.

Marsden, W. (1989) 'All in a good cause': geography, history and the politicization of the curriculum in 19th and 20th century England. *Journal of Curriculum Studies*, 21 (6), 509–26.

Marwick, A. (1970) *The Nature of History*. London, Macmillan.

Maw, J. (1993) The National Curriculum Council and the Whole Curriculum: reconstruction of a discourse? *Curriculum Studies*, 1 (1), 55–74.

McGovern, C. (1994) *The SCAA Review of National Curriculum History: A Minority Report*. York, Campaign for Real Education.

McKiernan, D. (1993) History in a National Curriculum: imagining the nation at the end of the 20th century. *Journal of Curriculum Studies*, 25 (1), 33–51.

Medley, R. & White, C. (1992) Assessing the National Curriculum: lessons from assessing history. *The Curriculum Journal*, 3 (1), 63–74.

Milne, A. (1973) 'Project Work at 'O' Level: A Review of a Recent Pilot Scheme' in R. B. Jones (ed.) *Practical Approaches to the New History*. London, Hutchinson.

Moore, R. (1975) History and Integrated Studies: surrender or survival? *Teaching History*, 13, 109–12.

Moore, R. (1982) History abandoned? The case for a continuing debate. *Teaching History*, 32, 26–8.

Morris, M. & Griggs, C. (eds) (1988) *Education – the Wasted Years? 1973–1986*. London, Falmer Press.

Nash, G., Crabtree, C. & Dunn, R. (1997) *History on Trial: Culture Wars and the Teaching of the Past*. New York, Alfred A. Knopf.

NCC (1990) *National Curriculum Council Consultation Report: History*. York, NCC.

NCC (1991a) *National Curriculum Council Non-Statutory Guidance for History*. York, NCC.

NCC (1991b) *Implementing National Curriculum History*. York, NCC.

NCC (1992) National Curriculum Council History Monitoring Conference Report. Unpublished Paper.

NCC (1993) *Teaching History at Key Stage 3*. York, NCC.

Nelson, M. (1992) First efforts toward a National Curriculum: the Committee of Ten's report on history, civil government, and political economy. *Theory and Research in Social Education*, 20 (3), 242–62.

Noble, P. (1990) Time to rectify past mistakes: the case for investment in primary history. *Teaching History*, 59.

Norris, S. (1996) *Reclaiming the Truth: Contribution to a Critique of Cultural Relativism*. London, Lawrence & Wishart.

North, J. (ed.) (1987) *The GCSE: An Examination*. London, Claridge Press.

O'Conner, M. (1989) 'Reflections From an Observer' in A. Hargreaves & D. Reynolds (eds) *Education Policies: Controversies and Critiques*. London, Falmer Press.

OFSTED (1993) *History Key Stages 1, 2 and 3: First Year 1991–1992: The implementation of the curricular requirements of the Education Reform Act*. London, HMSO.

O'Keeffe, D. (1986) *The Wayward Curriculum: A Cause for Parents' Concern?* Exeter, Social Affairs Unit.

O'Neill, C. (1994) Implementing Key Stage 3 History – the view from the north west. *Teaching History*, 75, April, 13–14.

Osborne, R. (1995) *The Politics of Time*. London, Verso.

Osler, A. (1994) Still hidden from history? The representation of women in recently published history textbooks. *Oxford Review of Education*, 20 (2), 219–35.

Ozga, J. (1987) 'Studying Education Policy through the Lives of the Policy-makers: An Attempt to Close the Macro–Micro Gap' in S. Walker & L. Barton (eds) *Changing Policies*,

Changing Teachers: New Directions for Schooling? Milton Keynes, Open University Press.

Pankhania, J. (1994) *Liberating the National History Curriculum.* London, Falmer Press.

Partington, G. (1980a) What history should we teach? *Oxford Review of Education,* 6 (2), 157–76.

Partington, G. (1980b) *The Idea of an Historical Education.* Slough, NFER.

Partington, G. (1986) 'History: Re-Written to Ideological Fashion' in D. O'Keeffe (ed.) *The Wayward Curriculum: A Case for Parents' Concern?* London, Social Affairs Unit.

Patrick, H. (1987) *The Aims of Teaching History in Secondary Schools: Report of a Research Project Funded by the Economic & Social Research Council.* University of Leicester, School of Education, Occasional Paper.

Patrick, H. (1988a) The history curriculum: the teaching of history, 1985–87. *History Resource,* 2 (1), 9–14

Patrick, H. (1988b) History teachers for the 1990s and beyond. *Teaching History,* 50, 10–14.

Patterson, D. (1994) Introducing and assessing National Curriculum history at Key Stage 3 in a 13–18 comprehensive school. Formative versus summative assessment. *Curriculum Journal,* 5 (2), 195–213.

Pendry, A. (1990) Dilemmas for history teacher educators. *British Journal of Educational Studies,* 38 (1), 47–62.

Phillips, M. (1996) *All Must Have Prizes.* London, Little, Brown & Co.

Phillips, R. (1991) National Curriculum history and teacher autonomy: the major challenge. *Teaching History,* 65, 21–24.

Phillips, R. (1992a) 'The Battle for the Big Prize': the creation of synthesis and the role of a curriculum pressure group: the case of history & the National Curriculum. *Curriculum Journal,* 3 (3), 245–60.

Phillips, R. (1992b) *History, Hegemony & the New Right: Implications for History Teacher Education.* Paper presented at the International Colloquium on Education: British and American Perspectives. Department of Educational Foundations, University of Wisconsin La Crosse, USA, September 29–30.

Phillips, R. (1992c) Time and the Sword of Damocles. *Welsh Historian,* 18, 10–12.

Phillips, R. (1992d) *The First Year's Implementation of Key Stage 3 History in the National Curriculum in Wales: an Evaluation Study.* Department of Education, University of Wales Swansea, Occasional Paper.

Phillips, R. (1993a) Teachers' perceptions of the first year's implementation of Key Stage 3 History in the National Curriculum in England. *Research Papers in Education,* 8 (3), 329–353.

Phillips, R. (1993b) Change and continuity: some reflections on the first year's implementation of Key Stage 3 History. *Teaching History,* 70, 9–12.

Phillips, R. (1993c) Reprieve from 'The Sword of Damocles'? *Welsh Historian,* 19, 11–15.

Phillips, R. (1996a) History teaching, cultural restorationism and national identity in England and Wales. *Curriculum Studies* 4(3), 385–99.

Phillips, R. (1996b) Informed Citizens: who am I and why are we here? Some Welsh reflections on culture, curriculum and society. Speech given to the SCAA Conference on Culture, Curriculum & Society; also published in *Multicultural Teaching,* 14 (3), 41–44.

Phillips, R. (1997a) 'National Identity and History Teaching in Britain: English, Northern Irish, Scottish and Welsh Perspectives' in A. Pendry & C. O'Neill (eds) *Principles and Practice: Analytical Perspectives on Curriculum Reform and Changing Pedagogy from History Teacher Educators.* Lancaster, St Martin's Press.

Phillips, R. (1997b) Thesis and antithesis in Tate's views on history, culture and nationhood. *Teaching History,* 86, 30–3.

Phillips, R. (1998a) The politics of history: some methodological and ethical dilemmas in elite-based research. *British Educational Research Journal,* 24 (1), 5–19.

Phillips, R. (1998b) Contesting the past, constructing the future: history, identity and politics in schools. *British Journal of Educational Studies,* 46 (1), 40–53.

Plaskow, M. (ed.) (1985) *Life & Death of the Schools Council.* London, Falmer Press.

Plumb, J. H. (1969) *The Death of the Past.* Harmondsworth, Pelican.

Price, M. (1968) History in danger. *History,* 53, 342–7.

Prochaska, A. (1982) *History of the General Federation of Trade Unions 1899–1980.* London, Allen & Unwin.

Prochaska, A. (1990) The History Working Group: reflections and diary in history. *History Workshop Journal* 30, 80–90.

Quicke, J. (1988) The 'New Right' and education. *British Journal of Educational Studies*, 26 (1), 5–20.

Ravitch, D. (1985) *The Schools We Deserve: Reflections on the Educational Crisis of Our Time.* New York, Basic Books.

Robbins, K. (1981) History, the Historical Association and the national past. *History*, 66, 413–25.

Robbins, K. (1990) National identity and history: past, present and future. *History* 75, 369–87.

Roberts, J. (1985) *The Triumph of the West.* London, BBC.

Roberts, M. (1973) 'A Different Approach to 'O' Level' in R. B. Jones (ed.) *Practical Approaches to the New History.* London, Hutchinson.

Roberts, M. (1988) Debate – History and the National Curriculum: A report on the first regional conferences and some suggestions for a strategy from now into the 1990s. *Teaching History*, 51, 32–3.

Roberts, M. (1990) History in the school curriculum 1972–1990; a possible dialectical sequence: thesis, antithesis, synthesis? *The Curriculum Journal*, 1 (1), 65–75.

Robinson, J. (1912) *The New History.* London, Macmillan.

Rogers, P. (1984) *The New History – theory into practice.* London, Historical Association.

Roy, W. (1986) *Teachers Under Attack.* London, Routledge.

Salter, B. & Tapper, T. (1981) *Education, Politics and the State.* London, Grant McIntyre.

Salter, B. & Tapper, T. (1988) The politics of reversing the ratchet in secondary education, 1969–1986. *Journal of Educational Administration & History*, 20 (2), 57–69.

Samuel, R. (1990) Grand narratives. *History Workshop Journal*, 29, Spring, 120–33.

Samuel, R. (1994) *Theatres of Memory: Past and Present in Contemporary Culture*, Volume 1. London, Verso.

Samuel, R. & Thompson, P. (eds) (1990) *The Myths We Live By.* London, Routledge.

SCAA (1994a) *Occasional Papers in History 1: The Impact of the National Curriculum on the Production of History Textbooks and Other Resources for Key Stages 2 and 3.* London, SCAA.

SCAA (1994b) *The Review of the National Curriculum: A Report on the 1994 Consultation.* London, SCAA.

SCAA (1994c) *History in the National Curriculum: Draft Proposals.* London, HMSO.

Scarth, J. (1987) 'Teaching to the exam? The case of the Schools History Project' in T. Horton (ed.) *GCSE: Examining the New System.* London, Harper & Row.

Schools Council (1972) *An Introduction to Integrated Studies.* Oxford, Oxford University Press.

Schools Council 13–16 Project (1976) *A New Look at History.* Edinburgh, Holmes MacDougal.

Schwarz, B. (1996) 'Introduction: the expansion and contradiction of England' in B. Schwarz (ed.) *The Expansion of England: Race, Ethnicity and Cultural History.* London, Routledge.

Scruton, R. (1980) *The Meaning of Conservatism.* Penguin, London.

Scruton, R. (1981) *The Politics of Culture & Other Essays.* Carcanet, Manchester.

Scruton, R. (1986) 'The Myth of Cultural Relativism' in R. Palmer (ed.) *Anti-Racism: An Assault on Education and Value.* London, Sherwood Press.

Scruton, R. (ed.) (1988a) *Conservative Thoughts: Essays from 'The Salisbury Review'.* London, Claridge Press.

Scruton, R. (ed.) (1988b) *Conservative Thinkers: Essays from 'The Salisbury Review'.* London, Claridge Press.

Scruton, R., Ellis-Jones, A. & O'Keeffe, D. (1985) *Education and Indoctrination.* Harrow, Education Research Centre.

SEAC (1991) *Teacher Assessment in Practice.* London, SEAC.

SEAC (1992a) *Specification for the Development of Tests in History for Pupils at the End of the Third Key Stage on the National Curriculum.* London, SEAC.

SEAC (1992b) *Teacher Assessment at Key Stage 3: History.* London, SEAC.

SEAC (1993) *Pupils Work Assessed: History KS3 (England)*. London, SEAC.

Seidel, G. (1986) 'Culture, Nation & "Race" in the British and French New Right' in R. Levitas (ed.) *The Ideology of the New Right*. Cambridge, Polity Press.

Seixas, P. (1993) Parallel crises: history and the social studies curriculum in the USA. *Journal of Curriculum Studies*, 25 (3), 235–50.

Sexton, S. (1988) *Our Schools: A Radical Policy*. Warlingham, Institute of Economic Affairs.

Shemilt, D. (1980) *History 13–16 Evaluation Study: Schools Council History 13–16 Project*. Edinburgh, Holmes MacDougall.

Shemilt, D. (1984) 'Beauty and the Philosopher: Empathy in History and Classroom' in A. Dickinson, P. Lee & P. Rogers (eds) *Learning History*. London, Heinemann.

Shepherd, J. & Vulliamy, G. (1994) The struggle for culture: a sociological case study of the development of a national music curriculum. *British Journal of Sociology of Education*, 15 (1), 27–40.

Shor, I. (1986) *Culture Wars: School and Society in the Conservative Restoration, 1969–1984*. London, Routledge & Kegan Paul.

Sieborger, R. & Alexander, N. (1996) *Minority and majority cultures – a South African perspective*. Paper presented at the SCAA Curriculum, Culture and Society Conference (London), 7–9 February.

Silver, H. (1990) *Education, Change and the Policy Process*. London, Falmer Press.

Skidelsky, R. (1990) *The Wrong Kind of Testing*. History Workshop: History, the Nation and the Schools: A Recall Conference, Ruskin College Oxford: Conference Papers.

Skidelsky, R. (1993a) *Interests & Obsessions: Selected Essays*. London, Macmillan.

Skidelsky, R. (1993b) 'The National Curriculum and Assessment: Choice or Collectivism?' in S. Lawlor (ed.) *The Dearing Debate: Assessment and the National Curriculum*. London, Centre for Policy Studies, 1995.

Skidelsky, R. (1993c) The future of history in the National Curriculum. *Welsh Historian*, 20, 4–7.

Slater, J. (1989) *The Politics of History Teaching: A Humanity Dehumanized?* Institute of Education, Special Professorial Lecture. London, Institute of Education.

Slater, J. (1991) 'History in the National Curriculum: the Final Report of the History Working Group' in R. Aldrich (ed.) *History in the National Curriculum*. London University, Institute of Education, Bedford Way Series, Kogan Page.

Slater, J. (1995) *Teaching History in the New Europe*. London, Cassell.

Smith, A. M. (1994) *New Right Discourses on Race & Sexuality*. Cambridge, Cambridge University Press.

Steele, I. (1976) *Developments in History Teaching*. London, Open Books.

Steele, I. (1980) The teaching of history in England: an historical perspective. *History Teaching Review*, 12 (1).

Storry, M. & Childs, P. (eds) (1997) *British Cultural Identities*. London, Routledge.

Styles, S. (1990) A race between education and catastrophe: the Final Report of the History Working Group. *Teaching History*, 61, 22–5.

Sylvester, D. (1994) 'A Historical Overview' in H. Bourdillon (ed.) *Teaching History*. London, Routledge.

Tate, N. (1986) *Countdown to GCSE History*. London, Macmillan.

Tate, N. (1994) Off the fence on common culture. *Times Educational Supplement*, 29 July.

Tate, N. (1995a) Speech to the Council of Europe Conference on 'The role of history in the formation of national identity'. York, 18 September.

Tate, N. (1995b) Speech to the Shropshire Secondary Headteachers Conference. Shrewsbury, 13 July.

Tate, N. (1995c) 'Why we must teach our children to be British'. *Sun*, 19 July.

Tate, N. (1996a) Introductory Speech at the SCAA Invitation Conference on Curriculum, Culture and Society. London, 7–9 February.

Tate, N. (1996b) National identity and the school curriculum. *Welsh Historian*, 24, 7–9.

Tate, N. (1996c) 'Why Learn?' Speech given to the Association of Teachers & Lecturers Conference, London, 22 June.

Teaching History Research Group (1991) *How to Teach, Plan and Assess History in the National Curriculum*. London, Heinemann.

Thatcher, M. (1979) 'Foreword' to H. Thomas: *History, Capitalism & Freedom*. London, Centre for Policy Studies.

Thatcher, M. (1993) *The Downing Street Years*. London, HarperCollins.

Thomas, H. (1979) *History, Capitalism & Freedom*. London, Centre for Policy Studies.

Tomlinson, S. (1990) 'The British National Identity' in S. Tomlinson *Multicultural Education in White Schools*. London, Batsford.

Tomlinson, J. (1993) *The Control of Education*. London, Cassell.

Tonkin, E. (1992) *Narrating Our Pasts: The Social Construction of Oral History*. Cambridge, Cambridge University Press.

Tosh, J. (1984) *The Pursuit of History. Aims, Methods & New Directions in the Study of Modern History*. London, Longman.

Truman, P. (1990) Teachers' concerns over the current vogue in teaching history. *Teaching History*, 58, 10–17.

Troyna, B. & Carrington, B. (1990) *Education, Racism and Reform*. London, Routledge.

Turner, J. (ed.) (1996) *The State and the School: An International Perspective*. London, Falmer Press.

Tyldesley, N. (1983) 'How to be a History Man': An analysis of the role of the head of department at a time of falling rolls. *Teaching History*, 37.

Tyldesley, N. (1993) A critique of the assessment arrangements for history in the National Curriculum: a response to Medley & White. *The Curriculum Journal*, 4 (1), 127–9.

University of Birmingham History Education Group (1993) The implementation of the National Curriculum in History. *Forum*, 35 (2), 48–50.

Wake, R. (1970) History as a separate discipline: the case. *Teaching History*, 1 (3), 153–7.

Walford, G. (ed.) (1994) *Researching the Powerful in Education*. London, University College London Press.

Wallace, M. (1993) Discourse of derision: the role of the mass media within the education policy process. *Journal of Education Policy*, 8 (4), 321–37.

Watts, R. (1992) 'History' in P. Ribbins (ed.) *Delivering the National Curriculum: Subjects for Secondary Schooling*. London, Longman.

Watts, R. (1993) Implementing the National Curriculum: term 1. *Teaching History*, 70, 13–17.

Wegner, G. (1990) Germany's past contested: the Soviet–American conflict in Berlin over history curriculum reform, 1945–1948. *History of Education Quarterly*, 30 (1), 1–16.

Wegner, G. (1992) Affirmation of a tradition: the German–American dialogue over the history curriculum in West German secondary schools, 1950–1955. *History of Education*, 21 (1), 83–96.

Welsh Office (1990) *National Curriculum History Committee for Wales Final Report*. Cardiff, HMSO.

Welsh Office (1991) *History in the National Curriculum (Wales)*. Cardiff, HMSO.

Welsh Office (1995) *History in the National Curriculum: Wales*. Cardiff, HMSO.

White, C. (1992) *Strategies for the Assessment and Teaching of History: A Handbook for Secondary Teachers*. London, Longman.

White, C. & Crump, S. (1993) Education and the three 'P's: policy, politics and practice. A review of the work of S. J. Ball. *British Journal of Sociology and Education*, 14 (4), 415–29.

Whitty, G. (1989) The New Right and the National Curriculum: state control or market forces? *Journal of Educational Policy*, 4 (4), 329–41.

Whitty, G. & Edwards, T. (1994) 'Researching Thatcherite Education Policy' in G. Walford (ed.) *Researching the Powerful in Education*. London, University College London Press.

Williams, M., Daugherty, R. & Banks, F. (eds) (1992) *Continuing the Education Debate*. London, Cassell.

Williams, N. (1986) The Schools Council Project: History 13–16 – The first ten years of examination. *Teaching History*, 46, 8–12.

Wright, P. (1985) *On Living in an Old Country: The National Past in Contemporary Britain*. London, Verso.

Yeo, S. (1990) The more it changes, the more it stays the same. *History Workshop Journal*, 30, 120–8.

Young, R. (1990) *White Mythologies: Writing History and the West*. London, Routledge.

Index